The Vanishing Peasant

M.I.T. Studies in Comparative Politics

Under the general editorship of Harold D. Lasswell, Daniel Lerner, and Ithiel de Sola Pool.

The Emerging Elite: A Study of Political Leadership in Ceylon
Marshall Singer, 1964.

The Turkish Political Elite
Frederick W. Frey, 1965

World Revolutionary Elites:
Studies in Coercive Ideological Movements
Harold D. Lasswell and Daniel Lerner, editors, 1965.

Language of Politics: Studies in Quantitative Semantics
Harold D. Lasswell, Nathan Leites, and Associates, 1965 (reissue).

The General Inquirer:
A Computer Approach to Content Analysis
Philip J. Stone, Dexter C. Dunphy, Marshall S. Smith, Daniel M. Ogilvie, 1967.

Political Elites: A Select Computerized Bibliography
Carl Beck and J. Thomas McKechnie, 1968.

Force and Folly: Essays on Foreign Affairs
and the History of Ideas
Hans Speier, 1969.

Quantitative Ecological Analysis in the Social Sciences
Mattei Dogan and Stein Rokkan, editors, 1969.

Euratlantica: Changing Perspectives of the European Elites
Daniel Lerner and Morton Gorden, 1969.

The Vanishing Peasant: Innovation and
Change in French Agriculture
Henri Mendras, 1970.

The Vanishing Peasant
Innovation and Change in French Agriculture

Henri Mendras

Translated by Jean Lerner

The MIT Press, Cambridge, Massachusetts, and London, England

Published in French by S.É.D.É.I.S., Paris, under the title
La Fin des Paysans, Innovation et Changement dans l'Agriculture
Française

Set in Linotype Baskerville by Eastern Typesetting Company. Printed
and bound in the United States of America by The Colonial Press Inc.

ISBN 0 262 13065 3 (hardcover)

Library of Congress catalog card number: 79–118349

Part 1. Change and Innovation in Peasant Societies

Part 2. The Farmer, His Enterprise, and Society

Foreword

The twentieth century produced the virtual disappearance of the farmer as a "social class" from the modernized countries of Western Europe and North America. As always, the most conspicuous thrust toward modernity was made in the United States. The astonishing fact is that this country now is fed by about 6 percent of its working population — a fraction that, if our national economic policy were more humanely and wisely geared to our world political role, could feed much of hungry humanity around the globe.

To comprehend the magnitude of this social transformation, we recall that when this country was founded over 90 percent of the world's population was engaged in agriculture. Even today, in the underdeveloped areas, over 70 percent are still agriculturalists (indeed, this figure is used by economists as a criterion of underdevelopment). The reduction of this social class to the vanishing point in the modern West is therefore a matter of historical consequence. Even France, still the largest agricultural producer in Western Europe, maintains this production with less than a third of its working force — a fraction that, as this study indicates on p. 235, is likely to decline to less than 10 percent in the next decade or so.

Henri Mendras has studied this momentous process in *The Vanishing Peasant,* a study that illuminates the historic roots of the process as well as its future prospects. Mendras is right to start with the question raised in 1896 by Gabriel Tarde: "Have we ever given a moment's thought to the life of this fossilized creature who crops up in books on ancient history, known as *the peasant?*" Mendras is right again — after close consideration of the theoretical and operational aspects of the disappearance of the peasant from modern society — to conclude with perspectives on the future.

It is this sense of the present as a transition from the past to the future which makes Mendras' book an especially valuable addition to the M.I.T. Studies in Comparative Politics. This series is animated by a conception of the policy sciences that seeks guidance on the great issues of public policy from analysis of past trends and conditions that improves our capacity to project future alternatives. Many of our previous volumes have focused upon elite and symbol studies, for we believe that comparative analysis of changes in the "composition and vocabulary of the ruling few" is a basic source of enlightenment in the policy sciences. Along with such studies, we are concerned with the "processes" of social change that reshape the environments that supply the "contexts" for political life as well as political analysis. To this subset of studies, Mendras makes a valuable contribution.

A special word of thanks is due Mrs. Jean Lerner, whose translation unites fidelity to the French text with alertness to the demands of good American prose style.

Harold D. Lasswell
Daniel Lerner

Translator's Note

It is the peasant as defined by Henri Mendras in his Introduction to this book who is in the process of "vanishing" from the French countryside.

There will always be men who till the soil and manage their farms, in France as elsewhere, but the farmer who is content to run a small subsistence farm in conformity with traditional routines and to live in a face-to-face society, seldom going "beyond the limited horizons of [his] own soil," (p. 14) is becoming rarer and rarer. And his "peasant soul" (p. 36) is disappearing with him.

Indeed, perhaps the "contented" farmer in general, the man who works hard but has no great ambitions in the contemporary sense, is doomed to extinction.

No translator ever had a better collaborator than mine, since I was fortunate to work closely with an author who knows English well. I believe M. Mendras and I are in agreement that the English version scrupulously conveys his intentions throughout.

I am grateful for further assistance and advice on various portions of the manuscript from Professors Edward Banfield and David Landes of Harvard University, Lovell Jarvis of the University of California, Charles Kindleberger of the Massachusetts Institute of Technology, and especially my husband, Daniel Lerner, also of M.I.T.

J. L.
Allegro in the Berkshires
April 1970

Abbreviations

A.N.M.R.
Association nationale pour les migrations rurales (National Association for Rural Migrations)

C.E.T.A.
Centre d'études techniques agricoles (Center for Technical Farm Studies)

C.G.A.
Confédération générale de l'agriculture (General Agricultural Federation)

C.N.J.A.
Centre national des jeunes agriculteurs (National Center for Young Farmers)

C.N.R.S.
Centre national de la recherche scientifique (National Center for Scientific Research)

C.U.M.A.
Coopérative d'utilisation de matériel agricole (Cooperative for the Collective Ownership of Farm Equipment)

D.G.R.S.T.
Délégation générale à la recherche scientifique et technique (General Commission for Scientific and Technical Research)

F.N.S.E.A.
Fédération nationale des syndicats d'exploitants agricoles (National Federation of Farmers' Unions)

F.N.S.P.
Fondation nationale des sciences politiques (National Foundation of Political Science)

G.A.E.C.
Groupement agricole d'exploitation en commun (Farmers' Organization for Communal Land Use)

I.E.P.
Institut d'études politiques (Institute for Political Studies)

I.F.O.P.
Institut français d'opinion publique (French Institute of Public Opinion)

I.N.R.A.
Institut national de la recherche agronomique (National Institute of Agronomical Research)

J.A.C.
Jeunesse agricole chrétienne (Christian Agricultural Youth Movement)

M.F.A.R.
Maisons familiales d'apprentissage rural (Schools of Rural Apprenticeship)

M.O.D.E.F.
Mouvement d'organisation et de défense des exploitations famil-
iales (Movement for the Organization and Protection of Family
Farms)

S.A.F.E.R.
Société d'aménagement foncier et d'établissement rural (Societies
for Land Management)

S.I.C.A.
Société d'intérêt collectif agricole (Associated Farm Interests)

Country folk! What a quaint, archaic expression!

"Fishermen, hunters, plowmen, shepherds: do we really understand the meaning of these words today? Have we ever given a moment's thought to the life of this fossilized creature, who crops up so often in books on ancient history, known as the peasant?"

Gabriel Tarde, *Fragment d'histoire future*, 1896.

Introduction: On the Study of the Peasantry

One or two billion peasants at the threshold of industrial civilization: this is the major world problem facing the social sciences in this second half of the twentieth century. The fears of Malthus are once again revived as the population of entire continents increases faster than the necessities of life. On a worldwide scale, agricultural overproduction is no longer a problem; food needs have become serious, and only management and production techniques appropriate to an industrial society can cope with the situation.

First to sound the alarm were the agronomists, the earliest to become involved. In the beginning the enormous agricultural potential of "underdeveloped" countries deceived them. It seemed that a few good techniques would suffice to double production in these backward nations, or even to increase it tenfold in some cases.

René Dumont, one of the pioneers, was astounded to discover that a technique, however good, is of no help so long as it is not accepted and put to use by the farmers. Experience proves that agricultural techniques are spread much more rapidly in the industrialized countries than in others. It is easier to double agricultural production in France or the United States, for instance, than to raise that of India by 10 percent; while for half a century Russia, though it accomplished great industrial feats, has had difficulty covering its food requirements. Paradoxically, agricultural countries are the least likely to feed themselves, and they often reach the point of begging their bread from their industrial neighbors.

What answers can the social sciences provide to these agonizing questions? There have been some historical surveys, renewed interest in problems of growth on the part of economists, several monographs by anthropologists, and some sociopsychological studies on attitudes toward change; but there has been no synthesis, no body of theory suitable for relating the policy of those who govern to the action of those in responsible positions. This explains why, in response to the assertion of the agronomist that "Black Africa is off to a bad start,"[1] the sociologist can only ask the question: "Can it get a start at all?"[2] — a rather disconcerting dialogue, and one that is likely to arouse dismay in honest men

[1]Dumont, 1962.
[2]Meister, 1966.

and humility in economists and sociologists. In order to learn how to help peasants all over the world adapt themselves to industrial civilization, so that they can feed themselves and prosper, would it not be best to study the example of Western peasants who have already made this transition?

I

The social sciences of the nineteenth century showed a surprising lack of understanding of rural affairs. All their efforts at analysis and interpretation were directed toward the industrial economy and urban society. Fascinated by the birth of the working class, by the prodigious efficiency of capitalist enterprise, and by the unique tool that money constituted, they lost interest in a social system that functioned without salaried workers or entrepreneurs or money. Yet this was the system that was dominant in the West a century ago and remains so in the world of today.

A few scholars who specialized in studying the peasantry continued the grand tradition of the agronomists of ancient times and the Middle Ages. But most of the writings of Mathieu de Dombasle, François de Neufchateau, Agénor de Gasparin, and Léonce de Lavergne, to name a few, only repeated what Varro, Columella, Olivier de Serres, and the Abbé Rozier had said years before. Being excellent observers, these nineteenth-century writers contributed much to the progress of agriculture; on the other hand, they could hardly revive the rural economy at a time when classical economists and utopian and Marxist Socialists were formulating an "industrial economy." For their part, Le Play[3] and his school attempted painstaking observation of peasant and working-class families, in order to understand their ways of thinking. They would undoubtedly have arrived at new perspectives if their desire for objectivity had not been turned aside by ideological concerns.[4]

Interested in reconciling the civil code and customary practices, jurists issued doctrines intended to analyze family farming, which should conform to family needs, economic imperatives, and agronomical exigencies.[5] The richness and subtlety of land contracts dealing with different forms of tenure and cultivation of the soil and with the distribution of its fruits testify to a thorough

[3]Le Play, 1879.
[4]Lefebvre, 1949.
[5]Juglart, 1958.

knowledge of technical and economic usages, customs, and social relations in farm regions. A normative science practiced by notaries and magistrates but little known to economists and sociologists, legal doctrine is the outgrowth of a type of observation and knowledge better-suited to productive sociological discussion than many descriptive studies.

From the Austria of Maria Theresa to Stolypin's Russia, great movements of agrarian reform in eastern Europe had their theoreticians and doctrinal champions. They can still be read today with benefit, especially if one is interested in underdeveloped countries. Rarely, however, do they prove a source of the elements of modern sociological theory.

On the other hand, the endeavors of the Russian populists to work out a truly rural economy based on such theories remains astonishingly modern after a half-century. It is a pity that such a promising intellectual enterprise should have been brutally smashed by precisely those political leaders it would perhaps have spared many disappointments. Tchayanov[6] tried to work out a system of peasant enterprise in which there was no place for money. His dual analysis of the Russian manorial regime, from the point of view of both the peasants and their masters, suggests possible ways of reconciling the exigencies of agricultural production and the necessities of the modern economy.[7] One can imagine what Soviet agriculture might be like if organized according to these principles.

These few isolated efforts to observe and understand the peasantry were all doomed to failure. They only helped convince the men of that day that the farmer still lived by the precepts of Xenophon and Hesiod; that everything had been said on the subject, and inquiring minds should turn to other areas.

At the same time, liberal economic analysis and Marxist theory were experiencing well-known successes. But both denied that the peasant economic and social system was unique and tried to break it down into categories and ideas based on urban industrial realities. This sort of intellectual annihilation of the peasantry deserves detailed analysis to show how it came about and what were its consequences.

[6]Kerblay, 1964.
[7]Tchayanov, 1924.

During the past century, the slow evolution of agriculture, unlike the accelerated progress of industry, gave the impression of reassuring stability and perpetual equilibrium. In contrast with the fever of industrial growth, the dependability of the peasant seemed eternal; the city and its industry absorbed men's energies, but the country continued to nourish bucolic dreams of peaceful happiness, security, and continuity. Anxious to permit humanity to live the enthralling adventure of progress while conserving the old rustic values, the idealistic socialists invented "harmonies" and "phalansteries," where, dividing his time and work between the fields and the factory, man might find total liberation and self-expression in the harmonious exercise of his diverse talents. It was agreed that the peasantry, respectful of the social order, of morality, and of religious beliefs, should feed the cities and make up the greater part of the battalions of industry as well as of the infantry.

Turmoil, revolution, progress were to be found elsewhere: in the city, where they attracted all those who wished for change. From this contrast was born the nineteenth-century idea that in agriculture nothing ever changes, that the eternal order of the fields will always be imposed on the farmer.

A century earlier, when manufacture was still artisanal, when the agricultural revolution was in progress, and the aroused peasants were preparing to burn down the châteaux, this image of agriculture and the peasantry would have seemed very strange. The improvement of agriculture was the great concern of the epoch.[8] In France the King set the example, while the upper classes applied themselves to the problem as it affected their domains, founded "agricultural societies,"[9] and consulted with each other on the best way to convince the peasants to improve their methods. In 1788 Rougier de Labergerie published his *Recherches sur les principaux abus qui s'opposent au progrès de l'agriculture* (Investigations of the principal obstructions to the progress of agriculture), which is surprisingly relevant to today's problems. Arthur Young's shock at seeing the primitive agriculture of certain regions, and his pleasure in visiting beautiful demesnes, illustrate the widespread progress being made.[10]

[8]Augé-Laribé, 1955.
[9]Justin, 1935.
[10]Young, 1789.

Following the British example, landowners both small and large began to enclose their fields for the use of their herds. No longer able to feed their animals without common pasture, the laborers and small peasants opposed this exclusive and individualistic form of property ownership. The "struggle for agrarian individualism" stirred up the whole nation and upset the equilibrium of village society.[11]

Most historians of agriculture in this country have admired the "French prudence" (*sagesse française*) that kept the nation from pushing the agricultural revolution of the eighteenth century to extreme social consequences and enabled us to conserve a large peasant class, while the British, yielding to the logic of the industrial economy, sacrificed their agriculture to the development of industry. In a way, France stopped in her tracks; she paused for a century and a half while her peasants, though slowly accepting technological innovations, remained peasants.

Today, the second agricultural revolution is upsetting every structure, and the dependable equilibrium has been disturbed. Agriculture, in its turn, is becoming "industrialized," and the French peasantry is being destroyed, one hundred fifty years later, by what we call industrial civilization. Suddenly we feel very close to the eighteenth century. We are rediscovering that nature can be subdued by technology, that agrarian history is marked by constant advances, innovations, and improvements, and that the farmers are living in turmoil.

We live essentially on ideas that were bequeathed us by the nineteenth century, and are today obviously anachronistic. It is important to revise these ideas and to look at the countryside with a new eye; otherwise we will remain blind to the great movement that is carrying the agrarian societies of the entire world toward a complete remodeling of their technology and their social equilibrium. The disappearance of the peasant in countries that have industrialized the most rapidly is due less to the force of economic circumstances than to the misapplication to agriculture of analytical methods, legislative measures, and administrative decisions that were not designed for it.

In countries such as England or the United States, where it was wholly subordinated to the logic of industrial society, agriculture

[11]Bloch, 1930.

remains an irreducible political and social problem, which seriously concerns leaders in Washington and London.[12]

In France a well-known example of this misapplication is the law of 1884 on unions, which was formulated entirely on behalf of the industrial unions and was extended to agriculture only because at the end of a legislative session one senator took it into his head to propose that the words "and agricultural" be added to the explanatory statement.[13] Thanks to this last-minute addition, the whole idea of agricultural trade unionism was able to develop substantially and serve important economic functions that were not intended by the legislator. Again, today we can observe all the difficulties faced by the extension of social security to the agricultural sector: legislation that is meaningful and equitable for salaried workers makes beggars of agricultural workers without settling their real problems. Finally, if France has not had a real agricultural policy for a century, it is in large part because she did not have the intellectual instruments for its conception.

Statesmen who make a profession of Marxism are as helpless as their "capitalist" colleagues: they may create *kolkhozes*, communes, cooperatives, or *agrogorods*, but they have difficulty in getting their peasants started, and agricultural production is the weak point of their economies. Curiously enough, it seems more difficult to produce potatoes and meat than to construct *vostoks* and *luniks*. Is it unwarranted to assume that the principal cause of this weakness is Marx's failure to understand the peasantry?

Neither Poland nor Yugoslavia, on the one hand, or India or Cuba on the other has yet demonstrated a solution to the so-called underdeveloped countries. The Chinese experiment is fascinating, but its success is not assured. The Israeli masterpiece is unique and therefore impossible to imitate. Is the problem not simply that the logic of industrial society is incompatible with the logic of traditional peasant society, and that to try to apply one to the other can obviously lead only to the destruction of the second?

The concept of an industrial society is today commonly accepted.[14] On the other hand, what are we to understand by

[12]Benedict, 1955; Higbee, 1963.
[13]Augé-Laribé, 1950, p. 134.
[14]Aron, 1962.

"peasant society?" A peasant society is a relatively autonomous whole at the center of a broader society.[15] If an agrarian society is completely autonomous and is not functionally part of a larger society, we would refer to it as a "savage" society, in the sense that the eighteenth century gave to this word (which seems more adequate than current terms such as primitive, archaic, lacking a written language or a history, and so on). If the rural communities do not enjoy relative autonomy in relation to the broader society, we would speak of farmers, local groups, occasionally of rural "classes," but not of a peasantry. In a word, the peasant is defined in relation to the city. If there is no city there is no peasant, and if the society is entirely urbanized there is no peasant either.

Peasant society is subdivided into local communities[16] that exist in relative demographic, economic, and cultural autarchy. According to Marx's famous image,[17] the French peasantry of the last century resembled "potatoes in a sack," each community being a social entity, each being unique although all the communities were of the same kind.[18]

Each community is a face-to-face group[19] in which everybody knows everyone else in all his aspects. Its social relations are thus personal and not functional or segmentary. The community unites peasants (independent farmers, stockbreeders, landowners, cultivators, or salaried workers and their families, and nonpeasants (notables,* artisans and merchants, and so on); but the dominant tone of the society is set by the peasants. Power belongs normally to the notables, who are in a marginal position between the local community and the broader society. The principal cleavages are often hierarchial in nature, according to a scale of socioeconomic prestige. If not, they can be of an ideological, ecological, or family nature in the larger sense: there is often no clear distinction between blood relatives and business connections. Finally, categories of age and sex are in general strongly individualized.

In communities as highly structured as this, everything contrib-

---

[15]Redfield, 1956a; Thorner, 1964.
[16]Redfield, 1956b.
[17]Marx, 1852.
[18]Arensberg, 1961.
[19]Maget, 1955.
*The word "notables" is used throughout this work to indicate persons of influence in the community, such as the mayor, the large landholder, the notary, or the teacher. (Trans.)

utes to the stability of the whole, and change can be introduced only by consensus, so slowly as to deny that it is change. These communities are not inflexible, but, except in a grave crisis, they evolve slowly to the rhythm of generations. Every innovation, whether it be technological, economic, or demographic, comes from the outside. In the words of Albert Dauzat, a man hardly to be suspected of prejudice on this subject, "The countryside has created nothing; everything comes to it from the city — dress, customs, songs. . . ." and one could add machines and technology.[20]

In such a social system, the individual does not have to adapt himself to new decisions or make decisions himself; neither does he have to express or reveal himself to others, who know him from every point of view. Hence he has a tendency to remain true to himself and to the image others have of him. Showing or expressing sentiments and personal opinions is not encouraged by the code of values and norms.

This archetype of traditional peasant society took various forms in Western Europe from the Middle Ages to the end of the nineteenth century. Today it is still an explanatory schema for understanding the logical functioning of rural communities now in process of being remodeled. Soon there will be only vestiges, so deeply eroded that it will be impossible to understand their place within structures radically alien to them.

In other regions of the world this schema can serve as a basis of comparison, and certain of its elements can be useful instruments of interpretation; but it would be dangerous to see in this a universal model for all agrarian communities dominated by a broader society. There would have to be many studies on different societies, leading to the construction of analogous schemas, before one could begin to inquire if there exists a single, ideal, and universal peasant type, and if the European peasant, with his variants, is only one of many species in a more extended genus.

II

The steam engine in large part imposed its logic on industry and, through it, on society as a whole.[21] A fixed source of energy,

[20]Augé-Laribé, 1955, Introduction and p. 147; Dauzat, 1941, p. 130.
[21]Bell, 1956.

it required the concentration of machines under one roof and
their combined utilization, so that work was subject to a fixed
timetable and hierarchical authority. Because it is immovable,
land requires that the machine must be mobile with respect
to the material being handled (cereals, arable soil, and so on)
and not the contrary, as in a factory. Natural biological mechanisms have their rhythm, which can sometimes be speeded up
but not radically modified. Space and time are the two essential
limitations on work in the fields that the steam engine could
not overcome. After several tries, steam tractors were abandoned[22]
and, as a result, the agricultural worker, a stranger to all
hierarchical authority, remained master of his enterprise, his
work, and his time. The social organization of agricultural production is totally different from that of industrial production.

Having escaped the first Industrial Revolution, and still awaiting
the third, the atomic revolution that will upset many natural
mechanisms, agriculture is today undergoing (somewhat late)
the second industrial revolution. In the case of the tractor and
the harvester-thresher, the internal combustion engine makes the
machine mobile over the immobile material and thus overcomes
the limitation of space. Progress in chemistry and botany
allows the rhythms to be accelerated and the crops to be
regularized and enlarged; the limitation of time thus becomes
widely flexible.

The agricultural revolution of the eighteenth century required
more than a hundred years to carry its advances into the French
countryside. It took place in the rhythm of a traditional society
that industry had not yet modified. While it brought social
change, supported and sometimes accelerated by political revolution,
the essential character of village society remained unaltered. After
a century of continual rural exodus, the present revolution in France
is reducing the number of farmers at the bewildering rate of
160,000 per year, both through the death of farmers without suc-
cessors and through the movement of young farmers into other
professions. Those who remain become correspondingly richer and
can meet the new exigencies of economy and technology, but not
without completely upsetting village society.

Equilibrium is being shattered: slow-moving agriculture is

[22] Faucher, 1954, pp. 82–88.

being shaken up so it begins to time itself to the pace of
industry, borrowing its sources of energy and its most recent
discoveries. In less than ten years, many yields have more
than doubled; the farmer who used to be satisfied with twenty
bushels of wheat per acre and four hundred gallons of milk per
milking now obtains sixty bushels and one thousand gallons.
Machines are multiplying: between 1946 and 1965, the number
of tractors in France has risen from about 20,000 to more than a
million. New techniques are developing directly from laboratory
research, rather than from the slow gropings of progressive farmers.
All agricultural production is dictated by the tastes of consumers
and the fluctuations of markets. Just as other sectors of production,
agriculture must submit to the rhythm of technological and economic change in industrial society.

The West has grown from a society of slow change to one
of rapid change. This is what Daniel Halévy has called "the
acceleration of history," a striking expression that masks rather
than describes the phenomenon, since it is the whole pattern
of society that has been radically transformed in order to
introduce change into the functioning of the social system. A
static, or almost static, equilibrium has given way to a dynamic
one, composed of continual disequilibria. Until recent years,
this break in rhythm had hardly affected agricultural societies
in France, a fact that probably explains why we speak today of
the "industrialization" of agriculture rather than its modernization.
The word evokes the image and suggests that in modernizing
in its turn, agriculture is going to follow in the footsteps of
industry; the path is marked out and need only be followed. But why
should twentieth-century farms follow the fate of the artisans and
factories of the early nineteenth century?

Having remained aloof from the first Industrial Revolution
and the capitalist system, agriculture is entering into industrial
society with premachinist and precapitalist social structures.
It is therefore reasonable to believe it can invent new forms of
economic and social management of production that perhaps
will then spread to other sectors.

Thus backward agriculture, free of all "industrial" heritage, can
now and then surpass industry and prefigure the future. It
offers to the sociologist a privileged field for analysis in which

it is possible to discern in current social structures the social survival of outmoded forms of production, and to conceive of structures that are more adequate to future forms of production and respond better to men's aspirations. This is what Naville suggests at the close of his impressive study of automation:

Working the land consists of preparing for the gathering of crops, conceiving and fashioning the conditions in which the harvest will ripen, automatically in the true sense of the word, which means spontaneously in its Greek etymology. The human hand announces, sets in motion, reaps, controls, and gives meaning to the result. It was a sign in agriculture as it will become again in the new industry. Indeed, industrial systems have many characteristics other than those of agriculture, but automation seeks to confer on them an autonomy that brings them closer to natural systems.[23]

For the past fifteen years, France has been a unique observation point, where almost all possible solutions have been introduced and tested. Thanks to the maintenance of traditional structures and the rapid introduction of progress, one can see that the most ancient forms of crop gathering and subsistence agriculture survive, while "industrial" methods of production prevail and radically new formulas for cultivation and management are being tried. The farmers' capacity for social invention and the rapidity of change keep the observer always one step behind.

Large, "modern" farms have always been managed "rationally." Even in the Middle Ages, great lords asked their stewards to keep accounts and their technicians to make experiments, introduce "novelties," and record good agricultural practice in books.[24] From Suger to Olivier de Serres to today's model farms, these examples have scarcely made an impression on the neighboring peasants; they remained faithful to their settled routine. Today the great "industrialized" farms are dispersed in all regions and are in a majority only in the Parisian basin. These cases will be taken into consideration here only as counterpoint, to illustrate the dominant traits of polyproducing* family farms, on which

[23]Naville, 1961, p. 8.
[24]Grand and Delatouche, 1950; Delatouche, 1956.
*The words "polyproduction" and "polycultivation" are neologisms in both French and English. These words and their variants are used throughout this work to refer to a system of "mixed farming" in which the farmer grows several different crops (as in subsistence farming) instead of specializing in one. Conversely, this specialization is referred to as "monocultivation." (Trans.)

our entire analysis is centered. In fact, it is the transition from peasant logic to economic rationality in the management of farms that sums up and symbolizes the conflict of civilizations and the transformation of the peasant into an agricultural producer. The great farms should engage the economist's attention, since they often furnish the major portion of a product (cereals, for example); the sociologist is more interested in the farmers than in their produce. The average French farmer has at his disposal about thirty-five acres, which he manages by trying to reconcile the proven principles of his routine and the new exigencies of economics and technology. Thus it is he alone who interests us here.

This famous peasant routine seems an irritating anachronism in today's farm regions. The interviewer no longer meets "routine-bound" peasants, but only old farmers who have renounced the pursuit of progress while the young outrun it or try breathlessly to catch up with it. Need we give examples?

Peasants have been reproached for their distrust of credit, yet indebtedness of agriculture has become a subject of major concern for those responsible for agricultural policy. Economists deplore the fact that farmers are overequipped with machinery of all sorts. Planners wished at one point to restrict imports of corn; in a few years they have obtained overproduction, without radically changing the agrarian structures that limit the farmers' movements on all sides.

In good economic theory, rural exodus is a necessary condition to agricultural progress; but it is not sufficient, since experience shows that it leads to the decline of rural regions. The best people depart, society begins to be closed and static, agriculture becomes fixed in its habits, and peasants look back with nostalgia on a lost past. Jean Chombart de Lauwe[25] showed that in the last century Aquitaine, declining in population, saw its agriculture stagnate, while Brittany, under constant demographic pressure, cleared the land, modernized its techniques, and branched out into entirely new products. Politicians and ideologists of the right or left, all of whom sing the praises of peasant virtues and the beauties of the rustic life,[26] were right

[25]Chombart de Lauwe, 1946.
[26]See Labat, 1919; Yole, 1930.

in opposing rural exodus as too simplistic an economic theory. For the past fifteen years, mechanisms have begun to work in the opposite direction, finally confirming this theory. All that was necessary was that a new generation of young farmers regain confidence in the economic future and in the nobility of the land as a profession. Profiting from the departure of their neighbors to expand, to equip and organize themselves, they can play the economic game of our industrial society; and they have decided to play it to the hilt, while at the same time seeking to modify its rules to their advantage.

The ease with which peasants formed in the traditional world can move in a modern world is a source of constant surprise to the observer. Provided that they enter into a coherent and significant economic game, "economic motivations" come to young farmers with disconcerting rapidity. Moreover, when they travel from their farms, these untrained country bumpkins show an amazing aptitude for creating new institutions that are perfectly adapted to modern conditions, such as C.E.T.A. (Center for Technical Farm Studies), S.I.C.A. (Associated Farm Interests), and M.F.A.R. (Schools of Rural Apprenticeship).* Under their constant pressure, modern methods of farm accounting have been introduced in France, and it is in response to their demands that rural economics has come out of its age-old lethargy.

What truth is more self-evident, what fact better substantiated, than the peasant's individualism and love of his land? He gives his life's blood to enlarge his fields, and then fences himself in on his property with fierce independence, like a petty king in his kingdom. Nevertheless for half a century it is in the area of agriculture that cooperation has known its greatest success. Buying and marketing cooperatives, mutual insurance societies, farm credit associations, Cooperatives for the Collective Ownership of Farm Equipment (C.U.M.A.), and the C.E.T.A.—no other sector of production can offer such a variety of cooperative organizations. Today some farmers are attempting the final step by joining their lands and grouping them into larger units where each product constitutes a workshop under the responsibility of one of the cooperating parties. Such experiments

*Schools sponsored by the Catholic Church, which young farmers attend one week of every three for a period of three years.

in "group farming" are not proceeding without difficulties, in the absence of legislation and established customs; for these pioneers must invent everything themselves until such time as economists, legislators, and public authorities have codified their experiments.

In devoting themselves enthusiastically to this total remodeling of their social and technical structures, the farmers have the feeling that they are making up for lost time and creating a place for themselves in the era of industrial civilization. Once the crisis of adjustment has passed, they hope in a confused way to rediscover the equilibrium their fathers knew. Having assimilated some new techniques and accepted some economic regulations, they expect to recreate a system of cultivation and independent farming as durable as the previous one. But modern technological civilization lives on continual change and dooms the quietude of immutable habits. Far from rediscovering traditional stability, the peasant will in his turn settle into the perpetual change of technological innovation and economic contingency. Furthermore, he is setting up, more or less consciously, the institutions that will help him to do this. Centers of management and rural economics study the evolution of markets and direct the management of farm workers accordingly. Services for agronomical research and agricultural extension complete the chain that progressively adapts the scientific discoveries of the laboratory so that they can be used by the farmer in his field.

Peasant values, so highly esteemed since the time of Xenophon and Virgil, and heretofore at the very heart of our Western civilization, will not be able to survive the shakeup of their ancient stability. The eternal "peasant soul" is dying before our eyes, just as is the patriarchal family domain founded on subsistence polycultivation. It is the final battle of industrial society against the last stronghold of traditional civilization. What we are undertaking here, then, is not simply a study of a new agricultural revolution but a study of the disappearance of traditional peasant civilization, which is a fundamental element of Western civilization and Christianity, and its replacement by the new modern technological civilization, which will often take on different forms in the country from those it presently assumes in the city.

III

The French countryside, as we have seen, now offers to the sociologist a sort of laboratory, where many "spontaneous experiments" lend themselves to highly varied analysis. The variety of local situations and the unity of overall conditions permit systematic comparisons in which each variable can be isolated as in a real experiment. The quickening pace of change throws into relief mechanisms of functioning and change that are usually obliterated by their slowness and the way in which they overlap within the general transition. Hence it is justifiable, on the basis of the French experience, to try to begin to answer the big questions put forth at the beginning of this work. In the chapters that follow we shall consider only the case of France, but the reader will want to inquire into possible generalizations and transpositions.

It is regrettable that we do not have a number of observation points in different regions of France, indeed all over Europe, where all the vicissitudes and manifestations of this deep change could be recorded. Within a few years there would have accumulated unique material for the study of social change. Our knowledge of the dynamics of rural communities would make decisive progress, which would result in valuable advice for all the countries of the world that will know similar upheavals. In the absence of broad systematic research adequate to the dimensions of the subject, the analyses that follow are supported by disparate facts of varying usefulness and significance.

For twelve years this research has been developing progressively, as events demanded, in studies and readings, travels, conversations with peasants, administrators, agronomists, and economists, and in other forms. With each step, as new ground, new problems and hypotheses were uncovered, it became more and more difficult to bring the undertaking to a conclusion. Soon it attracted other researchers and became a collective project. Today it is running away from its initiator to become the work of a team, and tomorrow it will probably be taken up by an institution.

Some inquiries conducted by the Division of Rural Sociology of the National Center for Scientific Research (c.n.r.s.),[27] works by historians, geographers, and economists; and a few outlines by

[27]See Appendix 2.

sociologists psychologists, and anthropologists[28] — this is meager
fuel for the aspirations that have been aroused. The author is
more aware than others that the arguments are supported
more by illustrations than by proofs, and that problems are
more often stated than analyzed or resolved, and he begs the
reader's indulgence for this lack, hoping simply that in another
twelve years our knowledge will have progressed so far that
he would no longer dare to write this book as he does today.

The general scientific outlook of the researcher dictates in great
part his choice of techniques, his manner of posing problems
in operational terms, and the treatment to which he subjects
his data. Consequently, for the reader and for himself, the
author should explain as much as possible his methodological
and technical assumptions, his theoretical postulates, and his
ideological and moral inclinations. It is up to the reader then to
judge in what measure the results, the conclusions, and the
interpretations are colored by all these prejudices.

Interviewing peasants is considered a difficult task. It is well
known that they never give a definite yes or no answer, that
they are always complaining, and that they carefully hide
their personal lives and feelings from all strangers. If asked about
their crops they are said to answer always: "For a good year
it's not so good, but for a bad year I can't say it's too bad."
Often they are even accused of lying or taking a mischievous
pleasure in misleading the naive person who tries to take an
interest in them. In short, duped or ridiculed, the interviewer
wastes his time and money on them.

The rural investigator is surprised to hear this widely-accepted
opinion. Although he is pitied for his difficulties in interviewing
such secretive people, he generally finds the peasants happy
to talk; often it is harder to stop the conversation than to
continue it. In a word, such a study is generally easier in the
country than in the city, provided some elementary precautions
are taken. The anthropologist suggests an ungenerous explanation for this seeming contradiction: the investigator makes the
peasants talk, it is true, but they say things that do not
represent what they think, and the data thus gathered seem to the
anthropologist unusable, or almost so. In his opinion, the

[28]Mendras, 1962.

behavior of the peasants must first be observed to be understood; he must not ask questions before he has acquired a great familiarity with their lives and with each one of them personally. He is convinced that only an anthropological study conducted by a highly-qualified researcher in a small community would result in valid data on traditional peasant societies, which are closer to "primitive" than to industrial society.

At this point, it is clear we are no longer discussing the pure technique of inquiry, but rather problems of epistemology and the sociology of knowledge, which are irrelevant. We must nevertheless ask one fundamental question, without trying to answer it here: is the sociologist, armed with his concepts and techniques, a product of industrial society? Can he exercise his talents profitably in other, particularly peasant, societies? In theory, the answer is not easy. In practice, the rural investigator must utilize his techniques of inquiry and take several precautions to assure himself a good reception.[29]

In his studies, the rural sociologist always owes a debt to the geographer and the historian and willingly acknowledges that it is a sizable one. To construct its syntheses, each discipline borrows from its neighbors, reducing them to the rank of subsidiary sciences, with the understanding that the roles can be reversed. Since the beginning of the century, historians and geographers in France have put together an important body of studies that have been the object of some very remarkable interpretations. There are detailed and meticulous works on each region, describing landscapes and the agrarian systems and seeking, sometimes in a distant past, for the origins of present conditions. Marc Bloch, André Deléage, and Roger Dion have all sketched bold outlines of the different agrarian civilizations that divide France. The social history of the countryside has recently made considerable progress, so that in any given region we sometimes know twelfth- or sixteenth-century society better than that of today.

Anthropologists are increasingly turning their attention to the peasant; they are no longer interested only in the strange customs of savage peoples. The Americans in particular have recently discovered, thanks to Robert Redfield and Conrad Arensberg, that the majority of mankind is peasant. This discovery seems ironically

[29]See Appendix 1.

naive to the European ruralist; he is frequently tempted to advise his overseas colleagues to read Olivier de Serres and look into the agriculture of the fourteenth century. But the studies that young American researchers have done all over the world suggest fruitful comparisons and reflections. The French have recently begun this work, particularly in connection with the African "peasantry;" anthropologists and folklorists in France are furnishing interesting data.

The syncretism of rural life makes any distinction between economics and sociology less meaningful than in other fields. The rural economist and the economic agronomist have at their disposal instruments of analysis that have been substantially perfected in recent years, and their researches steadily keep pace with those of the sociologist. The latter finds that he is often reproached for being "too much an economist," but how can he be otherwise? And if he is awkwardly so, he begs indulgence.

It is undoubtedly hazardous to try to bring order into such disparate materials by combining them with the precarious results of isolated pilot studies. Moreover, French farm regions in the midst of revolution continually outrun the analyst and observer. Finally, the social sciences are progressing at a staggering speed. On a theme as vast and shifting as this, with such uncertain instruments, the time for a synthesis has not yet arrived.

However, there is a moment in research when it is time to pause and draw tentative conclusions, to catch one's breath before embarking on a new course. To state a few ideas with precision, establish some distinctions, describe mechanisms, pose problems, advance theses and sometimes hypotheses; to submit the whole to the criticism of colleagues and suggest it to the ardor and curiosity of other researchers — such are the immediate scientific ambitions of this outline. Tentatively renouncing the building of a theory of the peasantry, it contents itself with adding "a few stones in the middle of the stream" that separates us from such a theory.

This choice explains and, let us hope, justifies the fact that the chapters that follow are directed toward the coherence of schemas and the logic of mechanisms rather than detailed analysis and rigorous use of techniques. For the moment it is especially important to state the problems well, if it can be done, and to bring into question the techniques of research. The researcher knows the risk he runs in delivering so imperfect and perishable a product; he cannot pretend to the glory of the moralist who engraves eternal maxims in marble. But this entire work inquires at the same time into both the destiny of the French peasantry and the universalism of social science.

The reader will no doubt be surprised, perhaps irritated, at being led by diverse paths to consider one after another perspectives and horizons sometimes too vast, sometimes regrettably truncated, and often badly circumscribed. But all the talent and uniqueness of the rural sociologist resides in the confrontation of points of view about a social phenomenon.[30] This ambition leads him to have recourse in turn to the erudition of the historian and geographer, to the reckoning of the economist, to the investigative techniques of the social psychologist, and to the analyses of the political scientist, in order to borrow their conclusions and tie them into one bundle that he arranges according to his own hypotheses, in hopes of understanding the phenomenon as a whole.

The first part of the book is concerned with clarifying the logic and coherence of traditional peasant society by showing how the confusion of roles, the coincidence of positions and organizations entails a personalization of relations and actions. Commanded down to the smallest detail by a moral imperative by which men's slightest acts are unhesitatingly judged, farm and social life is organized into temporal frameworks that are experienced but do not permit of an accounting. This patterning of roles, organizations, and social groups is profoundly resistant to innovation, which it accepts only when disguised in the form of slow social change. The introduction of hybrid corn into a district of the Basses-Pyrénées furnishes a typical illustration of this relation between innovation and change. It shows how much the present-day farmer, formed in the mold of traditional society, is disoriented by an innovation presented to him without consideration of the social consequences, because he perceives that the ultimate result is a complete upheaval of his system of economic, social, and moral life.

The second part analyzes the reactions and attitudes of this traditionally formed farmer toward the economic, social and political mechanisms of modern society. The old moral and temporal

[30]Mendras, 1962 and 1967.

frameworks prove to be inadequate to the management of an
agricultural enterprise, but economic rationality furnishes
only a partial set of criteria for determining the many new choices
imposed on the heads of family enterprises. Transformations in
the circumstances of these heads of enterprise, and the uncertainty of their future, make these choices still more risky. Indeed,
the multiplicity of agricultural organizations and the new relationships being established between economics and politics allow
the transfer of decisions to new decision-making institutions, but
this process carries with it grave consequences for the liberty
and responsibilities of the individual.

If the analysis, exceeding its proper theme, ventures into
conjecture about the future, it is because the farmers' anxiety,
born of these upheavals, is too pressing to remain totally
unanswered. Besides, having announced the extinction of the
peasantry, one is forced to wonder uneasily what a world
without peasants would be like. At this point, when the situation is
unsettled and nothing is fixed, it is permissible to speculate on the
structures of agriculture in the industrial society of tomorrow.

The utopias of the great nineteenth-century visionaries were
hardly realized, except as experiments in some towns of the
American West. They nourished nonetheless the thinking of an
entire century and animated legions of idealists who remain a
credit to their times. To imitate them by outlining an agricultural
"harmony" of the twenty-first century is a presumptuous aim;
but what would a sociologist amount to if, having dissected and
analyzed a social body, he did not become concerned with its
future and the well-being of society and mankind?

Part 1. Change and Innovation in Peasant Societies

"The peasants of the past died 'old and satiated with life' because they stood in the organic cycle of life, because their life had brought to their declining days all the meaning it could offer, and because there were no more puzzles they would have liked to solve. Thus they could consider themselves 'satisfied' with life. Civilized man, on the contrary, situated in the midst of a civilization constantly being enriched with ideas, knowledge and problems, may become 'weary' of life, not 'satiated' with it. In fact, he can never grasp any more than a minute part of what the life of the spirit produces that is new. He can only grasp something provisional, never the definitive. That is why death is for him a meaningless occurrence."

Max Weber, *Wissenschaft als Beruf,* 1919.

1. Forces and Mechanisms of Change

The apparent stability of traditional peasant societies did not rule out all innovation. The perfecting of implements, the introduction of new strains, and the improvement of methods of cultivation form an essential chapter of all periods of agricultural history. Societies that are ostensibly the most static are the product of a long evolution based on experimentation, on setbacks , and on advances. The mechanisms by which technical and social change are introduced into such societies have seldom been described and analyzed. Anthropologists and archaeologists study the diffusion of characteristics and artifacts; social psychologists amass studies on attitudes toward change and on the communication of ideas and innovations; historians determine the date of the appearance of a technique or the formulation of an institution or custom; philosophers of history investigate the causes of the rise and decline of civilizations; and economists are only beginning to discover the principles of growth. But the basic dynamics of large-scale societies, like those of local communities, remain largely unexplored.

Transformations in the economy and the rural societies of Europe since the early Middle Ages would furnish ample material for such research. How did Carolingian Europe give rise both to the scholarly agriculture of the twelfth century and to the movement toward urbanization that characterized the later Middle Ages? How did new botanical strains and modern methods of farming come into currency during the sixteenth century? The agricultural revolution of the eighteenth century has been the subject of many studies, yet how much do we know about the slow but radical transformation of the farm regions of Europe in the nineteenth century? Are there sufficient data to enable us to put into proper relationship such things as technical advances; the clearing of the land; agrarian systems and structures of production; demographic trends; institutions and customs; social groups and their hierarchies; and economic, legal and political power? Would it be possible to construct parallel analyses of the interaction of these within village societies and in the broader societies that surround them? Just such an enormous project was undertaken by Georges Duby[1] in a history that runs from the manorial economy of the tenth century to the scholarly agriculture of the fourteenth.

[1]Duby, 1962.

Carolingian Europe was entirely rural: there were no cities, only farm regions populated by peasants grouped in villages around the manors of *seigneurs*. These lords constituted the entire surrounding society, and they were themselves hardly more than warrior-peasants. The personal and direct bond of man to man was the foundation of the system. The lord "housed" his men on his land; that is, he gave them estates and in return expected personal services and their promise to cultivate the reserve.* The farmer fashioned his own tools, most of them wooden, from the shovel to the swingplow. They provided him with a primitive and not very profitable means of cultivation; the yield of cereals was hardly more than two or three times the seed.

The meal consisted of bread with a few roots, vegetables, or dairy products, a combination known as the *companaticum*. The *companaticum* of the lord was a little more abundant and varied than that of the peasant, but everybody subsisted in the same manner. The lord kept one or two blacksmiths in his "court" who manufactured the farming implements. There were no water mills, only hand mills, to grind the grain. The one real source of wealth was the men who improved the land; so that the more men the lord had, the further his domain could extend. But since it could only grow to a certain point, the rich lord possessed several manors; and he led a nomadic existence, moving from one to another to consume the produce on the spot and supervise the management of each. Thus Charlemagne traveled from one *villa* to another. In order to codify his instructions to his stewards, he ordered the drafting of the capitulary *De Villis*, a real agronomical treatise and the ancestor of the *maisons rustiques*. Such is the simplistic schema that can be constructed from a study of this "simple" society: personal bondage, subsistence cultivation, small and autonomous communities.

The lord who was a good manager concerned himself with increasing the number of his dependents; when they became too numerous for the village they drifted off to clear the forests. The eleventh and twelfth centuries saw a simultaneous increase in the area of cultivated land and in peasant population. This period also witnessed

* Reserve and demesne are used to designate that portion of the manor from which all produce went to the lord, as contrasted with tenures, the produce of which was divided between the lord and his tenants. (Trans.)

the development of tools, seeds, and techniques that made it
possible to obtain better yields. Implements grew in number and
efficiency: shovels, spades, and swingplows were now made of
iron, and harrows came into use. The horse collar and the water
mill gained acceptance. Plowing became more frequent, particularly
June plowing, which was warmly recommended in the capitulary
De Villis as a means of destroying weeds and maintaining moisture
in the soil.

   In the thirteenth century, English agronomists proposed yields of
eight to one for barley, seven to one for rye, six to one for leguminous
plants, and five to one for wheat. On one plot of land the harvest
could vary by as much 100 percent from year to year. In some
soils wheat never yielded more than three times the seed, but in
others, with careful cultivation, it could yield twelve times. The
little manure available was jealously reserved for the garden. With
trifling differences these would be the yields of Western agriculture until the eighteenth century, at which time manure and
fertilizer would permit a new increase. In the years from the tenth
to the twelfth century, then, agriculture had made considerable
progress. This enrichment was accompanied by radical change
in rural society, which became diversified and functionalized. A
man who went off to clear a piece of land was no longer under the
thumb of his lord; often he was set free, although he still paid rents.
The value of the stock of implements and livestock grew; demographic expansion diminished the value of men and increased that
of the land, which yielded more as it was better cultivated. The
population increased while the dimensions of the family plot
became proportionately smaller so that on the average the former
increased four times while the latter shrank to a quarter of its size.
The lord maintained the right of eminent domain and imposed
taxes. Thus the personal bond was progressively replaced by
economic and fiscal ties.

   The perfecting of implements — particularly the appearance of the
plow, which required a strong team — brought the beginnings of
social differentiation among the peasants. Those who had a team
and a plow were plowmen and those who had only their strong backs
and their spades were laborers. An increasing number of
artisans moved from the château to the village and worked for
peasants, providing them with the tools they needed. The great

lords who had seen their domains settled and extended now
entrusted the job of management to stewards, who collected the
rents and took special interest in the maintenance of the reserve.
The *corvée** gave way increasingly to the use of full-time
salaried labor. As seigneurial taxes multiplied, they required
collectors. Since the lord no longer rendered justice, he was replaced
by judges. Thus an entire class of feudal middlemen was born.

Among the lords themselves arose a distinction between the small
lords, who remained attached to the manorial system and close to
the peasantry, and the great ones, who were absent increasingly
from their lands. As they became richer, clever peasants and middlemen tried to raise themselves to the rank of nobility, and gained the
acceptance of the small country squires. Within the Church, likewise,
curates, canons, and monks took their places on this social scale in
process of formation.

From the moment that the soil no longer simply nourished men, and
skillful cultivators could extract a revenue from it, it took on
economic value. It could be bought, sold, and pledged. Demographic pressure increased its scarcity and its value. The landholder in difficulty could borrow a sum against a perpetual rent
annuity, and the creditor thus acquired a sort of lien on the land
that would someday assure him of the privileges of lordship. The
landholder who enlarged his manor easily found salaried workers
among the landless peasants. Since it was no longer consumed
on the spot by the lord's "court," the agricultural produce of the
demesnes was sold, giving rise to trade. The noble and the
wealthy developed a taste for luxury, beautiful clothes, and
high living.

To keep pace with them, the herds grew and took over new
pastures, while artisans multiplied in the growing cities. Generally
the herds belonged to city butchers, merchants, or lords. For some,
agriculture and animal breeding became an economic activity
from which they expected a good return. Alongside the peasantry,
there appeared veritable agricultural entrepreneurs: substantial
peasants and small country squires, managers of large domains
and middle-class inhabitants of the rising cities. These men devoted
careful study to their work, reread the ancient agronomists, and

---

* A form of forced labor under which the peasant had an obligation
to perform certain work for the lord. (Trans.)

established the technical and economic principles of profitable management.

This brief macrohistorical outline brings into relief the interaction of technical, demographic, economic, social, and psychological characteristics that made it possible for the Carolingian manor, so simple and primitive in its techniques and its social organization, to develop within two hundred years into the brilliant and complex society of the twelfth century, already extensively urbanized and employing most of the agronomical, economic, and legal techniques of modern agriculture and economics. It shows, moreover, to what extent all these elements are intimately and subtly connected in peasant societies. The smallest technological change, the least demographic pressure, act upon the equilibrium of the entire system, bringing movement and reorganization in their wake, and this movement, once started, follows its own dynamics until it constructs a totally new system.

However, though we can see the interplay of forces and the relationship among characteristics, the means and mechanisms of this prodigious "growth" are not equally apparent. Sources for this period are too rare and too scattered to lend themselves to closer analysis. Georges Duby, however, has succeeded in analyzing the growing importance of money, and cites some very provocative examples of the role of merchants and solicitors in small towns.

But, everything considered, the initiative for change appears to have lain chiefly with the lords, both lay and religious. From the king to the lowest lord, all noblemen were landholders and farmers. Many of them were concerned with the improvement of their domains and made use of distant connections in order to introduce innovations on their properties. Six centuries after the time of Charlemagne and the *De Villis,* Charles V asked Jean de Brie to draft the *Traité d'Estat, Science et pratique de l'art de bergerie* (Treatise on the State, Science and Practice of the Art of Sheepraising). His chancellor, Pierre d'Orgemont, was proprietor of a manor at Gonesse, where he had raised a flock of 600 sheep. Among his innumerable activities, Suger was a very progressive farmer who kept careful accounts on the increase in revenue resulting from any innovation. Albert the Great set up a plan for an orchard and in 1245 constructed the first known hothouse. In 1213, the Vicomte de Rohan received nine Arabian stallions from the Sultan of Egypt. In 1337 the herds of the Dame d'Olivet included sheep and a bull from Spain. These are only a few of many examples.

Delatouche[2] suggests that the mode of cultivation constituted an excellent "extension method," to use a modern expression. Not only could the seigneurial reserve play the role of a "model farm," but its cultivation through use of the *corvée* made it a real "school of practical application":

In a community subject to the rule of many, lacking a leader of vision, and singularly dependent upon precedent, communal practices constitute a strong brake on initiative for progress. It is entirely different when these practices are the result of discipline imposed by a master who wishes to improve cultivation, one who possesses real power and is willing to make use of it. Then such practices permit his initiative to be applied and generalized almost automatically. To promote the practice of June plowing, Charlemagne used something more than propaganda based on the calendar. On lands that were farmed collectively, his directives applied to the reserve; executed by those liable to the *corvée*, they served the peasant as an example for his own property, an example that he had no choice but to follow, restricted as he was by the amount of work and the extent of the area to be tilled. (p. 155)

Thus we can see that the relaxing of feudal bonds, the decrease in the size of the reserve, and the increase in the number of small autonomous farms that began in the thirteenth century were not favorable to the progress of agriculture.

In a study of the peasants of Languedoc covering the period from the sixteenth to the eighteenth century, Le Roy Ladurie[3] provides a striking counterproof that confirms Duby's analysis. Throughout this period, the average yield of wheat remained very low (between three and four and one-half to one); it did not begin to rise until the end of the eighteenth century, and not until the time of the Empire was it to reach a ratio of between five and eight to one on the best lands:

In other words, it happened that society contracted at the end of the seventeenth century while the economy became closed and static and finally fell back to its base level because this economy could not augment or renew its resources. These included not only its precious metals, but also its good land, limited by definition, and (for want of such land), its technical advances, so pitifully small in the sixteenth and seventeenth centuries. To pursue a hypothesis previously stated: if the yield of grain had increased by several degrees between 1500 and 1700 (as it was to do in the course of the eighteenth century), if it had been possible to plant the vineyards

[2]Delatouche, 1956.
[3]Le Roy Ladurie, 1966.

heavily and continuously (as was to be the practice almost every-where from 1760 to 1870), or to irrigate liberally (as the Catalans would after 1720), then the society of Languedoc would have been able, simply by augmenting its cadastral revenue, to handle the population increase and the disintegration of large estates, as well as the addition of new taxes. (p. 641)

At the end of the fifteenth century, men were scarce and fallow land abundant. The manors were reconsolidated and men, being better nourished, were less sensitive to epidemics. These conditions permitted rapid growth at the beginning of the sixteenth century; population jumped, but the economy did not follow at the same speed. This caused a contraction after 1530; not only Languedoc but all of Western Europe experienced a shortage of capital, a drop in salaries, accelerated parceling of the land, and so on. The wars at the end of the century prevented a recovery.

After 1600 began a period of "maturity." The death and birth rates were almost equal, growth in population diminished, and the population curve approached the horizontal. There was a rise in income from money and land (usury, the tithe, seigneurial and royal duties, and so on); this enabled the state, which had become more powerful, to undertake large-scale wars:

The mentality of the landed gentleman outweighed the initiative of the entrepreneurs. Agronomists became agrarians. In some respects society tended to freeze into social immobility, and the paralyzing consequences of this joined with the Malthusian effects of technical immobility. (p. 635)

In certain regions, the middle class and the aristocracy were engaged in settling and improving rural areas, since they had more capital available for these investments. This was the case particularly in the regions around Dijon[4] and Paris.[5] On the other hand, most agronomists and politicians (often Protestants) who were concerned with social and land reform and technical progress did not make themselves heard, and brought about no important changes: e.g., Olivier de Serres[6] and Laffemas,[7] Sully, and, later on, Vauban.[8]

At the end of the century, beginning in 1680, farming became less profitable and total agricultural production receded to its sixteenth century level. For the first time in two centuries, population decreased

[4]Roupnel, 1955.
[5]Mireaux, 1958; Venard, 1957.
[6]O. de Serres, 1605.
[7]Le Roy Ladurie, 1966, pp. 439–441.
[8]Vauban, 1707.

in its turn as a result of unemployment, poverty, and famine. Not until the middle of the eighteenth century and the years of the agricultural revolution would it be freed from this iron collar. Why were not the techniques recommended by such men as Olivier de Serres adopted in their time rather than later in the eighteenth century, along with others? The answer lies in general history rather than rural economics: the logic of industrial society came into play, with its corresponding system of values and world view.[9]

In the absence of more general studies of this order, the precise analysis of the introduction of a new crop or technique in rural societies permits a new approach to the old problem of the peasant's routine. In two illuminating articles, Faucher and Bloch[10] have shown that when a new crop can be introduced into the system without destroying its equilibrium, there are few cases in which "resistance to innovation" is not lowered. In support of this contention Marc Bloch cites the well-known example of the water mill, which, although known in antiquity, did not become widespread until the Middle Ages, a time when rye, probably brought from the nomadic civilizations of the steppes by the great invasions, was gaining rapid acceptance among the Meroviagian peasants. Similar to other cereals, though hardier than wheat, rye did not modify the established techniques and made it possible to seed certain land for the first time, thus increasing the area of the land under cultivation. It was widely adopted and became the principal food of the entire rural population, particularly in central France, where it reigned almost supreme.

Similarly, Daniel Faucher shows that the introduction of corn into the southwest in the seventeenth and eighteenth centuries was slow and gradual, and aroused no opposition:

Its cultivation presented enormous advantages. It could serve to feed men, and its yield was far superior to that of wheat. Its tops, leaves, and ears provided abundant fodder for the animals and permitted the expansion of animal breeding and an increase in fertilizers. It could be combined with wheat to partially eliminate fallow land, the ground lying fallow no more than half a year between the harvest and the planting of the corn. (p. 97)

However, two centuries passed before the biennial wheat-fallow rotation gave place to the wheat-corn rotation, even though the

[9]Hazard, 1953.
[10]Bloch, 1948; Faucher, 1948.

latter threatened neither the alimentary equilibrium nor the system
of cultivation; on the contrary, it enriched one and intensified
the other.

But the introduction of a new technique almost always has
unexpected consequences, and corn brought on a rupture in the
unity of rural civilization in southern France, by differentiating
Aquitaine from the Mediterranean Midi:

> Henceforth the peasantry of the southwest would have a charac-
> teristic attitude. . . . After the intellectual shock provoked by the
> introduction of corn, it fell again into passivity. . . . The peasant
> of the southwest abandoned one 'routine' only to fall again into
> another. (p. 98)

We shall show below how much he hesitates to leave that routine
today to accept hybrid corn and all the technical, economic, and
social consequences that it entails.

During the same period, the Midi also showed reluctance to
accept the mulberry plant, so highly praised by Olivier de Serres.
It was not until the upheavals of the end of the eighteenth century
that it began to spread into some regions. Like corn, it could be
integrated into the traditional system of cultivation. Planted at the
edge of the fields, it did not occupy any land; and the breeding of
silkworms provided work in the slow season. Like corn, it
supplemented the system of techniques without modifying it; but,
while corn strengthened the alimentary system, silkworms, which
were a speculative crop, opened subsistence polycultivation to the
national and international market. Any collapse in this market
brought on repercussions in all the producing villages. Imports of
silk from the Far East precipitated a crisis that forced silk
growers to revert to one of their traditional alimentary products,
i.e., wine. This they converted into a commercial crop easy to
dispose of in urban markets, which were expanding as a result of
the development of railroads. With some impetus from phylloxera,
subsistence polycultivation declined little by little in favor of the
monocultivation of the vineyard.[11]

Thus, from crisis to crisis, the Midi entered into the modern
economic cycle, while the southwest remained a peasant society
supported by subsistance farming, with the consequences that
Faucher has indicated: relative impoverishment of landholders and
small farmers, demographic deficiency, and above all "a sort of

[11]P. Clément, 1953.

intellectual languor that resists innovations." It is not our intention here to compare the social, political, and moral results of these two evolutions. Some will praise the foresight of the Aquitanian and pity the Languedoc peasant for his vicissitudes; others will feel contempt for the "languor" of the former and admire the latter's vitality. The sociologist is content to stress the fact that a different technical choice at the outset finally brings on radical changes in the entire society.

It is understandable, then, that the peasant, vaguely aware of the social import of the slightest technical change, hesitates when faced with any innovation. Marc Bloch has clearly demonstrated that the agricultural revolution of the eighteenth century was fought by large farmers against the "routine" of the small peasant, who showed little receptivity to the idea of increasing either national production or that of his own farm.

He knew the uncertainty of the market, the fluctuation of prices. . . . His principal concern was to keep more or less intact his traditional standard of living. In practically every case, he judged his fate to be linked with the maintenance of ancient communal restrictions, which lay heavily on his fields. These practices presumed fallow ground. To eliminate fallow ground was to eliminate the common pasture, which, on land under triennial rotation, opened a third of the cultivated soil each year to the herds of the entire community. Deprived of this facility, many farmers would not have known how to feed their animals. In short, most of the peasants feared the great social upheaval that seemed the inevitable result of new methods. In this they were not wrong. If they had known more about what was happening at the same time on the other side of the Channel, they would have found their worst fears confirmed. The agricultural revolution was accomplished in England much more rapidly and completely than in our country, but at the cost of crushing a whole segment of the rural population.[12]

The peasants of the Ganges valley, according to a study by McKim Marriott,[13] are reluctant to utilize the water brought to them by an irrigation project because they see clearly that this project will chiefly benefit the large landholders, and that it will make them dependent on agricultural experts and officials. In the end, "the canal seems to them a government strategy to extract more work and money from them." They know, moreover, that their houses would have to be scattered over the land to enable

[12]Bloch, 1948, p. 109.
[13]Marriott, 1954.

them to supervise irrigation by day and by night; whereas they are used to living in grouped villages which resemble fortresses, because the outside world seems to them to be full of danger, and they are afraid to go out at night into fields peopled "by wicked spirits and terrible bandits." Consequently, although they are fully aware that their interests lie in perfecting irrigation techniques, the project is unacceptable to them because of the radical upheavals it would introduce into their social organization.

On arriving in this village, McKim Marriott was struck by the number of techniques and crops that had been introduced during the last two generations: carrots from Asia, mustard seeds, mechanical seeders, and so on. These innovations had sufficed to double the population in one hundred years. Apart from the proposed collective irrigation network, a better utilization of manure or the use of selected seeds would have permitted an increase in the subsistence level. But these two innovations were unacceptable to the peasants because they could not be integrated into their system of techniques. Manure was the only available fuel; the new wheat produced a better yield in grain but the cows refused to eat its straw. Obviously cows, like men, must eat, and women must have something with which to make a fire in order to cook.

Thus the historian and the anthropologist[14] show us that in normal times, in a peasant society, the mechanisms of change are very slow, and an innovation is really accepted only when it no longer appears "new," having become integrated into the existing system. This is true even in the United States, though to a lesser degree.[15] When it is the result of a skillful adjustment among different techniques, the system of production assures the entire social system of a precarious alimentary and demographic equilibrium. Therefore one cannot be modified without calling the other into question. It requires at least a generation for an improvement to be introduced and completely integrated into the system of cultivation until it becomes a part of the technological heritage of the group. Then the son learns it from his father as he learns other things. In the end it can be said that innovation

[14]Anthropologists' works on this subject are numerous. For examples of an early and a recent treatment, see Redfield, 1950 and Mair, 1965.
[15] Miner, 1949.

has no place in these societies: as long as something is a novelty it remains peripheral to the system, and once it makes its place in the system it is no longer a novelty. Change is accomplished by rejecting innovation as such.

Historians point out that all agricultural progress, particularly that of the eighteenth century, has been the work of elements foreign to peasant society. We have mentioned the role of the great lords and the stewards of manors in the Middle Ages. In the sixteenth century, "botanical gardens" became stylish and played an important experimental role: in 1536 Rabelais, then in Rome, sent his patron the seeds of lettuce, melon, and various other plants, with advice on how to cultivate them correctly.[16] In the seventeenth century, it was often the urban middle class that gave new strength to agriculture and contributed to its progress. The influence of "postmasters" is common knowledge. Gaston Roupnel has shown how families of the legal profession in Dijon brought new population into Burgundy and introduced wine growing there,[17] and Marc Venard has analyzed the influence of the Parisian bourgeoisie on agriculture in the surrounding regions.[18]

During the eighteenth century the agricultural revolution was often directed against the peasants, and they accepted it only very slowly in the course of the nineteenth.

The rural mass followed the movement with great reluctance, often showing deliberate opposition at the outset. Traces of this resistance underlie agronomical literature to this day. Agronomy has in some way held a grudge against the peasantry for this.[19]

Moreover, agronomy did not concern itself with the peasants, for the most part; ancient, medieval, and modern agronomists did not write for the farmer, but for the landholder, who, in the words of Olivier de Serres, did not want "to be classed with illiterate peasants."

In this connection, Augé-Laribé has gathered evidence to show that in recent times no invention has ever been produced by peasants in a peasant society:

[16]Augé-Laribé 1955, p. 16.
[17]Roupnel, 1955.
[18]Venard, 1957.
[19]Bloch, 1948, p. 108.

These men, so ingenious in perfecting the details of execution, do not invent. All the great changes that have benefited them or that they have suffered have been imposed on them from the outside, by the cities.

And he recalls the words of Cattaneo: *"L'agricoltura rationale nasce nelle citte."*[20] (Scientific agriculture is born in the city.) Redfield was therefore correct in stating that the peasantry is defined in relation to the city or to an elite, and that as long as there is no city there is no peasant.[21]

The study of traditional village society demonstrates why, as a rule, peasants could hardly be innovators; all the weight of tradition and the entire social system has prevented it. The nonpeasant landholder, on the other hand, could, thanks to his marginal situation, fill the role of initiator and experimenter with new ideas.

The "traditional" peasant can never question tradition, which he takes for granted as the normal way to live and work. On the other hand, the squire, whether noble or middle-class, who has received an education and come into contact with the study of history, science, and the humanities, knows that elsewhere there are other "traditions," other ways of doing things. If he agrees to remain faithful to his tradition, it is through deliberate traditionalism and refusal to change — unlike the traditional peasant, who would not know how to be "traditional" or "antitraditional," but merely assumes a tradition that presents him with no questions or problems.[22]

Of course the contrast has never been quite as radical as this in French society. Even in the last century, squires were in many respects peasants and often submitted to village tradition as did their neighbors. The latter, for their part, were not so isolated from the external world that they could not imagine other ways of behaving than their own. In certain regions they applied their ingenuity to improving upon details; for example, in the vicinity of Toulouse, where the gardens were continuing experimental grounds for inventive cultivators. But these experiments, just as those of the medieval scholars, did not become either a science or a technique; and all the great agronomical advances came from

[20]Augé-Laribé, 1955, p. 147.
[21]Redfield, 1956.
[22]Weil, 1953.

the outside.[23] It continued to be true that the peasants, countryfolk at heart, hardly went beyond the limited horizons of their own soil. The notables, on the contrary, lived in the external world as much as, and sometimes much more than, they lived in the world of the village. They read newspapers and magazines and maintained relations with their social equals in neighboring regions. They often spent the winter months in town, enlivening scholarly circles, which often took an interest in agriculture just as in literature and archaeology. Within their own districts, their social role led the squires quite naturally to take an active role in the *comice*,* where they met other enlightened farmers of the region, the veterinary surgeon, and the officials responsible for furthering agricultural progress. Though they did not share Homais' religion of science, their studies had often taught them a respect for science and a certain confidence in its progress. The best of them took pride in experimentation and participated in the scientific movement of the period in one field or another.[24]

Furthermore, their way of life demanded that the squires draw monetary revenue from their lands. They had to maintain a household, pay for their children's studies, and often spend the winter in town. They employed numerous salaried persons. Hence they were the only ones, in some regions, who did not live under a system of autarchy. Those who were not satisfied with the revenue from land rents sought to supplement it by profitable speculation, often becoming the major dealers in cereals and the only stockbreeders who owned profitable herds. Hoping to augment their revenues, they were quite naturally led to improve their methods of cultivation. In a word, those who were not content with the rents from their farmers and *métayers*† were already firmly situated in a market economy and therefore sensitive to economic inducements; while all their neighbors were still operating in an autarchic economy in which the essential thing was to feed oneself.

Finally, agriculture being an "art of the locality," there is no new

[23]Faucher, 1962, pp. 123–134.
* A local jury that awards prizes and medals to the best farmers for their experiments and products. (Trans.)
[24]For a description of a nineteenth century agricultural *comice,* see Flaubert, *Madame Bovary.*
†Tenant farmers obligated to pay part of their rent in produce. (Trans.)

advance, no matter how well-tested elsewhere, that does not have to prove its value in each part of the country, not to mention in in each farmer's field. An innovation must be entirely acclimatized before it can be safely introduced in a particular agricultural environment. Only the squires worked on an economic margin sufficient to allow the risk each experiment entailed: to buy machinery, fertilizer, or seeds that might prove useless, to compromise the income of a field and all the work it required by attempting something that might prove disastrous. Unlike the squire, the small peasant usually did not have such a margin. If he had saved some money, he preferred to safeguard it, rather than to stake it on an agricultural investment which, unless it was in land, seemed to him to be risky. He hesitated to gamble on an experiment the crops he needed to feed his family or his animals. Only repeated success year after year could convince him to try an innovation in his turn, by which time it was no longer, properly speaking, an innovation. As we have said above, the peasant really accepts an innovation only if it is taught to him by his father along with the most traditional techniques.

Such is the sociological significance of the peripheral and innovating role of the notables. Belonging to the outside world as much as to the village, they could introduce any change they wished on their own property. If it turned out to be useless or injurious, it would not penetrate the village; if it proved to be profitable year after year, it would be integrated into the common experience before it ever reached the peasants. Furthermore, inasmuch as the notables filled a "paternal" role with regard to "their" peasants, progress was aided by the confidence that they inspired.

This entire analysis shows how difficult it was for the average peasant to be an innovator. To question the tradition inherited from one's father and accepted by one's neighbors, to be familiar with the advances achieved by scholars in the cities or by ingenious farmers in neighboring regions, to sense the need for change although it might disturb the mediocre but dependable equilibrium, to have the economic and intellectual means to risk experiment — all these circumstances were rarely combined. And if, by chance, this did occur because one peasant was richer, better educated, more imaginative, and more ambitious than his neighbors, not only they but in fact the social system as a whole could be counted on to react in such a way as to make him feel that his undertaking was improper.

When a peasant tried a new idea, he created a veritable scandal. Did he think he was cleverer than his father, shrewder than his neighbors, more educated than the notables, that he dared to do what they had not thought of doing? His act was in some way an insult to others, who were certain to respond by mockery, malevolence, and all the weapons of social control in order to make him show respect for the traditional norms of a face-to-face society. All this was intended to check his impudence, to cure him of his delusions, so that things would return to normal and everyone would be reassured of the undisputed value of tradition, which was to be preferred to any kind of progress.

Aware that he risked creating a scandal, the innovator was always careful to hide his experiment from his neighbors, not so much to be the only one to reap its benefits if it succeeded as to spare himself questions and reproaches. And it was only when the experiment was completely successful, when its results were certain and indisputable, that he dared to reveal it to others, whether as an entirely natural thing, merely a matter of course, or as a small revolution that he alone was able to undertake and carry on successfully, thanks to his "ideas," his particular methods, or his contacts with the outside (such as an engineer or a relative who had left for the city). And this placed him in exactly the same position, the same role as the notable: because he was different, marginal, he could flout tradition.

This explains why for centuries there have been excellent progressive farmers whose example was neither seen nor imitated by their neighbors. All those concerned with furthering agricultural progress relied on the proverbial "drop of oil" effect, without reflecting that, if progress really behaved like a "drop of oil," all of France would be populated with excellent farmers — since there is no district that has not had, since the eighteenth century, a good farmer, a model farm, or a school of agriculture. Still these "drops" of progress have hardly made a spot on the rural fabric.

Since one must be different from the mass to experiment with change, conversely the mass thinks that no change can be beneficial, or even possible. It is the other person, with his particular potential, who changes; it is never "I" because I do not have the same opportunities. "He" can do this because he is a rich and educated notable, or simply because he knows somebody who has taught him and has given him the financial means (subsidies, for example); but under normal circumstances — "ours" — it is out of the question.

So it can be said that in traditional society innovation was a luxury of the rich denied the average peasant. Wealth was measured in capital, not in income. An innovation was thus all the more appealing if it increased this capital, which was a mark of prestige. An example previously cited[25] illustrates this point: the farmer in the Massif Central who refused to replace his eight thin cows, who were poor milkers, by five thoroughbred animals. In this region, families are ranked on the village social scale according to the number of cows they own: five good dairy cows can provide a better income than eight worn-out hacks, but with eight a man is a "big shot," and with five he is a small timer — an important consideration if one wants to marry off a daughter. Any progress that increases the external signs of wealth is more easily accepted than another type. Thus the tractor is preferred to chemical fertilizers, despite its price and the costs it involves. René Dumont[26] tells us that in Tchad "manure is often piled up in high barrows. Explaining to the chief of a neighboring district how it might be used, I received an answer something like this: 'I am old and I will soon die. When passersby see this mound they will say to themselves that I was a great chief, for I must have owned a large herd if it could leave such a pile of manure!' The usefulness of this fertilizer as a commemorative monument had until then escaped me," concludes the disabused agronomist.

Since progress was linked to prestige and embodied by the notables and the rich class, it was natural that some peasants should want to measure themselves against these persons and share their prestige by behaving similarly. In certain regions where the squire and the notables were the recognized and accepted leaders of village society, the peasants tried to imitate them, showing confidence in them by following their example. Conversely, in regions where this paternal tutelage was endured impatiently or rejected violently, to do as well as those who

[25]Mendras, 1958, p. 15.
[26]Dumont, 1954, p. 100.

prided themselves on belonging to the elite was a way of opposing them, declaring oneself their equal, and thus denying their superiority.

From the eighteenth century on, there were proposals for making use of all members of the elite in order to hasten progress. Tocqueville[27] cites the example of a farmer who suggested having the curate read short technical agricultural treatises from the pulpit on Sunday and bestow awards on the best farmers. He concludes: "The farmers themselves, ordinarily very resistant to regulation, are led to believe that if agriculture is not improved the fault is principally the government's, because it does not give them enough advice or aid." It is remarkable how up to date this thought appears today. Clearly, the problem is not new.

The history of the nineteenth–century agricultural *comices* would furnish an excellent illustration of these mechanisms, since their chairmen were almost always notables who, with the support of the administration and the veterinary surgeon, sought to single out "good" farmers. Later, teachers filled the same role before turning it over to modern "extension agents." But there is a radical difference between these extension agents and their predecessors. Peasants followed a notable's example because they had confidence in him or acknowledged his competence. The universalistic authority of science succeeded the particularistic, personal and social authority of a "father." Of course, the *monsieur* of the old days was educated, and today one extension agent may inspire greater confidence than another, though they may be equally learned.

The peasant, a product of traditional village life, is by nature quicker to recognize the authority of science when it takes on the aspect of a social authority. Studies whose results are analyzed in the following chapters furnish excellent illustrations of the various possible combinations between these two "authorities." Moreover, the mechanism of change is essentially collective and social in nature: innovation must be integrated into the common routine of the entire village in order to be accepted. Hence a peasant is never inclined to be the only one to do something unaccustomed; on the contrary, he is carried along by his group. Extension work that is based on the assumption that it can be more effective when directed toward individuals is misguided. A

[27]Tocqueville, 1955 edition.

single individual has great difficulty in making decisions, as psychologists have shown and recent experience has confirmed. Agricultural progress has been much more rapid when it was the act of groups and institutions (e.g., C.E.T.A., experimental stations, etc.).

Ideology and politics also enter the scene and play a decisive role in the introduction of change. It is obviously no coincidence that Homais had such complete faith in science, or that a certain county-seat bourgeoisie who believed in progress took on more and more importance in the political representation of the farm regions at the end of the nineteenth century. Science can serve as a banner for social progress in its battle for power against traditional conservative elites.

Until now we have assumed that the notables filled the innovating role assigned them by their marginal position in peasant society. But it often happened that, on the contrary, they were primarily interested in keeping the society they headed as it was. More respectful of tradition than the peasants themselves, or simply neglectful of agricultural problems, they judged what had always been done to be good, and considered any new idea dangerous, whether technical, social, or political in nature. In this case, those who would have liked a share of the power, the "rising middle class," quite naturally made themselves champions of change, which they called "progress."[28]

This struggle of power- and prestige-holders with their would-be conquerors was a contest between two categories of nonpeasant notables: either aristocrats and bourgeoisie or two strata of the bourgeoisie itself. Daniel Halévy has described this transition on a national level as a passage from the "Republic of Dukes" to the "Republic of Notables."[29] It was only a reflection of the transfer of power going on in the districts, of which Roger Thabault has given a striking example in his historical account of his village of Mazières-en-Gâtine.[30] The whole history of agricultural organizations can be summed up as a long rivalry between the conservative squire and the radical deputy.[31]

The peasants took part in this struggle and were in some

[28]Yole, 1909.
[29]Halévy, 1937.
[30]Thabault, 1945.
[31]See Chapter 7 (including translator's note on "radical," p. 196).

respects its object, since the protagonists liked to think that they were "representing" or "serving" them.[32] They also tried to profit from it by lining up behind one or the other, according to his ideological tendency and his effectiveness in helping the village by bringing it various benefits. An interesting chapter of social history could be written on the way in which the peasants used their different local elites as instruments of intercession before departmental and national authorities as a function of political circumstances. This would explain the local reversals of opinion, which indicated not a change in political attitudes but a local reflection, an instrument of the political party in power which made one person seem in a better position than another to obtain favors.

In strongly hierarchical peasant societies where the nonpeasants were of little importance, the battle could be joined between the two upper social strata of "big shots": for example, an aristocracy of old peasant families and a group of average peasants recently become wealthy. Some regions did not witness a marked stratification; there were rich peasants and poor ones, with no deep social cleavage between them. The struggle for power thus set rival families against each other, together with their relatives and connections.

To simplify the analysis, let us assume that the power that a traditional and traditionalist aristocracy has held for several generations is being disputed by a group of "upstarts," or *"arrivants,"* (newcomers), as Jean Yole calls them. A technical innovation will probably find a readier welcome among this group than among the former, and once accepted by one group it will inevitably be discredited by the other. If it is accompanied by some advantage (some kind of subsidy or aid), and if it can be expected to be profitable, the members of the rising elite will naturally have an interest in helping their relatives and friends to profit from it. In welcoming the innovation, they will automatically declare themselves part of the clan of "progressives," while the reactionary clique will inevitably regard the innovation with the same scorn that their leaders feel for any change.

Any technical innovation, and progress in general, takes on political significance as it enters into the play of village rivalries. Though neutral to the expert and the economist, a technique

[32]Neufbourg, 1945.

becomes a political stake when it penetrates the village. It is good or bad according to who accepts or rejects it. Moreover, it is transformed into a powerful instrument for reinforcing a clique's loyalty, an ideological symbol that gives grounds for hurling imprecations at "obscurantist reactionaries who want to maintain the peasantry in its miserable subjection;" or, quite the opposite, for blasting "the irresponsible leaders who want to win the favor of the people by turning them away from their ancestral traditions." In this manner, in Africa, coffee becomes "white" and cotton "black;"[33] in France the unions were white and the cooperatives red; and we shall see below how a strain of corn can seem to some people a vehicle of clericalism and American imperialism.

This politicizing mechanism of technical progress can be seen in all peasant societies, and, no doubt, elsewhere. William M. Williams has given an excellent description of it in the Welsh village of Gosforth.[34] There the gentry have tried in vain to oppose modernizing farmers as they equip and enrich themselves and mock the "gentlemen" who cannot keep up their estates but think they are important because they hold all the club presidencies.

In former colonial countries, Western civilization as a whole was linked to technology to form a symbol of social struggle. Often the group on top, being in contact with the colonizers, initiated technical and social "progress." And naturally the rival group was scandalized by this Westernization and the abandonment of tribal, local, or national traditions. McKim Marriott has given an excellent description of this situation in India. In the villages studied, the Brahman caste was Westernized and urbanized to the point of abandoning a portion of its power in the village to the caste immediately below. The latter established its authority by redoubling religious austerity and social traditionalism to the point of borrowing the distinctive behavior of the Brahman caste.[35] This situation is not the most common in the third world; often literate people who have gone to Western schools are opposed to traditional chiefs in the farm regions, just as the farmers of Gosforth oppose the gentry. But it shows clearly that in the restricted face-to-face society of a village the roles can be

[33]Dampierre, 1960.
[34]Williams, 1956.
[35]Marriott, 1955.

reversed without changing either the meaning or the rules of the game; this is true in the most widely different climates and civilizations.

In the majority of traditional peasant societies, prestige is measured by two standards: the degree of conformity to tradition and wealth in capital. It has been sufficiently demonstrated above, in connection with technical innovations, that every effort toward change imperiled the peasant's prestige and position; and that only maximum prestige, surpassing in some way the village standards of measurement, permitted the notables to increase their prestige and authority by experiments that would have discredited the most respected peasant.

And so it is with all things. It is in embodying the traditional values as best he can that a person increases or maintains his authority in traditional societies — which does not mean that in some regions a certain form of deviance, an independence of spirit and behavior, cannot also attract respect and esteem. However, the prestige of the nonconformist is never as great as that of the conformist. Moreover, since the individual's position and reputation are normally derived largely from his family, he is judged by all the known members of the family: those who are living, who belong to several generations, and the dead who live in the memory of the village. The total position of an individual, his status, combines many more assigned than acquired positions. Consequently the individual is hardly able to modify the expectations of others, nor does he desire to.

Born into a conservative family, he will be conservative because others expect it of him and because every attempt on his part to escape his assigned role would meet with lively resistance on the part of the entire community. His whole life is passed in conforming to other people's image of him, according to his situation in the village. The son of a nonconformist family must himself be a nonconformist, and every effort on his part to become conformist meets with the incredulity, indeed the mockery, of the village. Thus he is obliged to be his father's son.

It is the same for the good farmer, the hard worker — or, conversely, the idler. If the individual comes up against so many obstacle to modifying his position, it is natural that most of the time he will accept the idea of faithfully filling the roles it entails. This rapid analysis suffices to show that the whole system of social control tends to dissuade the farmer from trying changes, which, as we have seen, always seem to him to be hazardous from a technical point of view.

While respect for tradition assured prestige, prestige was largely founded on the possession of capital, particularly landed capital. In a society of peasant landholders, the size of the estate determined the family position, and the social scale coincided quite closely with that of property ownership — or, to a lesser degree, with that of the land under cultivation by tenants, farmers, or *métayers*. Once the material subsistence needs were satisfied, every surplus in production was to be turned into capital, either in money or land or livestock.

The income was hoarded or invested, not spent. Consumption was not admired, and to spend too much was looked upon with disapproval, except on such rare occasions of conspicuous consumption as weddings. Even on these occasions a man sought to show his wealth, his capital, rather than his income. He would use his savings, i.e., his capital, to provide a beautiful wedding. In fact, in an autarchic economic system the very notion of income has no significance, since one consumes what one produces.

Money is normally considered a form of capital rather than a medium of exchange. Indeed, we can say it is a substitute for land and, like land, it is highly prized and relatively rare, since transactions are very infrequent. Thus one can say that money was all the more valuable in the eyes of the peasants because it was not very useful to them as an instrument of exchange. Under these conditions, increase in income could not be an indicator of economic activity.

Man worked in order to live, and if he contemplated working harder or better it was above all in order to be able to save money and increase his capital. Now the link between a particular task and the increase in *capital* is singularly indirect and uncertain, whereas *income* is more directly linked with the task — in the form of salary, for instance. Consequently, in an autarchic and relatively stable society, the individual has no reason to change his system of production since he has not, properly speaking, an "economic motivation." If demographic pressure increases, he clears the land, cultivates it more intensively, eats less well, or he moves elsewhere; but he does not seek to modify the system of cultivation.

The middle class and the nobles were the only ones who were sensitive to the economic argument because they were situated partially outside the peasant autarchy, which knew yet another intruder: taxes. The increase in seigneurial taxes at the end of the eighteenth century was certainly one of the causes of the introduction of commercial production into subsistence polycultivation, for example, the mulberry and the silkworm in the Midi near Languedoc or the madder in the Comtat Venaissin. Through these two subterfuges, the economic argument penetrated traditional peasant societies, where the economic agent had no economic choice, just as he had no choice of techniques.

The absence of choice at this level and in this sector of life is clearly a fundamental characteristic of these societies. A balanced system of cultivation and an autarchic economy need never be questioned by the farmer. They are for him basic facts comparable to the facts of nature, which he can sort out and make use of more or less effectively but would not dream of modifying. The transformations which do slowly come about are the result not of individual decisions but of a long social process which puts into play numerous collective mechanisms that function without full awareness on the part of individuals.

Both society, which is slow to change, and personality, which is more concerned with constancy than with flexibility and adaptation, find themselves disoriented when they must fit into the rhythm of an industrial society in rapid transition. Institutions and social and psychological mechanisms must be modified, personality structure reorganized. But these transformations are always very slow to happen; today in France the two societies exist side by side and the peasantry must pass from one to the other in a few years. Those who have been formed in the traditional world find themselves entirely disoriented by this and see only dangers and uncertainties beyond the beaten path of their fathers. To get out of the rut is to plunge into adventure without feeling armed to pursue it.

2. Work, Time, and the Land

The traditional peasant tilled the field he had inherited and learned to cultivate from his father. He knew all the most minute details of this field: the composition and depth of the arable layer, which often varied from place to place; its rocks, humidity, exposure, relief, and so on. The result of long years of apprenticeship, work, and observation, this knowledge, which he alone possessed, was the basis of his skill as a farmer. Moreover, he felt as if he had "made" his field and knew it as the creator knows his creation, since this soil was the product of his constant care: plowing, fertilizing, rotating crops, maintenance of fallow ground, and so on. Without going into the sentimental ties that bind the peasant to his land, let us merely point out here how important this personal knowledge of the field is to the peasant's skill: if he is the only one who is thoroughly familiar with his field, he is also the only one who can cultivate it properly; consequently, nobody else can help him do so.

If he acquires a new field he will have to go through a new apprenticeship, lengthy and delicate. Getting to know this new acquisition well brings into play a whole set of attitudes and psychological mechanisms: a man knows both the good qualities and the faults of what he owns, while he overestimates those of what he desires. This explains the serious obstacles involved in land consolidation among small landholders.[1]

This attitude, perhaps exaggerated but well-founded, obviously results in a refusal to believe that one can possibly know the chemical, biological, and physical characteristics of a particular soil merely through scientific methods of soil analysis. Merely on the basis of a few soil samples, an expert who has never seen the field undertakes to measure its "possibilities" and suggest improvements — in other words, to know the land better than the man who has prepared and cultivated it since his youth. One cannot imagine a more radical contrast between particularistic empirical knowledge and universalistic scientific knowledge.

Moreover, the diversified influence of microclimates combines with the peculiarities of the soil to individualize each piece of land. Though one can take samples of the earth, it is more difficult to keep meteorological records for each plot of land, as they would have to

[1] Coutin, 1953.

cover many years in order to be valid. Empirical knowledge, inherited from his father and supplemented by years of observation, here gives the peasant a skill that is difficult to replace. He alone knows that a certain field, seemingly well exposed, is really cold, or that a certain pasture, though quickly dried out in the summer, furnishes excellent grass very early in the spring, and so on.

Aware of the infinite diversity that characterizes the French countryside, the ancient agronomists taught that agriculture is an "art of the locality" and that the data established scientifically must always be minutely controlled and adapted to the characteristics of the site. In so doing, they were only translating into rational terms the deep sentiment of the peasants, whom they knew well and from whom they inherited a large part of their "science."

The idea that each bit of ground is unique and that intimate personal knowledge of it is the first requirement of cultivation remains a limitation that modern science cannot completely eliminate. And it is natural that the peasant, brought up traditionally, tends to overestimate this uniqueness and give more credit to his knowledge than to the precise data with which the expert can furnish him. This attitude is further strengthened by his sentimental attachment to his property, for what one loves is always unique. The peasant's love of his land is a hackneyed literary theme that does not easily lend itself to sociological or psychological analysis.

All agrarian civilizations have assigned a high value to the land, believing it could not be compared with other possessions. Whether it was a gift of God or an embodiment of the group, it had only one equal: woman. All the sexual symbolism attached to the land reinforces the analogy. It would be tempting to draw parallels between the feminine qualities attributed to the land and the economic talents expected of women in different rural societies. Perhaps we would find that the more the land is treated as a factor of production, the more are women's sentimental and "feminine" qualities valued, and vice versa.

Ancient Mesopotamian law[2] had codified this personification of the land as a heritage that was inextricably tied to its possessor. It was in some way a bond of kinship that no one had the right to break; the land was like a member of the family. If exceptional circum-

[2]Cassin, 1952.

stances necessitated transferring ownership of a piece of land, a legal stratagem was used to avoid violating the principle or breaking the bond: a clod of earth from the field was thrown into a stream, and as it dissolved the field was made symbolically to disappear. Thus the purchaser took possession of virgin land, which, fictitiously, had belonged to nobody.

Historians, geographers, and anthropologists have pointed out the differences among civilizations that they have encountered. According to Redfield, who gives a classic description of the ideal peasant type, it is characteristic of peasants the world over to attribute a sentimental and mystical value to the land.[3] The one exception is the Mediterranean peasant, whether he be of Latin,[4] Greek,[5] or Arabic origin. According to Jacques Weulersse:

Syrian land has been given neither love nor labor. The *fellah* cultivates it, of course, but reluctantly; and he can not make it provide more than the immediate necessities of life. He works for himself and not for his land; he does not feel that the land exceeds and extend him ... As a matter of fact, few peasant populations manifest such a weak feeling for the land, such a paradoxical scorn for things of the earth.[6]

And as Pitt-Rivers sees it, "the absence of a mystical attitude toward the land betrays the system of values of a population which lives in the city, from which it goes out to cultivate the land without any real love for it."[7] Thus it could be said that the urbanized farmer of the Mediterranean regions already has the rational and economic view of his field that the accountant and the economist seek to inculcate in modern farmers: it is capital, a means of production, and nothing more.

In most French regions the farmers are still, from this point of view, "real" peasants. The sentiments that tie them to their land have until now been the subject of only one pilot study of a limited region: the reader will find below its hypotheses and major conclusions.[8] It is enough to point out here how impossible it is to isolate the land from its entire natural setting, human and social. For the farmer the word "land" evokes simultaneously the soil he works, the farm that has supported his family for generations, and

[3] Redfield, 1956, p. 112.
[4] Banfield, 1958.
[5] Mendras, 1961; Friedl, 1962.
[6] Weulersse, 1946, p. 173.
[7] Pitt-Rivers, 1954, p. 47.
[8] See Appendix 2, No. 6.

the profession he follows, as well as the peasant condition and the whole body of the nation's farmers. During an interview he jumps from one meaning to another without seeming to realize that these meanings are separate and distinct; and at the same time he says repeatedly that the sentiments evoked by this word are ineffable, that they exist but cannot be expressed. To make them understood, he calls on the interviewer's experience: "If you're from the country, you know what I mean."

On the other hand, a big farmer from the Paris basin can refuse to purchase the fields he works because it is economically more advantageous for him to rent them and invest his capital in livestock and machinery. During an interview, his "economic rationality" is visibly in conflict with his "peasant sentiments," as when he seeks to justify his refusal to buy his land by showing his contempt for it: "It's a poor piece of land where a man wouldn't want to settle his family." Or again, by reducing it to nothing: "This piece of land is like any other . . . nowadays the land doesn't count any more. . . ." To reduce to naught or curse the land one refuses to own betrays sentiments similar to those the "peasant" feels but refuses to express. However, other farmers are able to analyze the origin of these sentiments, if not their content, in astonishingly lucid terms: "To know one's land, to improve it, takes a long time! And the more you know it, the more you become attached to it." Such statements, almost evangelical in tone, are an admission of the fact that sentiment and ownership go together: "What belongs, belongs . . . a peasant is a proprietor of the land . . . .When a man is a proprietor, he has a feeling and a concern for the land." As opposed to the big farmer, and contrary to all economic analysis, a small proprietor can state: "Rented land is expensive and amounts to nothing."

Thus the peasant has a deep conviction that his field is unique because he is the only one to know it, to love it, and to own it: knowledge, love, and possession are inseparable. And even when the farmer behaves in a rational economic fashion with respect to land as capital, his feelings for the soil are no less diffuse or deep; he identifies it intimately with his family and his profession, thus with himself. It can be said that these feelings are largely the product of a historical situation that is on the way to extinction, and that they will outlive it by some years. Moreover, they are already disparaged by the ideology that the new generation is fashioning for itself. Young people think that the cultivators should be relieved of land ownership, and that the latter should be considered solely as a factor of production, by farmers as well as by public authorities and capitalists.[9]

Traditional agricultural economics made land the essential form of capital and the one sure source of wealth. In agricultural systems based on vegetable production, animal breeding was often a luxury and the means of production were reduced to one team and sometimes even to a few implements. As a result, a farm was above all an area to be cultivated, a piece of land, as the language clearly shows: *terre* (land), *domaine* (domain), *héritage* (estate), and *exploitation* (farm) were synonymous. In a self-sufficient economy, agricultural production served to feed the people and only surpluses were sold to pay taxes and seigneurial duties and to procure the few commodities and services that were not to be found in the village. It was important only to produce, not to sell. The result, obviously, was that the possession of land was the basis of the social hierarchy and the sign of prestige.

Moreover, all of agrarian history can be analyzed as a struggle on the part of the peasantry for total possession of the land through liberation from seigneurial taxes and collective obligations. This liberation was accomplished legally by the Revolution, but it began in the Middle Ages with the struggles of peasant communities to break feudal ties, and continued throughout the nineteenth century and up to the present day with the parceling of the great noble and bourgeois estates and their repurchase by independent farmers and owners of neighboring estates. Under the legal and economic system of the past, the farmer was assured of the survival of his farm, and therefore of his family, only if he owned the land. Furthermore, history had taught him that ownership of the soil was the necessary condition of complete social and political independence. Whoever worked someone else's soil was always, in one way or another, the debtor — indeed, the servant — of the owner.

In a word, the entire technical, economic, social, legal, and political system gave high value to the land and made it a unique asset, without equal. It is clear that the working of a piece of land without a break from father to son enhanced its value further and gave it a personal and sentimental tinge. However, this "sentimental" aspect is

[9]See Chapter 7; Tavernier, 1966; and Debatisse, 1963.

probably secondary, while its social foundations are primary; the disappearance of the latter will bring about that of the former. Opposed to the whole traditional current of thought, this hypothesis can be easily put to the test by psychological and sociological studies, as new social and legal structures adapted to new technical and economic conditions spread into more "peasant" regions. On the other hand, the young generation of farmers, as it grows older, will perhaps tend to compromise between its new rational economic ideology and that of its ancestors. If it is true that liking and attachment come with age, and if the new legal and economic system that young people are hopefully seeking holds disappointments in store, many of those who claim not to feel these traces of sentiment for the land are likely to find some meaning tomorrow in the attachment they reject so brutally today.

In order to make more fruitful the land he considers unique, the peasant employs traditional techniques that are organized into a system of cultivation and technology tried and proven by generations of his ancestors. At the same time that his father taught him about his field, he taught him his ways and his techniques. In certain regions the agricultural system attained its equilibrium and a high degree of perfection toward the end of the Middle Ages. The introduction of plants from the New World served only to complete and refine it, without modifying either its economy or its logic.

At the heart of a complex system gradually formulated over the centuries and constantly under improvement, the interdependence of different techniques is particularly delicate. Moreover, there are structured, reciprocal ties that link the agronomical knowledge of a society with the implements and techniques at its disposal, its natural environment, and the structures of this society itself. Agronomists and geographers have described numerous systems of cultivation and have singled out this idea and defined it as "a combination of crop cultivation and animal breeding, a manner of working the land, and a combination of farm equipment forming such a complementary whole that an overall average of resources is assured each year, and each element of the system is linked with the others by reciprocal relations."[10]

Crop rotation has been the fundamental element of this combina-

[10]George, 1956, pp. 70–84.

tion since the disappearance of different forms of temporary cultivation and fallowing. Where these remain they are anachronisms, or responses to a very special natural environment. The rotation of crops makes it possible to avoid wearing out the soil, by alternating cleansing cultivated plants with nitrogen-fixing and forage crops. A free choice of plants and the possibility of lengthening or shortening the cycle give a certain flexibility to crop rotation, but it must nevertheless respect the basic rhythm needed to conserve the fertility of the soil.

The improvement of crop rotation and the disappearance of fallow land have been the great agronomical triumphs of the past two centuries. Advances in pedology and chemistry will now permit the farmer to escape from this restriction and to cultivate the same plant on the same soil for several years in a row by furnishing the soil, through chemical fertilizers, with the elements on which the plant thrives. The modern farmer who, using enormous machines and refined fertilizers, produces corn on the same soil year after year without having to combine it with any other cultivation or stockbreeding, reminds us curiously of the Indian peasant who, with the aid of his planting stick, plants his corn each year in a portion of the forest where the weeds have been newly burned out. Cultivation no longer moves about and the burning out of weeds has been replaced by fertilizers, but the relation between man and the soil still remains one of repetitive monocultivation. By contrast, the family polyproducer works on different plots, skillfully combined into one crop rotation, which is itself integrated into a system of cultivation. Hence the advances of modern agronomy contradict the perfecting of peasant agriculture.

The same turn of events can be seen in the relationships between cultivation and animal breeding. Relatively independent in ancient agricultural systems, they have been closely linked by agronomy in recent centuries. In the past, in most regions of France (and today in parts of the country using archaic systems of production), sheep, goats and cows were usually raised in great herds; these grazed on vast pasture land independent of small peasant farms, which were devoted essentially to vegetable production and the raising of small animals such as poultry and hogs. On these small farms, draft animals often accounted for most of the large livestock; when the cows were harnessed, draft and milch animals became indistinguishable. Small flocks of sheep and goats wandered along the roads and in the uncultivated spaces, the pastures or the fallow land, and there were continual disputes between breeders and farmers.[11]

For the past century, agricultural progress has resulted in large part from the fact that animal breeding has been gradually introduced into these farms and integrated into their system of cultivation. Dairy cows yielded their function as draft animals to oxen and horses, and later to tractors; they consume the artificial fodder grown on the fields, to which they in turn furnish fertilization by their manure. The current trend, which consists in integrating the natural meadows into a very long crop rotation, is the final outcome of this evolution. At the same time, better transport facilities, improved agronomic methods, and bookkeeping systems have again caused a tendency to confine intensive cultivation to the best acreage, beef and dairy production to stables and meadows (along with stock pens), and the breeding of stock to the pastures.

The whole art of the good peasant consisted in operating within as wide a range of cultivation and animal rearing as possible, integrating these into a system in which the byproducts of each could be utilized to the maximum for the others; and which, through diversified speculation, furnished security against inclement weather and uncertain harvests. Thus the efforts of successive generations of cultivation were in contradiction with the feeling that every change risked disturbing the established equilibrium, that it was hazardous to introduce the slightest innovation, since it might upset rather than improve that equilibrium.

It has long been observed that time does not have the same value in the country as in the city. Gulliver had difficulty explaining the usefulness of his watch to the Lilliputians, and since he said that he undertook nothing without consulting it, they concluded that it was his God. The ritual of the time clock at the entrance and exit of a factory could probably lead a modern Usbek to the same observation. In fact, the temporal frameworks in which the farmer lives, thinks, and makes decisions are not only imposed on him by natural cycles and atmospheric conditions; they are also, and perhaps principally,

[11]See Sclafert, 1959, *passim* and pp. 167–180.

the heritage of traditional civilizations.[12] It is not our task here to determine in what measure nature has imposed its own time on these civilizations, nor how they have been able to mold it to their needs, but simply to point out the dominant characteristics of time and duration in French peasant societies, in order to clarify certain attitudes of contemporary farmers.

Before the advent of the clock in rural regions, the principal instrument for the measurement of time was the calendar, which fixed the essential dates of the agricultural and the religious year, often somewhat confused. In their study of ancient religious and magical calendars, Hubert and Mauss were able to single out certain essential characteristics of the representation of time in traditional societies.[13]

These ancient calendars do not measure time as do modern ones, which divide the year into months and days of equal length. They impart a "rhythm" to the year by interrupting its continuity with festivals and crucial dates. As a result, time is at least as much a qualitative notion as a quantitative one: its parts are not indefinitely divisible into units of equal size. Each subdivison, extending between two festivals or two dates, is conceived as a whole that has its own unique existence and that consequently cannot be cut up into smaller units. These subdivisions can be considered as alike even if they have clearly different duration; thus quantitatively unequal durations are perceived and experienced as equal, and conversely, equal durations are experienced as unequal. "*Tasuait, tasuait*" ("the moment is a moment"), says the Kabyle peasant; in other words, each unit of time is an indivisible block in juxtaposition to others.[14]

One cannot go so far as to say, however, that time is not a quantity, only that it is not a *pure* quantity, homogeneous in all its parts, always uniform and exactly measurable. In making judgments about time, there are considerations other than capacity, opportunity, continuity, constancy, similarity. Units of time are not units of measure but units of a rhythm in which the alternation of diverse elements leads periodically to the same thing. In a word, the calendar is "the code of time's qualities." The principal functions of ancient almanacs was to indicate the auspicious and inauspicious days, the periods most propitious for certain enterprises, the moment when a certain plant

[12]Friedmann, 1966, pp. 22–25; Febvre, 1942, pp. 426–434; Gurvitch, 1958; and Evans-Pritchard, 1940, pp. 94–108.
[13]Hubert and Mauss, 1929.
[14]Bourdieu, 1963, p. 59.

must be sown to assure a good crop, the day when laundry must be done if it was to be good and white, and so on. The fact that each day was designated by the name of a saint undoubtedly contributed to the tendency to individualize and personalize it in some way. It had its own life and a unique identity: St. John's Day was not at all the same as St. Martin's or St. Nicholas' Day.[15]

In other words, one could say that time was less an abstract notion capable of giving dimension to human life than a series of experiences undergone. And for the farmer, whose work is directed by the seasons and atmospheric conditions, the spread of modern calendars and the notion of time they convey has not replaced the ancient idea. In autumn we plow and in summer we harvest, but since the season can be "early" or "late" we don't do the same work at the same time for two years running. While in a certain region all the sowing must normally be completed by All Saints' Day, in some years it continues past St. Martin's Day, either because the harvest was begun late or because it was too damp (or too dry) to go into the fields at the usual time. Thus time as experienced is never completely synchronized with calendar time. The proof of this is that the dates which limit these units (particularly the dates of transfer of rental premises) have varied from region to region and were especially variable in the wooded regions. Naturally the introduction of new techniques (the threshing machine, for instance) has led to the modification of some of these dates.[16]

For that matter, what is the exact meaning of the word "season"? Certainly the four seasons have importance in breaking up the peasant year. But the season is also the state of development of the vegetation: we often designate the different periods of work by this word. Yet the sowing season, the haytime, the harvest-time — to cite only the most clearly defined — do not have the same duration from year to year, nor from region to region, nor even from farm to farm. They vary with atmospheric conditions and the system of cultivation. Indeed, they tend to form indivisible units, unequal in length but perceived as equal in value. In the end, then, the season means its product, i.e., the crop, and men generally say that it has been a "good year" or a "good season."

The salary of farmhands and day laborers is probably the best

[15]Rivière and Maget, 1943.
[16]Maget, 1942.

index of the value assigned to time by agricultural practices
of former days. It is one of the rare cases in which money, a uniform
quantity, has served to "measure" time, which is a variable unit. The
salary of a seasonal worker who hired out for the summer from St.
John's Day to All Saints' Day was almost as high as the salary of the
man hired by the year. The four summer months had almost the same
"value" as the entire year. The day laborers were well aware of this,
for they remained unemployed all winter and had only one hundred
or one hundred fifty days of employment per year. In some respect,
then, work was the measure of time.

The study of agricultural calendars[17] reveals both a jumble of
rhythms that obliterates solar months and the importance of lunar
cycles, which serve to make this time scale complete. Only detailed
studies will enlighten us on the relations among these different units
and rhythms, and how they are perceived and experienced in each
rural society in France.

The week is probably the best-established unit and the one most
often experienced as such, especially if Sunday is different from the
other days. In regions where religious observance is widespread,
the social life of the entire week is organized around the Sunday
Mass — especially in districts in which homes are far apart, where
it is the principal occasion for leaving the farm and meeting
one's neighbors. Elsewhere Sunday is the day of rest, which is
enough to distinguish it in societies entirely work-oriented, even
though, in animal-breeding country, the daily care that animals
require does not always permit a completely different use of time on
Sundays than on other days. Today the penetration of "leisure time
activity" into country life tends to give a proper value again to
Sundays. It is no longer simply the day of no work and renewed
social contacts; it is becoming the day when people do something to
distract themselves. While true for men and especially for young
people, this observation is much less apt for women. Their household
tasks are often made heavier by the need to prepare a better Sunday
meal, by the accumulation of tasks considered restful (for example,
mending) and occasionally by going to Mass and helping the men
with their chores. Nevertheless, for them also, Sunday is different

[17]Many local studies, notably by geographers, include analyses of the
calendar of farm chores.

and strongly marks the weekly rhythm.

Despite this apparent regularity (six days and Sunday) the week could not be an unvarying unit since it is composed of days, units of duration which vary essentially in relation to the length of the solar day and the total work to be accomplished. One sleeps much longer in winter than in summer, and the hours of intense summer work contrast with the relative inactivity of winter. It used to be impossible to work at night in the fields; for, according to the Greek proverb, "the dawn laughs to see the work done at night." The rising and setting of the sun are today no longer the inevitable limits of the outdoor day; the day can be extended far into the night, thanks to the headlights of the tractors and harvester-threshers. And indoors, in the days when one had to economize on the feeble available means of illumination, the glimmer of the firelight gave the farmer only enough light to occupy his long winter evenings with conversation, weaving baskets, hollowing out wooden shoes, or shelling chestnuts. Nowadays electricity makes all inside work possible, in the stables as well as in the house, in winter as in summer. Thus technical progress tends to accentuate the natural and traditional inequality of the daily rhythm by prolonging the long summer days without increasing the number of chores to be done during the short winter days.

Moreover, this rhythm is neither regular nor predictable, since the work is dictated by atmospheric conditions. Depending on the state of the sky, one autumn day can be as different from the previous one as from a winter or summer day. If the ground permits and the season is drawing on, the farmer will spend more time plowing than he normally spends harvesting in the summer. On the other hand, if he cannot go out into his fields, he will be reduced to chopping firewood or repairing his tools. A day in a particular month in a particular season can in one year represent sixteen hours of plowing and in the next year six or eight hours of odd jobs or care of the animals.

Despite its extreme variability, the day remains a "unit" because it extends between two nights. The basic ambiguity of this always-variable unit of value should be thoroughly examined; a study of its subdivisions would surely be helpful. In many regions, the winter day is divided in two and the summer day in four parts: the snack at ten o'clock and four o'clock is a summer custom for breaking up a day which is inordinately long. In regions where each half-day normally includes its share of tasks on the farm and in the fields, the subdivision of days into quarters separated by meals is symmetrical with reference to the break for lunch at noon: the quarters are (1) care of the animals, snack; (2) work in the fields, lunch; (3) work in the fields, snack; (4) care of the animals. These subdivisions are variable according to the time of year and depend on the daily unit, which gives them their value with respect to the season and the work. For women, the difference between morning and evening is more marked.[18] Except during the summer, when they have to go out and help their men in the fields, the morning is always devoted to unchanging daily tasks: feeding the animals, preparing the children for school, housekeeping, and cooking. The afternoon, on the contrary, is a "free" time in the sense that it is employed in a weekly task which changes from day to day: laundry, ironing, and so on. Moreover, the daily schedule can be adjusted, which gives the woman a feeling of choice and hence a sort of "freedom." Although the weekly order is rarely violated, doing the laundry, ironing, gardening, and watching the herds introduce into the daily schedule a variety to which women prove very sensitive, according to Marie-Thérèse de la Rivière.

A survey made by the French Institute of Public Opinion (I.F.O.P.) among the rural population shows that women have the feeling of being subjected to the pressure of time to a greater degree than do men, while the opposite is true in the city.[19] In fact, women's tasks are more numerous, more limited, and more subject to deadlines that mark the rhythm of every moment of the day: the men want their coffee, the children have to get off to school on time, the meals must be ready on schedule, there are dishes to be washed before starting something else, the children come home from school, etc. Rural women also seem to be less cut off from the outside world than men, who are entirely absorbed in their work in the fields. Hence they are naturally more in contact with the "urban" concept of time.

This analysis, though brief, is enough to show the complexity of the temporal rhythm that presides over the life of polycultivating farm families, but we must not overlook more specialized activities. It is clear that the winegrower lives within a framework of "linear" time, closer to that of the cities. But what can be said of those who rear

[18]De la Rivière, 1961; Appendix 2, No. 27; Girard and Bastide, 1959.
[19]*Sondages,* 1953.

animals, and particularly of herdsmen? What concept of time does
the shepherd have, who brings his flock back to the sheepfold every
evening? Or the shepherd who spends many solitary months in
the mountains, moving his grazing sheep from pasture to pasture?

As mechanization became general, the concept of technological
and urban time invaded agricultural work and introduced into it
the new unit of the hour. This concept came first with the
threshing contractor, who asked to be paid by the hour; soon the
farmer who came with his machine to plow his neighbor's field did
the same; and today young farmers, mindful of how profitable their
tractors or harvester-threshers can be, keep a notebook in which they
carefully record their hours of work and the liters of fuel burned.
For the first time abstract time, made up of equal units, has entered
into agricultural work. It is tending gradually to modify the time
scale of an ever-increasing number of tasks. Though the process
of replacing one concept of time by another can be seen through
many easily-measurable indices and hence can be observed by the
sociologist with exceptional clarity, no study has yet been
conducted on this subject.

Hourly time already existed in country life. Every farm kitchen
displayed proudly a clock with a long pendulum, and most of the
farmers had pocket watches. According to the French Institute of
Public Opinion, 47 percent of farmers did not carry a watch on their
persons in 1953 (compared with 34 percent of the population as a
whole).[20] In dail life these instruments served to indicate the
progress of the day more than to fix the time exactly or indicate the
beginning or end of some activity. Witness to an external civilization,
they were employed to "tell time" only when in contact with this
civilization, when one must be "on time": to send the children to
school, to catch the train or bus, to attend a meeting. And in the
latter case, if it was an appointment with neighbors or other country
people, everyone knew it was not necessary to be punctual.

Today, on the contrary, as meetings become more frequent all the
time, young people particularly want them to start punctually in
order not to "lose time"; this is one of the indices which reveal the
passage from the peasant to the modern concept of time. In the
past, since the means of transportation were slow, people would go to
town for the day or half a day if they had a meeting. The meeting

[20]*Ibid.*

began when everyone had arrived at the city hall, the cooperative, or the school. People took advantage of the trip to do other errands or to chat with each other. Now they take the car or the motorbike in order to arrive in time for the meeting and leave immediately afterward if work is pressing. This change in customs was surprising to the rural researcher who went from a French village to an American one in 1950;[21] today it can be observed in every French village.

One must not, however, conclude from our analysis that this concept of "flowing, dreamy" time,[22] vague and slow-moving, was of no value whatever. Just as the Mediterranean peoples, in particular the Greeks, like to "while away the time," so too Mexican peasants are always ready to put off till tomorrow what they can avoid doing today. Most French peasants, on the contrary, do not allow them-selves to waste time. Time is so closely connected with the work experience that wasted time is wasted work; it is laziness to put off till tomorrow what one can do today. These two examples suffice to show how dangerous it would be to settle for a simplistic contrast between two extreme types. In each civilization the notion of time is closely linked to the system of values and the organization of daily life. In France we would have to undertake a study, region by region, to try to explain why some have rapidly accepted certain elements of modern time and others have proved more resistant.

Psychologists have demonstrated how closely the representation of time is linked to that of space.[23] In agricultural work the relation between these two dimensions is particularly evident. Ancient measures of surface area bear witness to this: the *journal* corresponded to the area one man could plow in one day (*journée*). Similarly, the estimate of distances was usually made in time: it is a two-hour walk to the village, or barely an hour by carriage. Curiously, the introduc-tion of modern technology has perpetuated this custom, since labor contractors compute their charges in tractor or harvester-thresher hours rather than in the number of acres plowed or harvested. When it was not measured in amount of time worked, space was

[21]Mendras, 1953, p. 135.
[22]Febvre, 1942, p. 426.
[23]Fraisse, 1957; Piaget, 1946.

measured in amount of work completed, for example in the quantity of seed used: the *sétérée* corresponded to the area sown with one *sétier** of seed. Even today the peasant familiar with metric measure usually refers to his work experience to evaluate the capacity of his field: "This meadow must be about one hectare, since I put in ten *doubles* (decaliters) of fertilizer."

The result is that space is not conceived, any more than is time, as an abstract area infinitely divisible into universal units. It is always a real and particular expanse perceived through a repeated work experience. This explains why the value of the *journal* or the *sétérée* varied from village to village in relation to the methods and customs of cultivation and the quality of the land. To illustrate, one does not plow the same quantity of land in one day by the swing plow as by the plow cart or spade; with the swing plow one does not plow the same area of heavy earth as of light earth; finally, in certain regions, some fields are sowed densely (more than ninety pounds of seed an acre) and others sparsely.

There are cases where space is measured in time, others where it is measured by the amount of work, still others where time itself is measured by the work. Logical empirical relations among these three "dimensions" of daily life exist in the experience of farmers in a given region. It seems to be well established that work was the principal measuring instrument which generally gave value to time and space.

Here we touch on the basic difference from the organization of factory work, where the arbitrarily fixed time schedule determines the beginning and the end of work periods. These in turn are divided into unvarying units: hours, minutes, and eight-hour days interrupted by lunch and rest periods in the shop. In the field, on the other hand, it is the task to be completed which determines the time schedule, always variable according to the progress of the work, the state of the sky, and occasionally even the fatigue of the worker. The farm worker, when he is the head of the farm, is master of his time: he fixes his own time schedule and work rhythm.

This freedom is predicated on weather and the work to be accomplished, and the choice is not made consciously and rationally

* Ancient unit of measure for corn, approximately two-fifths of a liter. (Trans.)

each day. A piece of work begun the night before must be pursued the following morning, and tasks naturally follow one another, according to an order dictated as much by nature as by habit. Each year a particular field is mowed after a certain other field, with no attempt to determine the maturity of the grass: "We always do it that way." And the beginning of harvest time or the haymaking or the sowing season is often a matter of collective behavior.

In communities of the past, a proclamation was made by the village assembly and all the farmers went out into their meadows, their cornfields, or their plowed lands on the same day. Today these community rules are no longer observed, but in some cases the habits acquired have survived them from generation to generation. In many villages, one can still see all the harvesters attack their cornfields on the same day, without prior agreement. Often community rivalry produces the same effect: as soon as the season starts, a real contest ensues among families, and the winner is the one who "works the hardest" and is ahead of the others. To be behind is to be criticized for laziness. Thus each year one family, almost always the same one, determines the timetable for the whole village by beginning every job first. This initiator role can fall to that family because of the situation of its fields, which makes them ready to harvest earlier than others, or because its social situation allows it to "set the pace" for the life of the village: "The Martins took out the binder this morning; we'll be behind if we don't finish the haying soon."

Thus during long periods, particularly when the work is pressing, the farmer, although master of his use of time, is in fact subject to a habitual schedule which he obeys as rigidly as if he were not the master at all. On the other hand, at moments of reduced pressure or relative inactivity, the farmer deeply feels his freedom of choice. In order to keep busy, he can spend more time in grooming and feeding the animals; he can take time and trouble in fixing a tool-handle or repairing his wagon; he can chop wood, trim his hedges, or clean out his irrigation ditches. We have already noted in the woman's daily schedule the alternation of mornings spent in doing repeated daily tasks with afternoons that hold a certain variety and a measure of choice. The succession of "strong" time, when the pressure of work is extreme, and "weak" time, when freedom and rest are possible, is no doubt one of the most characteristic traits of temporal rhythm as experienced by the farmer.

The worker's perception of duration of time is certainly very different in "strong" and in "weak" periods, yet no psychological studies on this subject exist. If it is true, as psychologists have shown, that everything that contributes to an increase or decrease in the number of observed changes has the effect of lengthening or shortening the apparent duration of time,[24] one can advance the hypothesis that the heavy tasks of summer seem shorter than winter's diverse occupations. Such a hypothesis could be confirmed by all the observations on the slowness of winter, although obviously these also express the languid feelings aroused by the dull season. As Bachelard says: "Time has no length unless it is too long."

But again we must distinguish between the feeling of the total duration of the period and that of the duration of the work itself. The period of heavy work can seem relatively short although the work itself at this time is felt to be very slow-moving. It is because there exists for the farmer no clear distinction between work and leisure or between production and consumption that time can have such different intensities. The sixteen hours of a harvesting day are sixteen hours of intensive and productive work; on the other hand, time passed in puttering with a tool or trimming a hedge should be considered as "active" leisure comparable to that of the worker who does odd jobs around his house or works in his garden after his hours at the factory. And what about such tasks as chopping wood for the kitchen? Are these "productive work" or activities linked to consumption and family life? When he occupies his evening in carefully reading his weekly technical journal for self-improvement, or his daily paper in order to determine the government's agricultural policy, does the farmer read his newspaper like a factory worker or employee? Or, on the contrary, is he the head of the farm who is informing himself so he can make decisions?

It is pointless to try to measure farm work the same way, with the same categories, as factory or office work. In this respect the farmer's situation is closer to that of members of the liberal or intellectual professions than to that of employees or factory

[24]Fraisse, 1957, pp. 216 ff.

workers. The modern technological concept of time, as we have said above, penetrates certain tasks of agricultural life more deeply every day, but it will never fill the same role as in industry.

The organization of work in an industrial shop rests on four basic factors: the factory hierarchy, in which the one who organizes and commands is not the one who executes; a very elaborate division of labor; modern "technological" time, conceived as an abstract, formless magnitude divisible into units as small as is useful; and finally, relatively uniform working conditions and instruments.

The minute and the second are the units of time employed by chronometers, which calculate time and motion. The work is regulated not only by the minute hands of the clock but also by the split-second hand of the chronometer. But we have seen that the hourly unit has hardly begun to penetrate agricultural life. One can work on a farm without a watch or a clock, and in any case only the hour hand is really useful. Hence it is difficult to organize the farmer's work without first teaching him the value of minutes and seconds. The Institute for the Scientific Organization of Farm Work (i.o.s.t.a.) has been occupied for many years in timing agricultural tasks, but its calculations are useful only in big "industrialized" enterprises which employ a large, specialized group of personnel, or for economists who are seeking analytical norms.

In order to give meaning to the scientific organization and timing of work the entire system of relationship among time, space, and work must be modified, so that the task no longer fixes the temporal limits but vice versa. Even today one cannot ask a farmer for a very detailed record of his work, nor a precise report of elapsed time. His figures deal with groups of operations — for example, the time devoted to plowing or to planting potatoes — and not with the timing of operations such as preparation of the implements, traveling time, and the different phases of active work on the plot of land. Indeed, the most progressive young farmers do keep notebooks where they record their daily activities faithfully, but this is in order to use machines "rationally" rather than to "rationalize" their own work. It is useful to account for the time used by machines, which cost something (amortization, fuel, etc.) but this appears to be out of the question for human work-time, which "costs nothing."

Nor is it applicable for draft animals, which go at their own slow pace. The rhythm of the animal was a determining condition of agricultural work. Oxen and cows were particularly slow. As for man's rhythm, it will retain its primordial importance as long as mechanized work does not supplant work with hand tools for most tasks; management studies show that, on an average, close to two-thirds of the tasks are still done with these implements.

Finally, at the risk of being repetitious, we must remind the reader that time does not have the same value in summer and winter. Chombart de Lauwe and Morvan observe that "in winter much time is available — too much, and of such a kind that one gets into the habit of filling the days with tasks of doubtful utility and doing them slowly in order to kill time, for lack of organized leisure activities. Thus one adopts a work rhythm which no longer seems to correspond to the needs of our century."[25] For all these reasons it is understandable that the most modern farmer keeps track of his tractor hours but does not bother to time his own motions.

Should he do so, furthermore, he would be liable to grave disillusionment. Economists agree that the norms they formulate are precarious, particularly because of the extreme variability of working conditions. Unlike the industrial worker, the farmer does not work in a space manufactured by man and organized rationally with a view to a better work output. Quite the contrary, he uses an essentially diverse and "irrational" natural space, subject to the caprices of the climate. In five days of sun, the topmost crust of the soil can become so hard that the productivity of beetroot weeders is diminished by half on a particular plot of land. The form of the plot has a decisive influence on the productivity as well; by quadrupling the length of the field without changing the total area, the plowing time is reduced by more than a third. The peasants are well aware of the time wasted in doing corners and turning the plow; they have always tended to lay out their fields in long narrow strips, especially in regions where the plowcart was the traditional instrument. The topography and the nature of the soil are just as important as the form and

[25]Chombart de Lauwe and Morvan, 1954, p. 59.

dimension of the plot. Finally, implements, machines, and methods of cultivation vary from region to region, and are not very standardized even today.

These various elements are found in different combinations according to the size of the farm. The large farms have larger fields and better-mechanized means. Economists have accumulated considerable data on this point. In the Châteaulin basin, sowing an acre of potatoes requires 345 hours of work on a farm of 20 acres, and only 274 hours on a farm of 60 acres; and yet the cultivation of potatoes from seeds is done almost entirely by hand (only 15 percent of the working hours are by machine). The difference is obviously much more marked for an acre of wheat, where more than a third of the work is done by machine: 63 hours on small farms, 35 on large.[26] Hence, under similar conditions, working time can vary by 100 percent depending on the size of the farm, although it is only small family farms that are under discussion.

These difficulties, which are due to astonishingly variable working conditions, should be mentioned but are not theoretically insurmountable. A larger number of studies could take more variables into account, and modern calculators can easily handle these data; hence it is not impossible to establish tables of norms sufficiently varied to be applicable to all cases. The real question is, what use would these norms be to the farmer? Would they show him that he spends too much time on this or that activity? In order to do something faster, he can either speed up his work rhythm and eliminate idle time or rearrange his shop and simplify his working methods.

In industry the calculation and acceleration of norms entail frequent disputes between employers and workers. The reduction of working time has important repercussions on the management of the business, since it is multiplied by the number of workers to whom it applies and the number of tasks they accomplish in an hour. In agriculture, on the contrary, the employer and the worker being one and the same man, an acceleration of rhythm very painful to the "worker" hardly seems profitable to the "employer," since in most cases his profit will remain the same. Moreover, the division of labor being much less organized, the

[26]*Ibid,* pp. 52, 53.

farmer accomplishes a succession of different tasks in one hour, so that there would have to be a series of norms for each activity of every man and not one single norm for the same task repeated a great number of times by many men. Finally, as useful as it is to accelerate the rhythm in summer, it would be out of place to do so in winter when there is too much time; yet how can we imagine norms that vary in relation to the seasons and the pressure of work to be done? They would no longer be norms.

On the other hand, on almost all farms experience shows that one could lose less time and simplify the work by setting up the different "farm factories" more rationally. By reducing the number of plots and bringing them closer to the farm, land reform would in some cases permit a considerable gain in working time; unfortunately such reform usually cannot be carried out without challenging the entire agrarian structure and the autonomy of family farms. The rearrangement of the buildings and the farmyard can frequently be accomplished without excessive expense and permits an appreciable gain in time, particularly in stockbreeding farms. Many farmers also could spare themselves trouble by simplifying their working methods. But here it is no longer a question of rhythm and temporal norms, of time and motion studies; it is a matter of rearranging working conditions or teaching the worker better practice. In other words, the farmer who has inherited buildings and a skill from his father would often see an advantage in reorganizing the former and improving the latter, but to do this he would have to have recourse to an architect and a master of apprentices, certainly not to Bedaux' timekeeper.

And here we touch on one of the fundamental characteristics of the profession. On a family farm, work discipline brings results for the worker with natural gifts, but it is up to him to set up this discipline in relation to these gifts and to impose it on himself. The capacity to define a discipline for himself and submit to it is the fundamental quality required of the farmer on a family farm. This is the conclusion of detailed studies by Chombart de Lauwe and Morvan:

The small farmer over forty years of age seems all but impervious to any rationalization of work. He prefers to work two hours longer every day rather than to discipline himself in order to gain a few minutes a day on the different operations to be accomplished in a day's time.

The difficulty or the distastefulness of self-imposed discipline in a particular piece of work is counterbalanced by the general work discipline that is imposed by the peasant morality; for peasants the supreme value is work, and zeal in one's work is the greatest virtue. Cépède states repeatedly that for the true peasant, a "brave" man (*courageux*) means a hard worker. Consequently the analysis of work independently of the worker hardly makes sense, and a purely rational, quantitative, and temporal analysis only serves to emphasize the extent to which work is a matter of morality for the agricultural worker: if he works hard he gains self-esteem and attains the esteem of others. It is in these terms that the farmer thinks of his work, and all of the foregoing analysis serves to emphasize the "rationality" of this "irrational" point of view.

In the management of his enterprise, the farmer regards problems of working time in a perspective comparable to that of the industrial employer; yet with this important difference, that he is subject to natural rhythms he can scarcely manipulate. But the comparison, however suggestive it may be, remains nonetheless as false as that of the farm worker with the industrial worker, and for the same reason.

For economists who have studied the problem of work on family farms, the essential problem is to assure the full employment of available manpower, on the one hand by increasing the tasks to be done in slack periods, and on the other hand by decreasing the tasks in peak periods. In this light they distinguish between immediate and less urgent tasks; and all their effort is concentrated on the latter. The farmers have responded to the same concern in oversupplying themselves with mechanical equipment. A machine that stores fodder, employed only a few days a year, may never pay for itself. It matters little that it permits the farmer to bring in the fodder in time to avoid being late for the harvest. Again this demonstrates, if there is still need, that, economically speaking, time does not have the same value every day of the year on a family farm. The result is that the establishment of a program of annual work, a necessary condition to economical management, involves considerable difficulty.

Kreher, and later Reboul,[27] suggested that the farmer follow his

[27]Reboul, 1957.

old habits but improve them by using the term "work blocks" for what he used to call "seasons." These are subdivisions of the year which take into account the number of days that vegetative cycles afford for accomplishing certain tasks and the number of days available for work on the farm during that period. In these subdivisions are comprised all the tasks relevant to the different types of cultivation and breeding — from which derives the term "block." In Germany one can distinguish six definite blocks, characterized according to the most important tasks:

(1) springtime sowing, reaping the winter catch crops*
(2) upkeep of cultivated crops, gathering the hay
(3) reaping the early cereals
(4) reaping the late cereals
(5) reaping the cultivated crops
(6) late autumn work

It is clear that each region of France will require a special delimitation of the blocks. "By comparison with the old method, which consisted in studying separately all the agricultural tasks, the system of blocks represents a considerable simplification, while being more exact," according to Dr. Kreher, "since it reflects the practical conditions more faithfully." There is no method for defining these blocks other than to study the actual practices of farmers. A large number of entries will make it possible by analysis to break down the season's work, to distinguish the tasks that are postponable from those that are not; then, keeping in mind meteorological data and work standards, to put the block back together by fixing limits and a precise content.

It is highly instructive to observe that, after long fumbling, the scientific organization of work in agriculture has come to abandon its imitation of industry's approach and take on that of the peasants themselves. The result is that it is no longer concerned with the working farmer, but proposes instead to aid the head of the farm to manage his manpower resources well. In fact, an improvement in management can bring an increase or an improvement in production and thus an increase in profit, which one could not expect of an acceleration in work rhythm, as we have said above.

The advance reckoning of his manpower needs that economists

*Plants cultivated between regular crops in a crop rotation. (Trans.)

propose to the good farm manager is conditioned by a jumble of natural cycles to which agricultural production will remain strictly subject so long as there are no revolutionary advances that permit effective manipulation of the biological processes. If specially compounded products are fed to chicks kept in coops, they can be developed into edible chickens within three weeks, whereas "farm" methods require three months. But cases of this sort are exceptional. The wheat sown in autumn is harvested the following summer, just as in the time of Hesiod, and we cannot shorten the period of gestation of a cow or sheep. Conditioned by the seasons, the vegetable cycles are immovable, except that one strain may be more adventitious than another.

On the other hand we can displace animal cycles; for example, we can obtain lambs when desired by putting the ram into the flock at the appropriate time, or we can make chickens lay eggs in December by giving them light and warming their roost. We can wean piglets at three or four days so that the sow can be mated again and serve her function of gestation continually. It is nonetheless true that the farmer has very little latitude in organizing the cycles of his different products in such a way as to distribute the mass of tasks to be accomplished in the most equal way possible over different periods of the year — especially since he must also bear in mind the state of the market, which gives the best prices to December eggs, as to all the early produce.

Annual or shorter cycles are very important, but one also must reckon with those that are longer. It takes three years to make a dairy cow, and two for a sheep. The annual vegetable cycles are in fact multiannual, since they are usually integrated into rotations. The triennial crop rotation remains the most widespread, but the cultivation of forage crops stimulates the lengthening of the crop rotations, which are frequently five or seven years long.

Moreover, the inequality of the crops makes it impossible to judge the profitability of a farm on the basis of one season, or even two or three. Only the ten-year average is significant. Let us remember that the farmer's lease is for nine years: three triennial crop rotations. And one of the fundamental criticisms leveled at tenant farming by agronomists is that in nine years a farmer does not have enough time to hope to enrich his lands. He

must have long years ahead of him to give the land all the care
it requires.

Finally, a tree takes at least thirty years to grow. Between the
three weeks of a chicken's growth and these thirty years, the
diversity of cycles in agricultural production is astonishing. It
furnishes an infinite variety of combinations among which the
choice is delicate, but decisive for the profitability of the farm. The
result is that the year and its subdivisions are the most familiar
units for the farmer in his role of organizer of his resources, while
he thinks of the management of his enterprise in terms of years
and series of years. We have shown that for the farmer as a worker
the hour has very little significance. Hence he lives in a time
characterized by particularly long duration and slight differentiation.

Bernot and Blancard were struck by the contrast they found at
Nouville between the long, continuous time of the peasants and
the short, disjointed time of the factory workers:

For the factory worker, work is measured by the hour and is
calculated by days in biweekly pay periods. For rural inhabitants,
and especially the farmer, work is measured by the year.[28]

In the end it can be said that the generation (thirty to forty
years) is the dominant temporal dimension of agricultural life,
for the transmission of family property from one generation to
another is the final reckoning, by which the good management of
the father of the family is judged without appeal. Can he settle
all his children and turn over his estate to one of them intact
or even increased in size? In the past there was no doubt that
this concern was paramount. Today technical progress and
economic circumstances move too fast and make this thirty-year
cycle somewhat illusory. But the farmers of today have been
accustomed to thinking in these traditional temporal frameworks.
For the researcher in Africa, "it is almost impossible to consider
the relation among present, past, and future as it is conceived by a
man whose expectations of life are inferior to ours."[29] For the
Berber peasant, verbs have only two tenses: the past and the
present-future, the perfect and the imperfect. The future exists
only as a function of the present. One can be prudent, forearm

[28]Bernot and Blancard, 1953, p. 328.
[29]Couty, 1966, p. 5.

oneself against the future; on the other hand, all forethought is useless, indeed senseless and impossible.[30]

The succession of generations was a fundamental rhythm of rural societies and contributed to a sense of temporal continuity based on perpetual renewal. We have shown amply that whether they are days or seasons, years or generations, all temporal units are "wholes" which follow each other, mingle, and always reproduce themselves identically. Under these conditions, time was certainly perceived by the peasants as cyclical in essence. To put it more imaginatively, the eternal order of the fields was the product of an eternal return of things.

The introduction of technological and economic change breaks this pattern, and time has a tendency to take on a linear aspect. The son will no longer do exactly as his father at exactly the same time. The dying father will have the feeling that he is leaving a farm in progress, hence unfinished, while in the past he took leave having "run the race," having "served his time," leaving to his son the task of carrying on. And this new linear view of time introduced by progress in its turn facilitates change and progress. A detailed study would undoubtedly throw light on the close relations between this transformation in the representation of time and the technological revolution of our day.

The feeling of the continuity of time, however, will probably remain stronger among farmers than in other social categories, in particular factory workers. Bernot and Blancard[31] have emphasized this very strongly: "Past, present and future are aligned with the family and the family assets." The family is a succession of heirs associated with the father. "For the factory worker, past and future time are less continuous with the present. Often he has never known his father." For farmers the future is a continuation of the present and the past; for factory workers the father's past is often totally different from the actual present and the future is the dream one has for the child, the "position" one wishes for him, without worrying about how he will achieve it. From present *facts* they pass to future *ideas*, and this lag between the idea of the life wished for and the fact of real life marks a discontinuity of time totally alien to the peasant. When

---

[30]Bourdieu, 1963, pp. 60–64.
[31]Bernot and Blancard, 1953, pp. 321–358.

he dreams of future progress on his farm, it is inscribed on present reality.

The importance of the family or of individual biography as an instrument for measuring time is also very characteristic of peasant experience. The peasant tends to date an external event in relation to an event in his personal life or a family memory: "The cooperative was formed the year of my first communion." This tendency obviously contributes to the tendency to personalize time and perceive it through actual experience instead of representing it as an abstract measure.

To family memories are added collective memories, making the collective recollection of a rural group extend into the near or distant past. In a passage filled with imagery, Bernot and Blancard describe the historical perspective of the people of Nouville. Alongside historical time there exists an unreal time, which is translated into stereotyped forms: that happened "in eighteen hundred and nothing" or "when Jesus Christ was village constable." Historical time begins with the Gauls, before whose era the country was covered by the sea. After the Gauls there were the Kings, then the Revolution, the war of 1870, the railroad (1875), the opening of the glass factory (1880), the turn of the century (1900) and finally the war of 1914, which marks for adults the beginning of their personal memories. This enumeration shows that collective memories peculiar to Nouville go back to 1870 and that beyond that people depend largely on vague schoolboy facts.

One could easily find regions in which collective recollection hardly goes further back than the living memories of the old people. This is the case particularly in Beauce, where already the last century has left the realm of memory and is lost in the vague mists of the past. In other regions, on the contrary, one talks of the Revolution as if it were yesterday and part of the everyday world. In Sologne, in the Vendée, peasant uprisings or the sale of nationalized properties during the Revolution continue to have the character of a recent past integrated into the present. Each family is still classified according to the position it took at that time. It would be instructive to employ research techniques to measure the relative length of the collective memory in different rural societies of France.

These few remarks on the relations among time, space, and work in traditional peasant life will suffice to show that economic rationality cannot be applied to agriculture as it is to industry. Abstract, invariable units, which can be divided and multiplied, are lacking here; we are still in the "universe of the approximate" rather than one of precision.[32] And it is not easy to see how abstractness can one day overcome all the combined peculiarities of the soil, the climate, the plant, the animal, and the man. The intimate knowledge of these peculiarities makes a good peasant, for whom no two pieces of land or two cows are the same. Moreover, since the work is not imposed by any external discipline, it is the worker's conscience that dictates the work. This is to say that a "feeling for the land" and "courage" are, for the traditional peasant, the fundamental professional qualities. A large open field of cereal cultivated by a fleet of big machines can be analyzed and managed like an industrial workshop, but not so a polyproducing family farm.

This no doubt explains why it is easy to organize the production of cereals in the framework of national programming in France, the U.S.S.R., or the United States, while stockbreeding, milk, and meat remain resistant to the hand of the planners. Zootechnicians are making such rapid progress in the control of physiological and biological mechanisms that the mass production of animals is today becoming possible. But as in vegetable production, this "industrialization" challenges the family structure of the enterprise that we have inherited from the technical advances of the past century.

[32]Koyré, 1961.

3. The Family and the Farm

The polycultivating* family farm is a structure of production unique of its kind in our industrial world. It defies the organizing principles of economic activity in other sectors. This contrast is what makes it so interesting to study: it throws into relief, *a contrario*, certain fundamental traits of a society to which it is alien, and perhaps allows us to understand that society better. In traditional agriculture, there is no division of labor, no separation between production and consumption, no distinction between economic and family life. The family and the enterprise coincide: the head of the family is at the same time head of the enterprise. Indeed, he is the one because he is the other. This is a purely intellectual distinction rather than a realistic analysis of his situation; in most of his activities the peasant is one and the other, and he lives his professional and his family life as an indivisible entity. The members of his family are also his fellow workers. The father usually directs the management of the farm, or is at least an advisor who enjoys the respect and support of the family. His wife busies herself with her own activities and shares much of the men's work. The children are apprentices and assistants wherever needed. Tasks are assigned by custom according to sex and age,[1] not by the organization of production according to the skill of the workers.

The position of the sons is particularly revealing. Their father teaches them their trade both in his capacity of father and in that of master of apprentices, with the result that the child never knows if a reprimand, a piece of advice, or a set of instructions belongs to everyday or professional life. The authority of the father is based on his position in the family as much as on his professional competence. The young peasant cannot derive from his apprenticeship any clear idea of what the farmer's trade is, or of the techniques of which it is constituted; it is part of a way of life he has learned from his elders, and of the position he was assigned at birth. For him, *savoir faire* (ability) and *savoir vivre* (good breeding) are the same thing: in his life as a child and an adolescent the technique of plowing is tied to the family field where it is learned, and integrated into a way of life just as are all the other "techniques" of professional and

*See translator's note, p. 11.
[1]Varagnac, 1942.

social life — language or the rules of polite behavior, for example. Every effort to isolate his activity as a farmer from the rest of the peasant's life violates a reality whose fundamental characteristic is syncretism, a reality that must be analyzed and understood rather than minimized.

Not only is it impossible to dissociate the role of father from that of farmer; the latter is itself of a complexity with hardly any equivalent in other occupations. In his polyproductive enterprise, the farmer assumes all the functions that elsewhere would be divided among several specialized workers and organized into a hierarchy of command.

For the peasant of the past, it was enough to know how to handle his hoe, his scythe, and his sickle and to drive his plowcart or swingplow. Manual dexterity and physical endurance were the essential qualities. For the farmer of today, who is still a manual laborer in more than half his tasks, these qualities remain essential. However, machines are multiplying, improving, specializing, and creating new tasks for man, and the machines must be prepared, repaired, adjusted, and operated. They increase the efficiency of the work and ease the hardships of the worker, but at the same time they complicate the profession by demanding new skills and mechanical knowledge. Aptitudes useful in the operation of a tractor, a harvester-thresher, a binder, and other equipment are becoming at least as important as strength and dexterity in the handling of tools. In short, the farmer is still the man with the hoe and must be at the same time a mechanic and tractor operator.

Only one skill is losing its importance: the art of breeding, training, and managing draft animals, oxen or horses. On the other hand, the breeding of animals for profit is becoming more and more scientific. It has always been necessary for the breeder to look after his herd and know it with a thoroughness that depends on the peculiar sympathy he develops through long experience. Today, in addition, he must be able to prepare a balanced diet and should know enough to call a veterinarian if he feels that his lack of experience makes a scientific diagnosis advisable.

Knowing how to handle implements and machines is enough to make a farmhand, but not a peasant, who must also know soil, plants, and animals. Pedology, phytology, and zoology are perhaps big words to designate the variety of agronomical knowledge that is necessary. The peasant had only the rudiments of this knowledge, the results of his father's experience and of his own work. It is what used to be called a "feeling for" the land and the animals, something that has always been necessary but is becoming more scientific and rational as techniques develop. The period of apprenticeship shows a gradual tendency to transform this traditional attainment and give it a scientific basis, thanks to certain aspects of physics, chemistry, anatomy, and other sciences. Soils, plants, and animals are too diverse for the farmer to be satisfied with a few manipulative procedures that have lost all meaning. The more carefully selected plants and animals are less hardy and more sensitive to parasites and sickness. To know which fertilizer to use and the right way to treat each case at each moment is no longer a question of habit or instinct but one of knowledge. While he is often obliged to resort to the expert's advice, the farmer must normally be his own expert. The rudiments of science are also useful for consultation with the veterinarian or the agricultural advisor.

If the family is large or the property extensive enough to require that one or two salaried workers be employed, the "employer" must know how to give orders, assign each one his task, maintain the rhythm of the work, see that the time schedule is respected, and supervise the work so that it is done well. In a word, he must be a good foreman. And the fact that he is the father and the husband makes his job no easier. He can certainly expect his son to be more conscientious than a hired hand, but by the same token the son will have a more independent spirit and character. Their very intimacy gives an emotional dimension to their work relationship. The clearly defined relationships of the salaried condition are simpler than those that exist between father and son, unpaid journeyman and eternal apprentice.

We have shown above that the organization of work is a discipline that the peasant can impose only on himself; it is not easy to impose it on his assistants. Certainly the work dictates the time schedule and the rhythm, but its urgency and the manner of doing it can be determined in varying ways, and the "employer," a hard worker himself, has only his personal, family, or employer's authority to make his wife, son, or employee fall into line.

Producer and foreman, the peasant is also seller and buyer. The fair and the market hold a prominent place in the social life of the traditional village. Since these activities are social as much as economic, it can be said, paradoxically, that the more autarchic the agricultural economy the more important are the fair and the market. They are occasions for meeting one's neighbors and relatives and finding out how things are going. The bargaining itself used to be a strictly ritualized social game, permitting the parties to prove their cleverness and cunning. For certain investments, notably cattle, knowing how to buy and sell at a good price was at least as important as knowing how to produce well, and some breeders were horse traders rather than farmers.

Today the fair is gradually being replaced by the merchant who stops at the farm to buy, and by cooperatives, to which the farmer turns over all of his produce. Face to face with the merchant, the farmer can always bargain, being free to sell or not to sell. But this freedom is less real today than it used to be. Once the peasant could return home with his cow or his sheep if he could not get a good price, and speculate on market fluctuations; he had no urgent need for cash because there was not much daily use for money in an autarchic economy. Now, on the contrary, he constantly "has his hand in his pocket." To buy necessities for his family and his farm, the farmer must sell whether the price is good or bad. On the farm, confronted by the merchant who makes him an offer, he is not really free to refuse. Without precise knowledge of the ins and outs of the market and unable to set several buyers into competition with each other, he finds himself at a disadvantage and must accept the conditions offered to him.

At the cooperative too, no discussion is possible. Rather, a new form of commercial regulation is in force, since the management of the cooperative is at least nominally in the hands of all the members. It is indeed true that most of the cooperatives entrust management to the skilled hands of a director. However, the farmer who belongs to a cooperative remains in theory a seller and a buyer, as was his father at the fairgrounds; furthermore, since the cooperative does the work of the middleman and the horse trader of the past, it replaces them in the economy.

Cooperatives of all sorts are multiplying, and more and more farmers are being called upon to accept responsibility for their direction. But to participate in the management of an important cooperative, even if only for the purpose of keeping informed, demands knowledge and time that average farmers do not have at present.[2] In any cooperative the management of the enterprise extends far beyond the framework of the traditional farm. As far as the economist is concerned, the farm is a "firm" and the farmer an entrepreneur. Liberal economics has built its models on this simplistic image, as false today as it ever was.

We have shown that in traditional self-sufficient polycultivation, since the peasant had few choices to make, the economic and technical management of the property was reduced to a few objectives: to avoid debts, to save enough to settle the children, to enlarge the estate if the occasion presented itself. The principles were those of domestic and family economy rather than of economic management of an enterprise. The only possible investment, the purchase of land, was made without any calculation for amortizing debts or increasing income. It was simply a transfer of capital from one form of hoarding (cash or livestock) to another, more highly valued by society.

Today, on the contrary, the peasant is gradually becoming an economic agent who chooses to engage in a particular speculation according to the technical means at his disposal and the returns he can anticipate. He invests in land, buildings, machines, livestock, fertilizer, and seeds, usually with the aid of credit in anticipation of profits from his investments. Economic reasoning, in the sense in which the term is used by economists and accountants, is entering farm management, often by devious and surreptitious paths that we shall analyze below. The farmer can no longer be content to manage his farm "as a good father" he must do so as a shrewd entrepreneur. To aid him in this effort, management counselors and centers for rural economics are springing up everywhere, while techniques of farm bookkeeping are constantly improving and spreading.

The growing complexity of machines and techniques of cultivation, the increased importance of marketing, over which the farmer must retain control, the penetration of an economic rationale into the management of the enterprise: these are evidence that the farmer's occupation is becoming more complex and diverse each day; and there is no division of labor to

[2]No study has been done on this subject in France, but there are many by American, Dutch, and Scandinavian scholars.

help relieve him of some of his tasks. He remains the jack-of-all-trades who must be competent in everything, as clever at handling the scythe and regulating a harvester-thresher as at reading a balance sheet from the cooperative or a booklet on zootechny. There is a visible contradiction between the growing complexity of the profession and the demands of traditional polycultivation.

The acuteness and inconvenience of this contradiction are diminishing, it is true, through the use of the various services for technical advice, jobbing, and marketing that are furnished by administrative, commercial, and cooperative organisms. These are multiplying plentifully, as witness the c.e.t.a., the c.u.m.a., management centers, the various cooperatives, and other organizations. But the real solution will involve much more specialized farms. In the meantime the farmer, torn between traditional needs and the economic and technical imperatives of progress, is deeply affected by this crisis in the survival of a form of agriculture that preserves its ancient structures at the same time that it is penetrating the realm of business management and adopting scientific techniques.

This tension is all the more painful because the farmer does not analyze or isolate each of his roles as we have just done, but rather lives them closely united, as they are in his daily experience. Hence it is impossible for him to distinguish the logic and the exigencies of each role and the expectations it arouses. The natural result is confusion in analyzing each situation, a jumble of motives and desires.

This confusion is brought to a head by the coincidence of family and occupation, which integrates all professional roles into the single, more comprehensive, and less clearly defined role of head of the family. Whether it be technical or economic, every decision concerning the farm also concerns the family, and vice versa, since one cannot be separated from another. If a farmer buys more hogs because the price is favorable or because it has been a good year for corn or beets, he is adding to his wife's work load and is anticipating a monetary return that will fall to her management. And so it goes. Growing children represent an increase in manpower, which must be used either by concentrating on products that demand more labor or by investing to augment his means of production. And his children have preferences that must be indulged; if they do not enjoy taking care of cows, the farmer will tend to change over to cultivation, regardless of the market conditions.

While in almost all sectors the production cell is distinct from the consumption cell, the family farm manages to integrate them, and to such a degree that one person finds himself alternately consumer and producer and sometimes both at the same time. The farmer's wife who gathers her eggs to sell at the market and puts some aside for a lunch omelette is obviously both one and the other.

That peasants have so much difficulty under these circumstances in distinguishing consumer credit from investment credit should not be surprising. Until recent years, borrowing money was for the peasant an admission of poverty and inability to meet obligations, whether to pay for bread, for fertilizer, or for a new tractor. Every outlay of money was an expenditure in the household sense, on which one had to economize if possible. It is normal that the most rational farmer cannot totally free himself from this way of looking at things when he manages the finances of his enterprise. Moreover, we must note that he makes a mistake analogous to that of the city housewife who asks herself, when she buys her washing machine or her refrigerator, if it is a "profitable investment."

His lengthy econometric studies on the wine market led Milhau to a similar conclusion: "The winegrower does not make the logical calculation of an industrial entrepreneur but rather the simple calculation of a consumer whose purchases, whether they be of capital or intermediate goods, are commanded and limited by the available income." In fact he was able to show that there was a strong correlation between the purchase of instruments of production (fertilizer, machines and so on) and purchasing power based on the previous year's crop; the correlation between the price of wine and such purchases is much weaker. A similar study of cereal production proves that the most significant correlation can always be established between the value of the crop for the year N and the quantity of instruments of production in use during the course of the year $N + 1$.[3] However, one cannot agree completely with Milhau when he states that the peasant entrepreneur reacts in the Pavlovian sense to economic stimuli while the "economist"

[3]Milhau, 1961, pp. 354–359.

entrepreneur is a child of Descartes in his obedience to the dictates of foresighted rationality. As has been shown, we are dealing not with simple responses but with a rationality just as Cartesian as the economist's, a rationality whose direct objectives are of a social and moral, rather than an economic, nature. Peasants furnish both an illustration and a unique field of investigation for the classic distinctions of Max Weber.[4]

In the final analysis, the survival and continuity of the family depend on those of the farm, and vice versa. Thus the father who knows that one of his children will take over the farm manages his enterprise differently from the one who has set up all his children in other occupations; and the farmer who wants to keep one son at home does his best to tempt him, when he comes of age, to remain and see that the "house" — the family and the farm — survives.

In all activities and sectors of society, the professional success of the father has repercussions on the position and prestige of the family. But everything is so closely tied together on the family farm that the father draws his professional reputation as much from his farm, his land, and even his buildings as from his technical skills or his economic successes. His "professional success," if indeed we can use such an expression, is measured as much by the expansion of the farm's means of production as by his family's standard of living. In the traditional peasant view, as we will show in a later chapter, the good farmer is the head of a large family who works successfully on lands sufficient to his needs. In other words, to be a good farmer one must be a farmer on a large scale, and hence high up in the social hierarchy of the village. Conversely, the prestige and social position of the family are normally among the concerns that directly motivate the farmer in each of his technical or economic choices.

This can best be illustrated by analyzing the diversity of attitudes and motives that move a farmer at the moment he buys a tractor. The economist thinks that small farmers are overequipped, and the troubled observer reproaches them for wanting tractors for show. (This explains, it is said, why red tractors, which can be seen from afar, sell better than those of other colors.) Perhaps this is true; still, the problem is not that simple, precisely because the peasant does not make his decision in relation to one single register of concerns, those of profitability or those of snobbism.

[4]Weber, 1962.

The untiring laborer at the handle of his plow, who spends the day in the furrow behind his team, is justified in wanting the alleviation of his hardships that a tractor affords in enabling him to sit while he plows and to do the job two or three times faster. If we stop to reflect on the fact that his work occupies his entire life, we can see that the tractor is not only an improvement in working conditions in the narrow sense but a whole new way of life. Other laborers, who have long leisure hours, do not make expenditures in their work, but since work and leisure are confused for the farmer, it is natural for him to make a nonproductive expenditure that gives a new flavor to his daily life. Man as a producer is not distinguishable from ordinary man, and the motivations of both, contrasted here analytically, blend and color each other reciprocally so that the shrewdest psychologist could not pretend to sort them out.

Moreover, the organization of work in peak periods is not easy on farms where the work force is limited to one or two men or where day labor is unavailable. It is thus essential for the farmer to be able to speed up the work during these periods. Although unemployed the greater part of the year, the machine justifies itself in the time gained by its use at critical periods. It replaces the seasonal odd-job labor typical of underdeveloped agricultural systems, a work force unemployed or paid to do nothing part of the year. When the weather is uncertain, it pays to do the work quickly. A wheat crop harvested on time and under good weather conditions will be of a superior quality and will suffer less waste. The monetary gain obtained in marginal situations is difficult to evaluate. In some years it can be considerable if a part of the crop is in jeopardy for lack of sufficient means, but it is difficult for the bookeeper to take this marginal profitability into consideration in his annual accounts.

Finally, some pessimistic experts fear that the tractor will have regrettable repercussions, notably excessive sinking of the soil. But in general the peasant feels that it enables him to do a better job, something every good worker likes to find a way to do. In short, the machine is a means of doing the work well, with less difficulty, and within the desired time, an assurance that can seem expensive in some years but worthwhile in others.

Though the manual laborer and the technician have their opinions on the purchase of a tractor, it is the head of the enterprise who will have to judge, in the last analysis, the profitability of the investment. This implies that he is a man of true "economic" mentality, that he has a clear realization of the meaning of capital, income, interest, amortization, and so on. Indeed, the rudiments of accounting are rapidly gaining hold today, thanks largely to management counseling. There is scarcely a farmer who does not know that a tractor must be in use for a certain number of hours per year in order to justify its purchase. But this formulation of the problem is much less precise and significant than a calculation of amortization; and if the farmer is content with it, it is because it permits him to assume the viewpoint of the consumer and ask himself not if the tractor will be paid for quickly enough but simply whether it is worth buying. In these terms, the internal debate between the worker and technician, on the one hand, and the head of the enterprise, on the other hand, will inevitably be decided in favor of the former, because the latter has implicitly renounced the purely economic rationality that should have been his.

This is all the more true because at this point of the debate the father of the family intervenes. He too has the right to an opinion and a deciding vote. His arguments, formulated on another level, have considerable strength. The son no longer wants to spend all his time "behind the cows;" if he cannot have a tractor, as his neighbors do, he would rather leave for the city. A machine to handle and to tinker with will give him a feeling of being "modern," and of keeping up with his school friend who has become a mechanic in town or in the city. How can the father explain to him that this beautiful machine creates the risk of running the farm into bankruptcy since he has not calculated the amortization? Besides, a farm never fails the way an industrial or commerical enterprise does. When by chance a creditor orders the foreclosure of his debtor's farm, the dismay and disapproval aroused testify that he is breaking the rules of custom. There is agreement on this point between the farm credit agency, which almost never resorts to such an extreme, and agitators ready to make a scandal of such an action.[5]

There are hardly any irreversible economic sanctions against bad management in agriculture. One is "slowly ruined," grows poor, cuts back; but the enterprise does not die till the day the farmer himself

[5]Dorgères, 1935, p. 7.

dies, and his son, discouraged, seeks other work. This explains why he must manage as a good father of the family rather than an experienced entrepreneur. In other words, he must think first of the family's interests, its security, its perpetuation, the education of the children, and so on, and must subordinate economic imperatives to these.

In the long run, family success consists in part of an increase in prestige, a move several steps up in the village hierarchy. And the father of a family cannot be indifferent to social advancement; it should even be his objective if he has a marriageable daughter. Prestige used to be measured by the acreage of the estate or the number of head of cattle. Today the ownership of a tractor is another decisive index. Or rather, this was so a few years ago; now the brand, the horsepower, the age of the tractor are taking on more and more importance as its use is spreading. By these signs it is recognized that the "business is going well," and they are signs that must be acquired even at the price of a decrease in income if one wants to preserve or improve his social position. After all, who would not approve of the father so desirous of seeing his daughter marry well that he would go into debt by buying a tractor he will never be able to pay for?

Let us point out that the working farmer and the technician speak approximately the same language as the father of the family; but in this language the head of the farm cannot make a clear, reasoned analysis of the socioeconmic situation or a "rational" decision that respects the imperatives of the economic game.

The chief of an industrial enterprise takes the advice of his directors (commercial, technical, personnel, and so on) and then decides alone, in the end, bearing in mind his financial possibilities. In a large firm his decision will have no direct repercussion on his family. When the industrial enterprise belongs to a family, the fate of one depends closely on the other; however, family life is not influenced by each and every management decision. Thus autonomy of decision is assured for the employer in his role of entrepreneur, and, thanks to this autonomy, economic mechanisms can function according to their own logic.

These are not the ways of agriculture. Of course, management counselors try to rationalize the economic decisions of their flock by urging them to keep accounts. Once the calculating is done, the farmer is free to sacrifice economic arguments to personal and family arguments if he pleases, but he must make this choice, they say, with full knowledge of the facts. Surely this is no more than a bookkeeper's delusion, a false rationality! On the family farm everything is both social and economic, and purchases of a tractor, a refrigerator, or a washing machine are all made according to the same procedure, allowing no opportunity for the economist to impose his point of view.

The example of the tractor has served as a good illustration for the preceding theoretical analysis. Any other management "decision" could be subjected to the same analysis and lead to analogous conclusions. Farmers, whether or not they are "peasants," are not a race apart; they have no collective "soul." They are simply in a situation that has no counterpart in other professions and that, by its nature, incites them to act as they do. To analyze their attitudes toward credit or money, to measure their resistance to the accountant's methods, to seek to inculcate them with "economic motivations" — all this betrays a strange naiveté with regard to an agricultural society in which almost all the farms, though they may show a deficit on the balance sheet, continue to prosper. A subsistence economy has its own logic and rationality, which economists should analyze before seeking to measure it by their own standards and to condemn without understanding.

As farms become specialized and are opened to the market, the role of producer will be different from the role of head of the family, manual labor will be subordinated to management tasks, and thus the farmer will acquire a knowledge of bookkeeping and an economic mentality. But this evolution, which is going on rapidly before our eyes, is accompanied by a total transformation of economic and family structures and cannot be accomplished simply by "educating" the farmers.

The farmer, while head of the farm, is not the sole decision-maker. The other members of the family — referred to until now as "concerns" of the head of the family — often have a word to say, sometimes make certain decisions independently, and always create, simply by their presence, a situation and a division of roles that act as a check upon the head of the enterprise.

The division of labor between the sexes is one of the fundamental facts of traditional peasant societies. Whether the cows are the responsibility of the women or the men, whether or not women work in the fields: these, among others, are the revealing indices of the allotment of tasks, a key element in the organization of the farm. In regions where the women assist the men in almost all kinds of work, without having to themselves any responsibility other than that of the farmyard, they are at the same time housewives and farmhands. Their influence on the management of the enterprise merges with their wifely influence on their husbands. Elsewhere, on the other hand, feminine and masculine activities are clearly distinct.

We do not have available any detailed study of the part played by women in farm management, and even with such a study at hand it would be very difficult to draw significant conclusions without taking into account the various personality traits and the conjugal history of each household. It is well known that there are farms on which it is the man who rules and others on which it is the woman; and it happens quite often that the woman is a better manager than the man. More and more frequently women keep the accounts, thus taking responsibility for one of the essential instruments of management.

When the feminine activities are clearly distinct from those of the husband, it is possible for each to do his part better. In practice, it can happen that each keeps his own accounts; Garavel found that this was the practice of a family in Morette.[6] In many regions money made from dairy and farmyard products is considered to be at the wife's disposal for the daily household expenses. Other income falls to the man for the treasury of the farm, for big expenses, and for savings. Here again, we would have to verify the extent of this practice and above all clarify the distinction between household and farm. Sometimes the analysis could be carried even further to inquire if each farm does not in fact shelter twin enterprises.

In Béarn, for example, under the traditional system of cultivation, the man occupied himself with cultivation and large livestock while the woman raised pigs and poultry. All the income came

[6]Garavel, 1948, p. 116.

from animal products: milk and meat for the man, pork and fowl for the woman. Thus both contributed equally to the family's consumable goods and to the commercial product. Corn passed from one sector to the other: produced by the man, it provided fodder for the pigsty and the farmyard. Obviously this transfer was not tabulated; hence it was impossible to measure the profitability of the two "enterprises." The man did not exchange money for his corn and the woman always earned a little money (perhaps not enough for her liking) by selling products without having to pay for the principal raw material. Healthy economic management would have called for two separate accounts that would take into consideration the transfers between two "firms," whose manifest economic autonomy was so intermingled that they seemed to be one single family farm.

This distinction, which is evident in the Béarn region, no doubt holds in other regions, since one often hears peasants complaining because their wives steal grain from the granary to feed the chickens. One informant has even assured us that his wife got up during the night to accomplish her larceny. This anecdote illustrates, if need there be, that the tone of marital relations has some bearing on the economic management of a farm.

Between father and son there no longer exists a clear division of labor, and it is well-nigh impossible to give the customary precise definition of their reciprocal positions. They work together most of the time, and their personalities confront each other in a continuing game in which it is impossible to discern the son's influence on the decisions of his father. It is true that young people are tending more and more toward a certain independence, thanks chiefly to their participation in various organizations. The J.A.C. (Christian Agricultural Youth Movement) and the Center for Young Farmers dispense new ideas, technical knowledge, and views on farm economics, all of which serve as fuel for the dialogue with the older generation. The father is sole head of the enterprise; the final decision is his, as is the responsibility. But if he lets himself be "led" by his son, the son becomes the real head; and if instead he shows resistance to such a reversal of roles, he risks creating painful family tensions.

The problem of the transfer of property from father to son has taken on a completely new aspect as a result of the acceleration of change. In some regions the allotment traditionally takes place during the lifetime of the father, who hands the management of the farm on to his married son, but in most places the father remains sole head of the family and the farm until his death. It sometimes happens that he feels himself outpaced by technological and economic change. Accustomed to oxen, he gladly leaves the tractor to his son. All the excitement about unions and cooperatives for the organization of markets means nothing to him. Under such circumstances the more sensible relinquish their leadership to the young: "We did what we thought was right in our time; now it's up to them to take on the responsibilities."

But such voluntary retirement is still exceptional. Most of the time technical innovations and economic difficulties result in a redistribution of roles within the family,[7] an unacknowledged diminution of the father's role in favor of the mother's. It is very difficult for a farmer molded in the traditional autarchic system to penetrate the mysteries of economic formulas and the workings of the market. He has learned how to make his land produce well and how to protect himself as best he can on the fairgrounds, but not how to orient his system of cultivation in relation to marketing outlets. Discouraged by these new tasks, he tends to confine himself to those that are habitual: work, and manual work in particular. He becomes more and more a laborer, abandoning his prerogatives as head of the enterprise to his wife or son. This does not happen without upsetting the equilibrium of family roles. Since the farmer's paternal authority is supported by his authority as head of the farm, the lessening of one brings on that of the other. How can a peasant be a father, in the full meaning of the word, if he is not a good peasant? Limiting his horizon more and more to the field where he works, he leaves to his wife the maintenance of contacts with the outside world. One is reminded of Jean Giono's statement: "The peasant women in the regions I have described are shrewder than the men."[8]

Closer to the children and the problems of their future, the mother feels a need to understand the new world that is intruding more and more into the economic and social life of the

[7]The entire analysis that follows is based on the studies of Marie Moscovici, 1960, 1961; and Appendix 2, No. 21.
[8]Giono, 1955, p. 149.

village. Thus she plays her traditional role of the teacher who must explain the world to her children in order to "socialize" them. In the past, religious beliefs, the moral code, and the rules of polite behavior made up the greatest part of what she handed on to her children. Today she seeks to furnish them with a picture of the larger society around them and of the way in which it functions socially and economically, so that they can move into it and make their way, whether they live on the farm or leave it. The economic and technical incompetence of the farmer must be compensated for by the greater social *savoir faire* of the mother of the family; and, as the father ceases to be the central personage, the family comes under the mother's authority.

If the mother loses hope that her children will have a decent life in the country, she turns their ambitions toward other occupations and other horizons. Then the farm, instead of being modernized, gradually loses its character of an economic enterprise until it is no more than a means of survival and subsistence. The result, obviously, is that all economic concerns of management are subordinated to family needs. The departure of the children transforms the farm into a retirement farm, until it disappears with the death of the parents.

This evolution, which is the most common course of events, feeds the rural exodus and permits the amalgamation of holdings, to the profit of those who have withstood a turn in their own fortunes. Instead of rigidifying in his role of manual laborer, the peasant can in fact accept the new conditions the world imposes on him and remold himself into a small progressive entrepreneur by taking advantage of all opportunities to modernize, expand, and meet the needs of the market. If he joins forces with his wife to assure good management, family and enterprise remain completely merged, but on a new basis: the wife is coentrepreneur and her entire maternal role in fact depends on her economic role. Thus the farm very nearly resembles a family business.

The wife often seeks to confine herself to the feminine tasks of housewife and mother, and a whole "feminist" cultural invites her to do so through women's magazines, radio, the movies, and so on. She wants to be like a city housewife and limit her farm tasks to the farmyard and the bookkeeping. The result is a new distinction between farm and family: the father produces and the mother consumes, exactly as in the city.

In all these cases, as in their variants, the position of the father is no longer as central and dominant as it used to be. Equaled or dominated by that of the mother, it is limited to its economic aspect, and even this is gradually subordinated to the influence of the mother and the children. Each individual, motivated by his particular concerns, comes to weigh in decisions so that we no longer know who makes these decisions or by what criteria.

This analysis of the farm as enterprise leads one to wonder if rural economists, accountants, and management counselors are not the victims of economic theory and appearances when they speak of family farms as "firms." The doubt becomes stronger when we try to disentangle the collective bonds that unite the farms of a given region. The quip of one rural economist that "an agricultural region is a group of farmers who make the same foolish mistakes" implies in fact that farmers do not make their technical and economic decisions independently.

In a rural society governed by tradition, this goes without saying, since the very existence of individual choices is doubtful. Everyone adheres to custom and cultivates according to a routine. The village feeds itself and furnishes the same products to the market in good years and bad years alike. But now that agrarian individualism is the property of the peasant, to be his own master and accountable to no one is the pride and ambition of the small farmer, while he never fails to lament the triumph of individualism within the peasant corporation. How can we explain, then, the fact that the majority of farmers in any region make similar choices, which, once tabulated, bear such a resemblance to a collective choice? Restrictive structures and situations direct these decisions, and collective mechanisms guide them. Unfortunately we do not yet have available any significant study of this process.

The fact that decisive economic choices are made at the bottom of the ladder by the rank and file worker is another characteristic of agriculture that radically distinguishes it from other sectors of production and poses delicate problems for all efforts toward economic planning and guidance. In fact there is not, for the time being, an intermediate step between the macrodecisions, made in Paris by political and administrative agencies, and the two million farmers who make the microdecisions. This is probably why agricultural planning continues to be regulated by price mechanisms, and not by control of output as in other sectors, in which there are intermediate echelons and the heads of enterprises command the activity of thousands, indeed tens of thousands, of workers.

It is somewhat paradoxical to confine the management of a sector of production as important as agriculture to two million totally independent farmers, lacking all economic competence, whose education is limited to elementary school. An average farm represents a capital of about forty thousand dollars. Its economic and technical management is infinitely more complex and diverse than that of a commercial or artisanal enterprise representing an equivalent capital, and yet the latter are rarely managed by employers lacking professional training. Some large farms of the Paris basin and the north, whose capital may amount to several million new francs, are often in the hands of farmers no better trained than these average farmers: an extreme case that clearly illustrates the anachronism of agricultural structures.

As long as the mass of these farmers remain faithful to traditional market products, there is need only for a few groups of specialized producers, organized into unions and cooperatives, who adjust the supply as far as possible to the demands of the market. But if the situation offers the more general inducements to which all farmers have some sensitivity, such as good prices, there ceases to be any security against fads such as those that have marked the past ten years (beets, corn, apples, and so on). And this happens because the peasant who abandons his routine knows no better than to follow the fashion of the moment: the product that pays well, the machine, the seed, or the technique that "everyone is talking about."

Unless extension agents and management counselors are themselves informed and guided painstakingly, they will only lend momentum to the very fads they are working against by advising everybody to do the same thing at the same time in most regions. The farmers, as we shall see later, are fully aware of this dilemma and state firmly that they will remain faithful to their routine because they do not want to be victims of fashion.

If the farmer is to make the adviser a true participant in his decisions, he must have already abandoned routine and taken some adventuresome risk — must, for example, have broken out of his isolation to become a member of a Center for Technical Farm Studies (c.e.t.a.), where he and his neighbors discuss their problems with a technician. Since the technicians at these Centers are hired and paid by the farmers, they belong in some way to the farms they advise, and can really share the responsibilities of the farmers.

In the absence of a detailed study of the collective decision-making mechanisms of farmers in various French rural societies, we must be content simply to note a few contrasts. Historians have compared the collective restrictions that influenced all aspects of the farmer's life in the villages of eastern France with the suspicious individualism of the small Breton farmer, who lives alone in the middle of his heritage at the end of his sunken road. During the eighteenth century the agricultural revolution broke the bonds of collective servitude and granted independence to the eastern peasant, who guarded it all the more jealously for having been too much a prisoner of the village community. But the fundamentally hierarchical society of the west retained its basic structures, which continue to weigh upon the peasant subject to its authority. As a result, the peasant of Lorraine is today clearly more independent of his group than the peasant from the Vendée. In mountain regions cooperative bonds have been kept very much alive, but the peasants of the southwest have always rebelled against any form of collective subservience.

The few available observations show that the progress of change is institutionalized and in some way ritualized. Certain people take the initiative, and they are almost always the same people. Later others follow their example in greater numbers. Finally there are backward ones and those resistant to all change, who are always left behind. In practice, everything happens as though a few individuals made decisions for the village or the district as a whole. This schema is obviously rough and oversimplified; yet if this "model" is accepted in principle, one sees that the farm as an independent "firm" and the farmer as an entrepreneur are fictions rather than realities. At most it could be said that, from the point of view of economic decisions, it is the small region or the group of farmers who form an independent unit, and not the farm. But the frontiers of these regions and groups would have to be carefully delineated before one could arrive at a meaningful analysis.

Until now, most of these collective mechanisms were latent, buried in the social system as a whole, and their agents were not clearly aware of them. It is the role of the unions, the cooperatives, and the c.e.t.a. to give an institutional form to such mechanisms and to make the peasants sensible and responsible participants. As these institutions develop, the region becomes less important, since the farmers of any one region are divided among many institutions according to their economic interests, their level of professional education, their political tendencies, and so on. To the extent that this trend asserts itself, the farms will lose their independence, and the "firm" will be a group of farms united by the g.a.e.c. (Farmers' Organization for Communal Land Use), the c.e.t.a., the s.i.c.a., or a cooperative. And to the extent that these institutions are specialized and their leaders are chosen with respect to their competence, agricultural production will come to be managed according to economic and technical criteria, whereas in the traditional system those who took it upon themselves to make decisions for the group did so because of their social position and their technical competence. The region was led by notables of economic, social, and political power rather than by those farmers best prepared to solve technical and economic problems.

These few reflections show how poorly the problems of classical economics and sociology are adapted to analyzing the structures and mechanisms of agriculture. The farmer is neither an employer nor a salaried worker, since he is both. His enterprise, which seemed the prototype of a firm in a competitive system, has neither an internal unity nor an external autonomy sufficient to permit its analysis by the economist or the sociologist as an individualized economic agent. The confusion of enterprise and family precludes economic logic from presiding over production policy; the erosion of the power of decision at the level of the rank and file worker makes all efforts to orient production perilous.

For his part the sociologist, though armed with ideas of role and status, has no real idea of how to use them to analyze a peasant society. When he describes complex roles precisely codified by custom, he tends to use the word in the sense meant by anthropologists.[9] But when he seeks to disentangle the motives of the head of the farm he artificially breaks a complex reality into facets and borrows the social psychologist's conception of role.[10] This uncertainty of the intellectual instrument best adapted to the effort to understand peasant societies in transition makes the sociologist cautious; for if he studies more traditional societies he turns into an anthropologist, and if he studies groups of modernized farmers he is quite naturally attracted by social psychology. And to understand precisely the passage from one to the other he would have to use the same set of conceptual tools.

For the economist, on the contrary, the question is settled; the present agricultural structures are condemned. But these very structures excite the admiration and enthusiasm of the moralist and the social doctrinarian, jealous defenders of man's independence and liberty who are appalled by the state to which he has been reduced within industrial structures. If the very concepts that are used to analyze the situation involve a final judgment, then the outcome is *petitio principii* rather than scientific understanding.

It is remarkable that jurists have understood, analyzed, and codified the spirit and basic meaning of the family farm more accurately than have economists and sociologists.[11] In industrial and commercial legislation all the rules apply to the enterprise in the interest of the enterprise and of economic life; in rural law, on the contrary, legislation is passed for the farmer on one hand or for the land on the other, and the enterprise that ties one to the other seems to merit less attention.

The legislator tries to assure good technical exploitation of the land by making contracts sufficiently long and by providing restrictions of such a nature that, for example, the farmer near the end of his lease does not tend to wear out the land. And he is concerned especially with the farmer and his family, to whom he wants to

[9]Linton, 1936; Nadel, 1957.
[10]Merton, 1966; Dahrendorf, 1960; Rocheblave-Spenlé, 1962.
[11]Juglart, 1958.

assure security and continuity, contrary to the common rules of our civil law. The tenant is assured of being able to preserve his farm against the will of the proprietor, who is no longer totally the master of his property, and the good father can give an advantage to his son and heir by transmitting to him the bulk of the family estate, to the detriment of his brothers and sisters.

All the efforts of legal doctrine in support of this legislation tend to reinforce social concerns at the expense of those that are economic. Jurists seem moved much more by a desire to maintain social structures and assure the stability of a social category than by the wish to create conditions favorable to the profitable production of alimentary agricultural products. In this they are certainly more "peasants" than the farmers themselves, who remain faithful to their social structures but want to play the economic and technical game of modern civilization.

By analyzing one innovation, hybrid corn, the decisions it entails, and all its implications we will be able to be more specific about this conflict between two logical systems of life and behavior. With one case and one particular decision, it is possible to analyze the interplay and the balance among the different elements dealt with in the preceding chapters. We will see in particular how the absence of an abstract, quantitative view of time and space combines with the absence of differentiation of roles and with participation in village society to create an incomprehensible economic situation, and to leave the farmer with a choice that he can make either in terms of individual morality or by yielding to the trends of fashion, but never by economic reasoning.

4. An Innovation: Hybrid Corn

Perfected in the United States, where it contributed to the wealth of the Middle West, hybrid corn was made famous by Nikita Khrushchev, who became its ardent propagandist. It was introduced into the southwest of France after World War II, but some time passed before it became acclimatized and the peasants were convinced of its superiority over varieties traditionally cultivated in the area, particularly the *grand roux basque*. If accurate statistics were available on the cultivation of the two types of corn, it would be very revealing to follow the progress of the hybrid, year by year, region by region.

Students of Basque and Béarnais agriculture are quick to suggest several hypotheses to explain why certain districts adopted the new variety more rapidly than others. Regions of grouped habitation, they say, are more likely to be favorable to the diffusion of an innovation than regions of dispersed habitation. In the former, people are continually side by side, living close together, and the progress of one cannot help but seem attractive to his neighbors; while in the latter, the farmer, isolated from the village, has little chance to see, compare, and become informed. This is to acknowledge by hypothesis that the neighbor's experience is the primary source of information and his success the most convincing argument. It is also to accept the fact that communications are more effective in villages than in hamlets and on isolated farms. But it appears that the diffusion of an innovation is accomplished according to a more complex psychological and social process. We attempted to verify the above hypothesis in the *département* of Basses-Pyrénées but the results were hardly conclusive; they tended rather to prove that regions of dispersed habitation have moved more rapidly than those of grouped habitation. Obviously, this index is insufficient; we must know whether the relationship that it shows is dependent upon some other variable, namely the cultivating traditions of these different regions.

Politics is also said to have some relation to the spread of hybrid corn, which would seem to be more attractive to Catholics than to Communists. We will see, in fact, that there exists a logical connection, although all efforts to compare electoral results and religious practice with figures on the adoption of hybrid corn have, unfortunately, met with failure. Certain "red" regions have sown the hybrid early, while very devout villages have resisted it for a long time. It is clear that this comparison could only be conclusive if it were made at the individual level and not by geographical units. In any case, it leads us to think that the link is not as direct or obvious as some local observers state.[1]

Wealthy parts of the country, satisfied with their lot, are less inclined to change than those not as well endowed. All the indications, all the cases that we know of support this hypothesis. For this study we have chosen the Nay valley, precisely because in 1960 it was one of the Béarnais regions slowest to abandon native corn, with which it had had great success. If enough statistics were available to provide an approximate estimation of crop yields and farm income by communes or districts, it would be possible to be specific about the connection between the profitability of agriculture and the farmers' readiness to change.

The scarcity of sources and the insignificance of these attempts at comparison oblige us to take up the analysis at the individual level, limiting ourselves, for lack of more complete material, to the data furnished by the survey conducted by Jean-Claude Papoz among one hundred farmers of the Nay valley.[2]

As far as agronomical technique is concerned, the replacement of native corn by hybrid corn seems very simple: the two are cultivated in practically the same manner. The hybrid should be planted earlier, with more space between the rows. The leaves need not be stripped nor the tops chopped off; this involves less work but results in less fodder. The most notable differences are that the seed must be purchased because it is produced by hybridization, that fertilizer must be used in large quantities (at a cost of about $24.00 per acre), and finally that the hybrid, more sensititve to atmospheric conditions and parasites, requires weed killers and anticryptogam treatments. It grows more slowly at the outset than native corn, and it must have very well-plowed fields to prevent suffocation by self-sown

[1]The control studies on which these observations are based are the work of Jean Duplex.
[2]Papoz, 1960, and Appendix 2, No. 3. In the following, the sentences in quotation marks are borrowed from the reports of the interviews. The interpretation of the results owes much to several discussions with Nathan Leites. His suggestions, for this work as for others, have been particularly fruitful, and I thank him wholeheartedly.

grasses. If these few precautions are taken, it produces a crop that averages twice that of the *grand roux basque*.

These improvements in cultivation are, we see, within reach of any farmer; and the costs of seed, fertilizer, and antiparasite products are small in comparison to the increase in returns. The superiority of hybrid corn is so obvious to the expert and the economist that Nikita Khrushchev's enthusiasm is more understandable than the hesitancy of Russian or Béarnais peasants, or even American farmers.

In the United States a sociological survey conducted in a part of Iowa[3] has revealed that ten years after the beginning of the first campaign for the hybrid variety, only about 75 percent of the farmers had planted it. In fact, an average of five years passes between the time a farmer learns about it and the time he decides to use it. In Iowa each farmer wanted to make his own experiments before coming to a decision. We shall see that the Béarnais peasants are less individualistic. But the complex mechanisms of collective decisions have resulted in about the same delay in the adoption of hybrid in the Basses-Pyrénées.

If everything were as easy for the farmer as for the agronomist, this delay would be much shorter in Iowa, in the Ukraine, and in Béarn. That the peasant does not have the same view of things as the agronomist was made evident from the outset by the statements of one of our informants, who exclaimed: "But, monsieur, they're going to kill agriculture in our region with this corn!" How can a farmer see a mortal danger in this corn when it is meant to bring an increase in his income? This is the paradox that we must try to clarify.

In 1959, ten years after hybrid corn had been introduced into the country, 19 farmers out of 100 who were interviewed did not cultivate hybrid corn (10 had never cultivated it, 9 had given it up after trying it for one or two years); and 36 cultivated less than 2.5 acres of it (Table 1). Thus more than half of the farmers had not really accepted the new strain. Finally, all but 16 of them continued to cultivate native corn at the same time, but generally over areas more limited than those devoted to hybrid (an acre, on an average): "We still grow a little of it."

The simultaneous cultivation of the two varieties facilitated

[3]Ryan and Gross, 1943.

Table 1. Acreage Planted in Corn

Acreage	Native Corn	Hybrid Corn
Do not cultivate corn	16	19
Less than 2.5 acres	58	36
2.5–6 acres	18	29
More than 6 acres	7	15
Total Farmers Interviewed	99	99

comparison; and since comparison was favorable to hybrid, it should have led to the rapid elimination of the indigenous variety. Yet this was not the case. The farmers continued for several years to cultivate both, although almost all of them (85 percent) agreed in their judgment that the hybrid gave a better yield. Yield was thus not a decisive argument. Seventy percent of the farmers found, on the one hand, that hybrid corn was too demanding in care, work, and various expenses it involved; and, on the other hand, that it did not serve exactly the same purpose as native corn, particularly in feeding poultry.

Hybrid is generally white while the *grand roux* is yellow, and in the southwest a fine chicken must be yellow. More important, it is claimed that one cannot make good *foie gras* except by stuffing the geese with native corn. One farmer's wife said: "If I give my hens hybrid, two hours later they're hungry and begin to peck, but native corn holds them longer." Specialists do not see much difference in the nutritive qualities of the two varieties, but the peasant women refuse to be convinced; they know that where poultry, and especially their livers, are concerned, only native corn gives good results. The proof of this is that on the market it sold at 10 cents more per bushel in 1959.

Agreeing on this point with his wife, the farmer finds also that native corn is "better looking" than hybrid. And often, in order to convince the interviewer, he would go up to the granary to find an ear of each type and compare them: "Look, this one is big, yes, but it isn't perfect at the ends; and above all, you see, the kernels are so close together that they're not round — they look shriveled, — while the ear of native corn is perfect, the kernels all golden and puffed up. This one's a good ear!" One does indeed have a better appearance than the other, and it is easy to understand that there is more aesthetic satisfaction in producing and harvesting it. In fact, it somehow looks healthier.

These aesthetic and nutritive qualities are obvious and convincing to the farmer. On the other hand, he is obliged to acknowledge, although reluctantly, that the ear of hybrid corn is fatter and the yield better. But there is some argument even on this point. On the market native corn is measured by volume, while hybrid delivered to the cooperative is weighed in quintals of 100 kilos each. This distinction seems to support the argument that the former is heavier than the latter, and that if the system of measures were reversed, the weight of the former would greatly exceed the volume of the latter. Discriminating minds have applied themselves to experiments in this area and have found only a minimal difference, but they have not succeeded in convincing others.

Another method of comparison consists of stripping two baskets of corn, which makes it obvious that one pail fills up with kernels more quickly than the other. Some have conducted experiments and found that a basket of hybrid that contained 87 ears yielded 37 pounds of kernels, while a basket of local corn that contained 130 ears yielded only 30 pounds. The only decisive method would be to weigh the yield of an acre of hybrid and an acre of native corn, but this is difficult; and besides, one could never be sure the two had been cultivated correctly.

On the Nay plain, well-tended Basque corn produced excellent results (63 bushels per acre). Hybrid, if poorly cultivated, can scarcely produce more; often it produces even less. Now, half of the farmers interviewed stated that there was no need to alter methods of cultivation when switching from one crop to another; one-third simply said more fertilizer must be used. One farmer asked: "Why add fertilizer just to make weeds grow and then have to use a weed killer?" It seems that, in general, farmers pay so little attention to the instructions on cultivation that they obtain a yield that is hardly 30 bushels more than that of native corn, while with normal care they could double that figure.

At the beginning, comparison was often impossible because many farmers took small portions of seed given them by neighbors (one farmer confessed that he had borrowed what was left in the seeder) and planted them in their vegetable gardens. To explain the good results, they could easily claim that "in the garden it yields more than in the fields." One informant even said: "I brought back one seed, planted it in front of the house, and nothing came up, so...." Conversely, other farmers, having obtained the seed without paying for it, did not want to spoil good land and sowed it in their worst fields.

Thus an argument based on yield is less convincing than it would appear. While it seems utterly impossible to discuss quality, quantity can be measured in various controversial ways. This is all the more true because the increase in quantity that is dangled before the peasant as a source of new income is bought very dear. It is often pointed out that "You have to buy this corn before you can harvest it." The native corn, on the other hand, costs only manure and hard work. Never knowing if the year will be good or bad, the peasant does not want to gamble, to put out money for a risky result. Besides, "a penny saved is a penny earned;" and "if we have to borrow from Farm Credit for fertilizer, then nothing doing!"

Finally, hybrid corn grows slowly at the outset, and the farmer who has sown his fields and put into them every care and every necessary expense is anxious to see the results of his efforts in the first shoots. If the sprouting is slow, he becomes worried and must suffer the mockery of the neighbor whose native corn "gets going" sooner. The first month gives an easy victory to the traditionalist. To the sarcastic "Look how your corn is rotting!" the innovator can only answer, "It's you who's rotting with your old ideas" while waiting for his corn to catch up. Only after several years does he have enough confidence in the hybrid to wait till it makes up for the delay and surpasses the Basque.

Other details further complicate matters. For example, hybrid corn is harvested later, so that the innovator, who has not yet gathered his crop when all the others have finished, risks being taken for lazy and hearing it said: "He has his ideas but he's a slacker." As another informant told us, "You let yourself in for trouble." Some find simply that the fields of hybrid are "sad" compared with local corn.

And besides, in the final analysis, why produce more corn? This question, surprising to an economist, is asked by most farmers. One informant said, "If I could raise even one more pig with this hybrid corn I'd do it, but my wife already has more work than she can do!" In the traditional system of production corn served essentially to feed hogs and poultry; the farmer sold very little, perhaps a few bushels at the market if there was a surplus; or he exchanged seeds with a neighbor. But that was all that left the farm. And now the farmer's wife cannot feed many more hogs and chickens, so her extra grain is wasted rather than used effectively.

To this argument it is easy to reply either that one can sell more or that one can reduce the acreage planted in corn and use it for another crop, since on a farm of about 25 acres an acre gained is very precious. But then the crop rotation must be modified. And since in any case the native corn is always saved for the poultry, hybrid corn is obviously superfluous on the farm, paradoxical as that may seem.

We have pointed out above that a new crop is accepted only on the condition that it can be integrated into the system of cultivation and can improve and strengthen it. This general proposition did not seem to apply in this particular case, since the crop was preserved while only the strain was changed. And until the new strain makes its place in the system, despite its great technical and economic advantages it is superfluous. From the agronomist's viewpoint, it permits concentration of the crop and therefore an increase in available space if needed. But as far as the farmer is concerned, it has no place either in the crop rotation or in the system of production and distribution as long as it has made no change in the traditional utilization of corn. And two-thirds of the farmers made no change in their methods after planting hybrid (Table 2).

Nevertheless 66 farmers out of 100 acknowledged that in 1959 the price of corn was "interesting," and only 19 did not admit it. The price was in fact set quite high at the time to encourage farmers to produce enough to stifle imports. But price was not, as we see, a strong enough argument to convince most of the farmers. They produced a small amount of it but decided not to take advantage of its benefits, for in order to do this they would have had to modify the equilibrium of their farms.

Table 2. Utilization of Corn

No answer	7
No change: sell less than one quarter of the crop	58
Sell a little more	12
Sell more than half the crop	12
Total Farmers Interviewed	89

To be specific, fat pork, which was a traditional product of the countryside, no longer sells well because it has ceased to appeal to the urban customer. In 1959 there would therefore have been no advantage in using corn that could be sold to fatten hogs. Only the most progressive farmers had reached this conclusion and decreased the number of pigs that they raised. This simple and limited modification of the system of production contradicted its "spirit," since instead of selling a "finished" animal product, like fat pork, which demanded work and care, one sold a "crude" vegetable product, i.e., corn. Moreover, not only was it not converted into meat, but it was not even husked, stripped, and dried, because the cooperative took the ears just as they were after harvesting. To a farmer worthy of the name, expert in his trade and imbued with the technical values and refinements of such a complex system of production, the direct sale of corn represents an obvious regression of the system and a negation of his skills, which it renders useless. It is easy to understand that a fine hog, the result of attentive and prolonged care, is an object of pride for his breeder, but that an ear of corn, even if very good, is not a "masterpiece" that likewise does honor to the skill and experience of its "creator." In this sense and on this purely technical level, one can rightly say that hybrid corn is "killing" Béarnais agriculture, as our informant feared.

If the problem were simply one of making room for a new and profitable strain, the foregoing arguments would explain the objections and the reluctance of most farmers and the refusal of some to change. But the experience of those who first planted hybrid showed the others that the corn itself was seldom enough, and that usually those who sowed it found themselves forced, a few years later, to introduce other costly modifications. In short, hybrid is the forerunner of a whole series of changes.

It is reasonable to produce hybrid only if one sells it in large quantities; hence it is necessary to seed larger areas than was once the practice. The differences between the methods of cultivation used for native corn and for hybrid corn are minimal; however, before effective weed killers had been perfected, repeated tilling was necessary to destroy weeds. Unless a farmer has an unusually large work force at this disposal, it is difficult to cultivate more than five acres without the aid of a tractor. Among the 52 mechanized farmers we interviewed, 43 had bought their tractors after adopting hybrid, while those who did not follow suit are still not mechanized.

It cannot be said that the introduction of hybrid corn on a farm brings about the purchase of a tractor, but the one is often followed by the other chronologically, a pattern that can be justified technically and explained financially if the increase in sales of corn is sufficient to pay for the tractor. Some farmers, however, have followed the opposite course: they have begun by mechanizing, often on credit, and gone on later to introduce hybrid, perhaps in order to pay their debts. In both cases the tractor costs money and increases the variety of possible crops, and therefore aids the extension of hybrid.

This extension leads naturally to the purchase of supplementary equipment. Regular seeding facilitates growth and tilling with the tractor, and the larger crop can no longer be husked by hand or dried in the granary. Huskers, dryers, seeders, and fertilizer spreaders are more in evidence among those who adopted hybrid several years ago than among others. Some of these machines far surpass the needs and potential of a family farm; the corn picker particularly is profitable only over large areas. If one does not want to be overloaded with useless equipment he must own the machine in common with his neighbors or join a cooperative. Half the farmers who were among the first to sow hybrid corn had bought huskers in cooperation with their neighbors.

Once a new crop has entered the system, it is advantageous to exploit it to the maximum in order to amortize the investment, a procedure that leads in turn to modification of the crop rotation. The old rotation gave an important place to wheat, and grassland accounted for the best pieces of land, notably on the plain bordering the Gave river. Given minimal care, the grass grew as best it could. Little by little mediocre yields impelled the farmers to reduce their wheatfields in favor of corn. An acre of wheat yields an average of 16 bushels, while the same area can yield 96 to 125 bushels of hybrid; yet at the time of the survey the two cereals were sold at the same price. The income from an acre is thus doubled or tripled by replacing wheat with corn.

Integrating the grassland into crop rotation by plowing and reseeding it with temporary forage crops after several years of corn also results in better yields of grass. The first who dared to plow a meadow on the banks of the Gave caused a scandal:

to reduce to mere fields meadows that had been coveted by landholders for generations and to plant them with corn that could be grown elsewhere was almost sacrilegious. Ten years after the first experiment was carried out, it still ranks among the most burning and controversial technical problems. A farmer to whom we mentioned it hotly rejected such an absurd idea: "What, *me* go plow up the meadows just to turn them back again into meadows?"

Cattle raising benefits from this exploitation: veal slowly gives way to milk, which is more easily marketed as the region becomes urbanized and industrialized. In this way the whole system of cultivation is transformed and oriented toward marketable staples: corn and milk. In the face of such upheaval the peasant hesitates. He is justified in his impression that in adopting the new system, he is setting in motion machinery which he will be unable to control or escape. He will be driven to become a modern farmer and to challenge the best-established ideas and values.

After all, the example of those who have taken the step is not very encouraging. The corn that was supposed to be so profitable has only caused them new expenses and obliged them to go into debt. And it is said that "it's not good to buy on credit," for then "you become a slave to the loan." True, these investments will perhaps be profitable in the long run; they are a gamble on the future. But to the man who bases his judgments on the past and the present, the operation hardly seems to pay for itself.

In addition to machines, fertilizer, a new crop rotation, and indebtedness, hybrid corn also introduces onto farms the agricultural extension agent, And many farmers say, "Advisers we don't need; what we need is hired hands." In the past, every peasant knew how to cultivate corn; he had always seen his father or his neighbors do it. Some of them, more skillful than others or possessing better lands, produced very fine crops. But all followed the familiar and dependable routine. More delicate than native corn, hybrid makes it necessary to relearn methods of cultivation from the beginning, with scrupulous attention to the instructions of experts.

But to the farmer these experts do not seem to be very sure of their techniques. They say one year to do the opposite of what they advised the year before, so that the farmer no longer knows where he stands, or whom to trust. This is easily explained. At the beginning, when seeders had not yet come into general use, extension agents advised planting in a square arrangement in order to achieve regularly spaced sowing, using a rod to set the distance, as was done in the past with native corn. The neighbors were amused to see the innovators return to their grandfathers' methods; that the new corn should be cultivated in the old-fashioned way was the subject of many a joke. Later, as seeders, tractors, and implements were improved, it became necessary to widen or narrow the lines and rows. Similarly, in the early years the advice was to plow just before seeding; later the same technicians said that it was better to plow several weeks before planting. Of course there was a reason: plowing made it possible to kill weeds at the beginning of their growth, but once an effective weed killer was developed in the form of simazine, it was better to let the soil be aerated between plowing and seeding.

Although the engineers undoubtedly have their reasons, it becomes impossible for the peasant to know good from bad. John says he was advised this way and Paul says he was advised to the contrary. Who is right? Which is the better expert? How can we tell? The peasant would willingly accept a new routine, well tested and proposed by someone he trusts; but whom can he trust? Besides, some technicians can be tactless and do considerable harm to the cause they are defending. One of them stated during a meeting: "You don't know how to get the best out of your land." This remark made the rounds of the village and the man who told of the incident concluded from it: "We don't need these quacks. We've always managed to be our own advisers!"

But in a more serious vein, if the farmer can no longer rely on a familiar and dependable routine he must trust an agricultural expert to tell him how to proceed. And if techniques are continually evolving, the informed farmer should constantly expect such an adviser to propose innovations, improvements, and changes. Thus he is no longer his own master and will always need a teacher to instruct him. This technical tutelage imposed by progress goes beyond matters of simple technique to create a psychological situation that reminds him of his childhood and schooldays. His father, who taught him the routine, is no longer there, but he has found a substitute father, and he has himself regressed from adulthood. His apprenticeship, which he had thought was completed, becomes perpetual. Several informants said proudly, "I'm not one to take others' advice," or "I don't need to be ordered around; I know as much about it as he can show me." And, as everyone agrees, "A gentleman like that can't tell us how to farm!" To repeat, a hired hand who can be given orders is preferable to an engineer who gives advice.

Finally, as we have said, it is not worthwhile to cultivate hybrid corn except to sell it, and to sell it in too great a quantity for the Nay market. It must therefore be given to the cooperative of Billières near Pau, which was built and organized by the corn growers' union. Billières is one of the showplaces of French agriculture, and it brought the commune of Pau a visit from Nikita Krushchev. In order to spare its members every inconvenience, the cooperative sends trucks to the farms to pick up the corn just after the crops are in, so that there is no need to dry or strip the ears. So much kind attention is disturbing to the average farmer, who is still an uncertain participant in the "cooperative" spirit. He is told that the immense silos at Billières are his, but he does not really believe it; and he feels himself a very small farmer indeed, powerless in the face of a large enterprise that he does not control and whose good or bad will can bring him prosperity or ruin. If tomorrow the cooperative stopped sending its trucks, or if it lowered its prices, what recourse would the peasant have?

Autarchy assured the peasant an admirable independence with regard to those in power. He is aware, with whatever degree of clarity, that by planting the new corn he is relinquishing this independence. Are not the men who extol this corn and direct the unions and cooperatives part of the powerful forces that he has learned from a long history to distrust? Fierce independence is the greatest pride of the Béarnais peasant, as of other peasants. While pretending to save him, hybrid corn threatens to destroy the peasant's unique attribute.

Rational arguments used by extension agents meet, we see, with objections just as rational on the part of the farmers. Each lives in his own psychological and social universe of motives and values. One of them sees the economic and technical advantages of a minimal change without feeling deeply its ultimate consequences, while the other is worried by these consequences because he is more concerned with his way of life as a whole than with progress in one detail. Nevertheless, despite these objections and anxieties, and others less specific which we shall point out later, hybrid corn has won the battle in the whole of the southwest as well as the Nay plain, as witness the fact that in 1958 eighty percent of the farmers were cultivating it.

Before the war there had already been an attempt to introduce a new Italian variety of corn into the southwest. Teachers propagandized the young by giving them packets of seeds and fertilizer and instructions on their use. On the occasion of a world conference on corn at Pau in 1934 there was an exhibit intended to facilitate comparison between Italian and native corn. But after a few years everyone had returned to local varieties. This experience had shown the farmers that there were other types of corn, in some ways superior to theirs; but at the same time it had strengthened their conviction that native corn was better, and better adapted to regional conditions.

Hybrid corn, an American strain, had been introduced in the southwest at the time of the Liberation, but it was not until about 1950 that a coherent popularization campaign was undertaken by agricultural services and professional organizations. A group of agricultural leaders — presidents of local unions and progressive farmers — made a study trip to the United States in 1951. Subsidies, seeds, and fertilizer were distributed to the farmers who agreed to plant the new strain. In 1952 a group experiment was set up: if ten farmers in a village were willing to participate in a test for three years, they would be granted subsidies and credit, on the one condition that they would agree to apply scrupulously all the new methods required by hybrid. The third year the efforts were prolonged by urging the farmers to plant temporary grasslands. Certain subsidies were given to the group — usually a payment in kind, such as a seeder — to serve as an inducement to work collectively and compare the results obtained.

The farmers who joined the game at that point changed their ways rapidly; most eventually bought machines, particularly corn pickers, in co-ownership, and even helped form irrigation cooperatives. These groups served as an example to other farmers, for whom tours and demonstrations were organized. Meanwhile the cooperative at Billières, constructed in 1954, provided for the disposal of the increase in production.

This intensive direct action was supplemented by written propaganda in different organs of the professional press, particularly the weekly *Le Sillon* (The Furrow), published by the Agricultural Services. The results of the survey (Table 3) show that the reading of technical journals and booklets is naturally more widespread among farmers who were earliest to adopt hybrid, but one cannot say whether reading these journals has moved them to adopt hybrid or adopting it has convinced them it can be to their advantage to read the journals.

Similar statistics are available for extension meetings (Table 4). Among the pioneers, 62 percent feel that these meetings were decisive in bringing them to try the experiment, and 30 percent have the opposite opinion; and the proportions are reversed among those who made the decision during the last three years. Responses concerning fairs and expositions are distributed in the same way.

By contrast, conversations with other farmers and observation of neighbors' fields assume much more importance as the cultivation of the crop spreads, fields of hybrid become a common sight, and conversations on the subject become more frequent. The pioneers remember having gone to see demonstration fields in other villages. Those who made the decision between 1953 and 1955 state that they did so without having seen fields of hybrid corn. After 1956, on the other hand, almost everyone could see the corn in his neighbor's field or elsewhere. The distribution of responses on conversations is comparable: those who decided between 1953 and 1955 remember less often than the others (50 percent as opposed to 70 percent)

Table 3. Reading of Journals and Adoption of Hybrid Corn

	Have Adopted Hybrid Corn			Have not Adopted Hybrid Corn
	1952 and earlier	1953– 1955	1956– 1958	
Read the journals	81%	55%	40%	21%
Do not read them	19	33	60	74
No answer	—	12	—	5

Table 4. Attendance at Extension Meetings and
Adoption of Hybrid Corn

	Have Adopted Hybrid Corn			Have not Adopted Hybrid Corn
	1952 and earlier	1953– 1955	1956– 1958	
Attended meetings	62%	39%	30%	26%
Did not attend them	30	61	68	74
No answer	8		2	—

that conversations had some weight in their decisions.

American surveys have stressed the fact that every farmer wanted to conduct his own experiment before deciding definitely. In Béarn the cultivated areas are generally so small that it is difficult to know which is an experimental and which is a "normal" plot; thus we must again depend upon the recollections and "feelings" of the farmers. As one would expect, three-fourths of the pioneers say they conducted tests, while only 40 percent of those who have recently decided give the same answer. Let us remember that half of those who have not switched to hybrid say that they have tried it and then given it up.

Table 5 clearly shows that the pioneer attempts took several years to spread like a drop of oil and convince the others. After the initial experiments, combined with a popularization campaign that was remarkably well conducted and supported by substantial funds, the corn had to be tested for five or six years by a large number of farmers before it was accepted by the majority. Once the trial period was over, most of the farmers came to a decision during the course of the years 1957 and 1958. Finally, even the most unyielding ones could no longer stay outside the movement. As one of them said: "By God, I had this hybrid corn forced down my throat!"

The relations between father and son within the family play a

Table 5. Dates of Adoption of Hybrid Corn

1952 or earlier	13
1953 to 1955	18
1956 to 1958	49
Have not adopted it	19
Total Farmers Interviewed	99

very important role in this process and should be taken into consideration in a more refined model. In Béarn more than elsewhere, the father maintains a strong patriarchal authority, and the son is of no importance beside him. He must be silent, particularly when a stranger is present. The father is alone responsible for the enterprise and the family, and he tends to think that "young people can have their fun, but when the crop is involved, that's a different matter."

The young people join organizations, in particular the j.a.c.; they attend meetings and invariably support innovations. But the proposal of changes by the younger generation is not the best way to assure acceptance by the old. Some of the young leaders of the popularization campaign did not get along well with their fathers and could not get them to take the course that they urged upon others. Some of the young farmers said, "If it had been up to me, I would have planted it [hybrid] sooner." Or again, "It was out of the question as long as my father was alive." One young man said in the course of an interview that he intended to drop native corn, whereupon his mother, who was also present, appeared shocked and spoke for the first time: "Do you really mean it?" The results of the survey confirmed that young people looked more favorably upon hybrid corn than did their elders.

The absence of a child on a farm often explains why the head of the enterprise has no interest in increasing his production. "When you don't have children you don't care about branching out," while "a family man wants to do well." One father explained himself thus: "I know that hybrid gives a better yield, but it takes a lot of fertilizer. I'm for it, but I'm old. If I had sons I'd push them, but I'm not going to break my neck just for myself." Another acknowledged that he took the step because "my son told me to." One son admitted: "It was hard for my father to get started, but when he saw the results . . . ." Furthermore, it seems that the parents are often more interested in stockbreeding, while the young people prefer cultivation, if it pays well, because it is less confining.

If we could take farm acreage into account, we could make the analysis more precise, but our figures are too limited to provide anything but general impressions. We questioned farmers who

Table 6. Productive Acreage

Less than 16 acres	25
16 to 24 acres	24
24 to 32 acres	25
32 to 40 acres	14
40 acres or more	11
Total Farmers Interviewed	99

owned a total of more than 12 acres distributed as in Table 6 among different categories of productive acreage, by which farm economists mean land used for agricultural production, i.e., arable land, acreage devoted to pasture, and acreage used for arboriculture and truck farming.

All farms of more than 40 acres switched to hybrid corn but after some delay. On the other hand, there were many farms of 32 to 40 acres that experimented with it before 1952. The last to make the change were the farms of 16 to 24 acres. The smallest farms (less than 16 acres) have followed a mean course; some even made the test before 1952.

The position of each category with respect to innovation can be characterized as follows (see Table 7):

–The smallest farms and next-to-largest farms (32 to 40 acres of productive land), being in the most critical situation, are the first to innovate.

–Owners of the smallest farms make the test with a view to obtaining the greatest possible yield from their land and strengthening the autarchic system of production; in some cases they drop hybrid even though the initial small-scale experiment has been successful.

–The next-to-largest farmers feel that to survive in a market economy they must be at the forefront of progress and must equip and extend themselves rapidly. They are the most assiduous readers of technical publications and the most regular attendants of meetings, but they are also least likely to conduct tests before deciding.

–The owners of average and large farms, unlike the others, look to the years ahead. It is the proprietors of the next-to-smallest (16 to 24 acres) who have no awareness of their critical situation; they have lost all concern with the future.

Table 7. Means of Information and Use of Tests, by Size of Farm

	Less than 16 acres	16–24 acres	24–32 acres	32–40 acres	40 acres and more
Read technical journals	44%	20%	44%	71%	45%
Have attended meetings	48	16	36	51	36
Have observed neighboring fields	76	83	56	35	54
Have made tests	60	43	63	42	72

It is possible to construct a hypothetical model for the diffusion of hybrid corn that will show schematically the role of each of these categories and the dynamics of the collective mechanism. The example posed by the experience of the pioneers and by the popularization campaign was observed first with skepticism, and later with interest, by all the farmers. Then a few big farmers, convinced by economic and technical arguments and by test results, made the decision and drew in their wake the mass of farmers: first the next-to-largest, then the average, then the small. The next-to-smallest dragged behind and seemed somehow disinterested in the progress of their farms.

One average landholder described this mechanism himself: "If a small farmer does experiments I pay no attention, if an average one does I think it over, and if a big farmer does I trust him." A small farmer also confirmed the above hypothesis: "I experimented for four years, but I didn't branch out. This year one of them [a large farmer] began, so I'm going to get started." Each large farmer decides for himself after he has weighed the pros and cons, while the small ones decide because of their trust in somebody else. The result is that the little ones unconsciously decide in relation to the situation and the motives of the large farmers, which are very different from theirs. Furthermore, a certain rancor, whether justified or not, can often be detected among the small farmers: "The big farmers didn't tell us everything," or "They told us we mustn't do it," or "They just said that to fool us."

Only a sociometric and historical analysis would permit us to put this schema to the test and refine it, since it is rarely observed in such simplicity. We would have to know exactly who speaks with whom, who has influence over whom, who observes whose field, and so on. In one village an informant was able to single out a small group of eight farmers "who tell each other everything," about twenty "who listen," and a dozen whom "you never see."

The introduction of hybrid corn has entailed distinctly different changes on small and large farms. On those of less than 25 acres, native corn was abandoned by only 3 farmers in 50. Each of the two types of corn occupies an average of one-sixth of the productive land, or a total of one-third for the two types, which clearly exceeds the average for the other categories. Only a few farmers claim to sell more corn than in the past. Among the majority, hybrid has come in some way to support native corn by permitting expansion of the pigsty and the poultry yard. It strengthens the autarchic system of production, which can thus be perpetuated for some time, especially if the family has supplementary nonagricultural income that provides for its financial needs. Two-thirds of the farmers have no tractors. Those who have bought them have placed themselves in a delicate situation; it is hard to see how they can pay their debts unless they do so from extraagricultural income.

On farms of more than 32 acres, the acreage planted in corn rarely exceeds one-fourth of the productive land, and this figure is as low as one-sixth on farms of more than 40 acres. On the other hand, hybrid corn occupies from two to three times more space than that of native corn, and close to half the farmers, particularly those who own between 32 and 40 acres, say that they sell more of it than they used to. Eight farmers out of 25 have already abandoned the local variety, and it seems that most of them own between 32 and 40 acres. These last are patently leaving the traditional autarchic system and orienting themselves toward the market, thus following the example of the owners of the largest farms (more than 40 acres), who had taken this new direction before the advent of hybrid corn.

Thus we see clearly that hybrid corn, like almost all technical innovations, tends to create a cleavage between those who can adopt it with profit and those who refuse to, or those who by adopting it only improve temporarily a jeopardized economic situation, or those who aggravate such a situation by making unwise investments. An example is the farmer with 12 acres who had just bought a tractor but said he did not have enough money to buy the seeds and fertilizer necessary for the cultivation of hybrid corn. But for most the stakes are set: since the income from traditional cultivation is decreasing and the price of corn is going down, it is more and more difficult to "get a start" and to make the necessary investments.

In sum, analysis of the changes brought about by the diffusion of hybrid corn shows that the farmers have a justifiable presentiment when they feel that it is not simply a matter of changing one variety for another, but that they are faced with a fundamental choice between traditional autarchic peasant economy and mass production for the market. Those who hesitate before this innovation, or who in accepting it wish to integrate it into the traditional system without modification, are dimly aware that hybrid corn is really only a token and a means to an end, and that they are in fact confronted with a new society and a new economic system. Unfortunately they do not know that all their efforts to reject these last cannot save them and will, in the end, be their undoing.

Thus once more it can be said with justification that hybrid corn is destroying native agriculture, meaning traditional agricultural and village society, because it is destroying small farmers and with them a whole system of stratification and a kind of society. The Béarnais village of the past is dying, and the people know it. As one of our informants said, "Within ten years, at the rate things are going, there won't be any more small farmers."

A technical change so inoffensive in appearance but with such revolutionary indirect effects is bound to be surrounded by rumors and mythological fantasies reflecting the deep anxieties of the farmers and the social and political tensions that it arouses. We have dealt with the real difficulties that the innovator may encounter on the technical level, but one could also make a sizable collection of all the tales that have been told about hybrid.

Some say with certainty that it "doesn't fatten up the pigs because it's just made of bran;" or, better still, that it "gives the pigs disease." Others believe that it "destroys the land." Elaborating on the process of cross-pollination and its possible effects on a field of local corn bordering a field of hybrid, his Béarnais imagination caused one farmer to worry: "I'll be involved in a lawsuit later on."

More simply, a crop that must be so carefully nurtured does not inspire confidence, for obviously "what's artificial is always artificial;" or "there's going to be sickness and it will spread to the native corn;" or again, "the native corn will be corrupted." In any case it is a fashion that will pass, as do all fashions, like Italian corn before the war. Farmers are frequently heard saying: "You'll see, we'll have to go back to native corn." So it is useless to start hybrid only to abandon it later: "We don't give a darn for what's in fashion."

Thus is established a comparison that sometimes takes on the form of rivalry between the native corn, with which the farmer identifies, and the other, a foreign breed brought in by the "gentlemen with eyeglasses" from the city, and from America at that. For, as we have said, this corn was imported from America and is generally called "American corn." Since Béarnais farmers have until now received only catastrophes from America — like phylloxera and potato bugs — their recollections and experiences lead them to think that the American corn carries epidemics or some other hidden evil.

It does not have the plump, dazzling health of the native *grand roux basque*. It looks ill, like city people. It is delicate; the proof of this is that it takes a long time to grow, that weeds are fatal to it, that it must be helped along by a large supply of fertilizer. For a long time many people said: "If we just did for our corn all that's done for the American, we'd find that ours would be better."

Some tried to convince themselves that the American corn, whatever people said, was neither superior nor better than the Basque. And in order to find out for sure, they set to work on counterexperiments and reverse tests. They cultivated the hybrid corn as they did the native, and the results were disastrous, clearly inferior to those obtained with local corn. Thus they "proved" that the Basque was "better" than the American. Some even pushed the scientific spirit to the point of trying to cultivate the Basque as one would cultivate hybrid, by adding a large amount of chemical fertilizer. The results were just as disastrous: the stalks grew too tall and collapsed, and the ears were no fatter. The idea that each must be treated according to its needs did not enter the mind of the experimenters. In opposition to such relativism, they concluded that chemical fertilizer, being harmful to native corn, was intrinsically "bad," and that consequently it should not be used with hybrid corn either, because something bad cannot give a good result.

Pushed to the absurd, these reverse experiments have given rise to a more widespread belief that the foreign corn will have to become acclimatized in order to be fully established. Some think it can never really become acclimatized: "You go find a shoot of vine in the Jura, you plant it here, and it doesn't grow. It's the same for corn." Another, less pessimistic, states: "I didn't use any fertilizer because the corn just has to get used to this country" — which amounts to wanting to give it a hard life, to make it undergo a training period, a rite of passage; for "the hybrid must prove itself under the same conditions as the Basque." In other words, it is up to the corn to bend to our habits of cultivation and local conditions; it is not up to us to change our habits for "this little gentleman who must be treated with respect." One of our informants pronounced definitively and without appeal the judgment underlying all of these comments: "Native corn is our corn; American belongs in America." And how can one admit that in Béarn an American product is worth more than a Béarnais? Would that not be nonsensical, and insulting to the Béarnais?

This moralizing manichaeism is coupled with a personification of plants that on the one hand allows a highly elaborate psychological identification with "our" corn, and on the other hand presumes a confusion between the system of moral values and the system of technical and economic evaluation. At the beginning of this chain of reasoning one borrows the expert's or the extension agent's point of view, devoting oneself to "experiments" meant to be as "rational" as possible and intended to verify genuine "hypotheses." But then these hypotheses come to be formulated in terms of moral values: there is good and evil, right and wrong. "Experimentation" can thus be interpreted only to the advantage of the good; it denounces and unmasks the evil that seems more attractive than the good.

The system of technical and economic thought based on return and efficiency, when viewed from this level, seems strange to the Béarnais farmer. Quantity has no value for him; it does not satisfy him as an argument. One farmer says regretfully: "If it weren't a question of quantity I wouldn't produce any more hybrid corn." Yet it is precisely quantity that is the decisive argument of the expert and the economist. Farmers discuss the technical aspects freely and frequently, but it seems that they discuss their financial and economic difficulties much less often, although these are normally the most decisive. Some indications lead us to think that if it had been possible to record conversations among farmers on the subject of hybrid corn, the arguments would have dealt mainly with the technical details of cultivation and the entire moral, family, and social context — that is to say, the difficulties, the inconveniences and the risks.

There is good reason to think that in the end, despite appearances, the Béarnais peasant makes his decision from economic motives and because at some point he feels forced to do so by the way things have turned out. But it is certainly not appropriate, in Béarnais peasant society, to talk money or management. In a civilization such as this, in which the art of conversation is highly developed,[4] certain themes lend themselves to discussion and others do not. It would be unsuitable to speak of matters too personal or intimate; to do so might uncover feelings or circumstances that should be left in the private domain. If this interpretation is well founded, it follows that the farmer never discusses the real reason for his decision, which he makes alone with his conscience. On the other hand, he develops a whole language to explain it, rich in wordy sentiments and technical details.

Once it has reached this level of emotional and sentimental reactions, there is only one step to go until the debate acquires a political coloration. This step is taken all the more easily because political life is so spirited in Béarn and because, by a trick of fate, "American" corn became a problem at the time that the extreme left was campaigning against the Americanization and "Marshallization" of France. Some militant Communists did not hesitate to state that hybrid should go home, together with Ridgeway. Inasmuch as the corn gathered its most fervent protagonists among young farmers from the Catholic movements, it entered all the more easily into the local political game, and it was altogether natural that the extreme left should campaign against it.

Thus the most ardent advocates of social progress found themselves opposing technical and economic progress in the name of national independence. In the end, by a singular logical turnabout, they showed themselves in the reactionary colors of defenders of traditional, precapitalistic, hierarchical peasant society — a paradox more apparent than real, it is true, since we have seen that hybrid

[4]Lefebvre, 1965, p. 150.

corn gave impetus to the proletarianization of the small peasant and caused the capitalistic system to penetrate into Béarnais agriculture. Here as elsewhere, Marxist theory met with some difficulty in accounting for the contradictions of the peasant's situation and disentangling the lines of conduct that are adapted to it. It must be realized, furthermore, that the political and syndicalist history of Béarnais agricultural organizations quite naturally induced farmers to look behind hybrid corn for political consequences and motives. Agricultural unionism in the Basses-Pyrénées had been dominated before the war by the strong personality of de Lestapis, a fervent Catholic, who influenced a whole generation of young militants who today hold responsible positions within the *département* and in Paris. In particular the president of the corn growers' union, who was one of the founders of the cooperative at Billières, is the spiritual hier of de Lestapis. The J.A.C. has also had a decisive influence since the war. Thus, whether he accepts or deplores the idea, a farmer can reasonably believe that there is a political network that has a preponderant role in everything that touches on agricultural progress, and particularly on hybrid corn.

The Church, for its part, has unequivocally allied itself with technical progress and economic success. One priest states as an obvious fact that "those who are not with us are the weak ones, those who are dying." And the Church is particularly powerful in the Basque country, rivaling its secular neighbors, so that a partisan wit can speak quite naturally of "curate's maize." Moreover, it is natural that hybrid corn and its sponsors should serve as scapegoats for the small farmer who is aware that he cannot keep up with modernization and that his farm is doomed. This explains very logically the hypothesis advanced at the beginning of the chapter, i.e., that Communists were against and Catholics for hybrid — a hypothesis that we have not been able to verify with the aid of the available data but one that has value as myth and has figured in the great debate aroused by American corn.

The history of agricultural organizations cannot be explained without reference to the political history of each *département* and of France as a whole, as we will see in a later chapter. The peasants know from experience that those who were willing to help them in the past had some ulterior political motive, that they hoped to acquire some influence through services rendered. It is entirely natural for them to believe that anyone who would extol the advantages of hybrid to them, give them advice and even subsidies, and bring trucks up to their doors to buy their crops must have some personal interest. Nobody goes to so much trouble without reason, through pure dedication. Such solicitude must hide something; sooner or later the farmer will have to acknowledge his gratitude to somebody. The young people, who have hardly any memory of prewar political history, are less suspicious, because they believe that today economics and technology are less closely dependent on politics. But their elders tend naturally to seek in the present what they have learned from the past. And when all is said and done, who can say they are not right?

The political danger is not simply ideological or electoral. It is much more direct for the farmer who is becoming increasingly dependent on the expert-adviser and the leaders of cooperatives and unions. One of our informants showed his concern in these words: "We're forced to keep records of everything; we're not free any more to think as we please." Anything that threatens his liberty, no matter how small, is very disturbing to a peasant who has taken centuries to win it.

In the village itself, such changes in agriculture bring into play a number of institutions and influences. If a farmer wishes to obtain a loan from the farm credit agency, his file must be examined by the district administrative council, the members of which are big farmers, precisely those whose fathers used to lend money to people in need. Now they give credit with state funds and no longer with their own, but they are the representatives of the families who have always controlled credit in the village. In the past, to ask for a loan was to admit that one could not make ends meet, and therefore to humiliate oneself. Bitter memories are aroused in an old man who sees his son take out a loan, even for the purpose of an investment that will be a sign of progress and enrichment. The people to whom one must turn are always the same. What is worse, in order to justify his request for a loan he must explain his purpose and open his farm to strange observers: "You have to declare everything and the whole village knows about it right away."

Finally, everything in the village has its political outcome. The best proof of this is that the young people, so set on technology and so scornful of politics, found themselves organizing electoral lists in the

municipal elections of 1959 and won mayoralties in the most progressive villages. If hybrid corn has led to changes in municipal
councils, then suspicions of its political connections are less dis-
placed than they seemed at first sight. Everyone knows that a
mayoralty is only a stepping-stone to all political careers. Thus the
same men reappear everywhere, and there is a justified fear
that if someone does not take vigorous action, they will acquire
control of the entire professional and political life of the
départements.

That a limited technical change has such direct political repercussions is new proof of the close interdependence of all aspects of
society in rural societies. On the technical level, hybrid corn must not
only replace local corn; as we have seen, it must also eliminate the
other cereals, since it permits doubling or tripling of yields and
pays for the investments. It was these arguments that extension
agents cited to urge farmers to abandon the cultivation of wheat,
usually without success and to the great dismay of "true" peasants.
One of the latter exclaimed: "But tell me, monsieur, of what use is a
peasant if he doesn't produce his bread?" These words reveal the
fundamental and total nature of the conflict between the ideal of
the traditional peasant, who farms to feed himself and assure the
continuity of his household, his farm, and his family, and the interest
of the producer, who seeks to produce the largest possible quantity of
the product that sells for the highest price. It is scandalous and
immoral that wheat, a cereal used to make bread, is worth less than
the corn that feeds the animals. There is something wrong in this,
though it is not clear what.
   Advances in cultivation also run counter to traditional ideas in the
amount of risk that they require. By customary methods of cultivation
one renders to the land, in the form of seed and fertilizer, a part of
what it has produced. Furthermore, one bestows on it all the attention
it can use, and expects in return that it will furnish a harvest more or
less abundant, according to weather conditions. Thus one has "laid
out" only his work, and the product saved from the preceding year:
"We use what we have and we don't buy anything." For the new
cultivation, on the contrary, one must buy seeds, fertilizer, and
weed killers, thus staking money on the chance of a return one is
never sure of: "We have to lay out money and we're never sure of

getting it back. It's like the national lottery, and I never played."
Is there anything more removed from the land than the lottery? It
is really a sacrilege to put them in the same category, and all the
professional and moral conscience of a true peasant rebels at the idea.

To earn money is certainly desirable; but on the scale of peasant
values, strengthened by years of inflation, money is not a dependable
value. Only land really has value, and thus a man must work it
well to enrich it, rather than branching out into hazardous specula-
tions that seem to bring a quick return but have no future.

Moreover, there is the claim that one profits when the price of
corn is favorable. But the prices at the market or the fair are set by
merchants and one must submit to them, whether good or bad,
as one submits to inclement weather. The farmer can hardly
take his animals back to the farm because he refuses to sell at a
low price. But he would not think of changing his system of
cultivation in the hope that the price will be different at the
next market. He produces what he must; he sells what he can.
Now hybrid corn, which is not beautiful, which is not cultivated
"as it should be," sells well. To decide to grow it, then, implies
that one is abandoning the mentality of a producer to take on that
of the merchant who speculates in prices. "Me, monsieur? I
never dreamed of speculating!" This expresses the dismay of the
peasant who considers himself honest because he is a producer,
rather than a mere merchant, who makes money on prices
without creating anything. One dares not say that commerce is
in essence dishonest but one thinks so secretly, and this is
what authorizes the honest peasant to be otherwise in the
marketplace: one must fight fire with fire.

It is pointless to insist further by showing how American corn can
be considered an agent of moral perversion and the expert
who proposes it a fiendish tempter. So it is said that here also,
in the deepest sense, hybrid corn threatens to destroy the
farmer in a pernicious way, by corrupting him and attacking his
moral integrity.

If prices could be counted on, one could earn a good living by
selling at the best possible price. But it was generally recognized
in 1959 that the price of corn was too high: if everybody began
to grow it, "what would they do with all this corn in the
cooperatives?" The price would go down, and once again the

farmer would be trapped. To this worry, which turned out to be justified when the price did begin to go down in 1960, the economist answered with his implacable logic: "Grow only corn on all your land, corn and more corn without crop rotation. With present-day fertilizers this is possible. On twenty-five or thirty-five acres at one hundred bushels per acre and at the present price, you will coin money. Ride as long as it lasts by investing to the maximum, enlarging and equipping your farm. When the price goes down, you can start another crop." This is the logical outcome of the system toward which hybrid corn leads: the total destruction of the traditional system of cultivation and its replacement by monocultivation, the end of independence and economic security for the peasant, who becomes a speculator. Intrigue and immorality.

If the farmer had received training or an education that would enable him to know and understand the elementary mechanisms of the modern economy, he could follow changes in the market and see ahead. He used to grow corn to fatten his pigs and geese, which he sold to people in Pau or elsewhere. He saw the whole process and could control it in part. Now he has to produce much more and send the raw product to the cooperative. At the same time, many regions of France that did not produce corn are beginning to do so. In Beauce, near Paris, though there is no Béarnais sun, corn is taking the place of beets. It is understandable that the question is asked: "What are they doing with all that corn in Paris?" "They say they're going to send some to Yugoslavia. Do they need it there?" Or: "With the Common Market we'll need even more." All these reflections betray a sort of dread among farmers faced with immense quantities of corn for which they can imagine neither a destination nor a use, and an anxiety among producers who see themselves contributing to this accumulation.

In order not to abandon all control over prices and outlets, farmers can group themselves into unions and cooperatives. Acting through public authorities, the union can assure that prices do not drop too sharply. The cooperatives stock surplus and look for prospective outlets. But these institutions, as we have said, are often as much a source of disquietude as the authorities themselves, and the farmer feels himself as helpless before one as the other. He rarely distinguishes between them, and as they become fused by his obsequious fear he begins to think quite naturally that hybrid corn provides a new way for the authorities and the administration to meddle in his affairs. He might even follow such reasoning as: "They tell me that with this corn I'll make more money. That's probably because they want to make me pay more taxes, since nowadays the farmer is just the tax-collector's tenant." Navarre has always tried to keep its distance from France, Paris, and their functionaries, and its people are particularly jealous of their independence.[5]

In a brief and revealing statement a modernizing farmer who had knowledgeably cultivated his hybrid corn summed up all the preceding: "This new corn makes us stop and think about the old routines." To this expression of approval he immediately added a reservation: "These Americans come around to pester us!" Another reasoned more moderately: "Always asking us to do better! You'd think we were condemned to hard labor!" Or, as still another put it: "Before, we lived better by producing less; today you work like a mule just to give to some other class of people." And the one who predicted the death of Béarnais agriculture meant exactly that; he ascribed it to hybrid corn without seeing the latter as the forerunner of the entire modern technological civilization that besieges on all sides a peasant civilization ultimately doomed by the exigencies of technical and economic progress. If America is the prototype of this new civilization, one can easily understand why the Béarnais reproach the Americans for coming "to pester them." They are a new incarnation of "the others," of "them," the "*ils*" whom the French, especially those in rural areas, continually berate for not "leaving us alone."[6]

Between the beaten track and adventure the French peasant, like many of his countrymen,[7] sees no middle path, for he has no means of information or calculation at his disposal for meeting the adventure to which technical progress and the market lead him. It is not certain that the past was as satisfying as is said,

[5]Lefebvre, 1965, p. 131 and *passim*.
[6]Wylie, 1957, pp. 206 ff; Bernot and Blancard, 1953, pp. 400–407; Leites, 1958.
[7]Leites, undated, pp. 560–667.

but it followed a path that had been traced by generations whose problems, risks, and hardships were familiar to him. Now, on the contrary, he must "branch out" without knowing exactly why nor how, trusting in experts and leaders whose interest lies more with "them" than with "us."

The term "branch out" *(see lancer),* so often used by farmers in connection with hybrid corn, expresses well the deep sentiments of the peasant, who has enjoyed a routine of delightful immobility, or rather, of daily movements that stir a man without displacing him, and who now sees himself suddenly plunged into a kind of violent and exhausting movement to which he must unreservedly give his all, with unpredictable outcome. The diver who for the first time leaves the secure and restful beach to throw himself into the immense sea, agitated by continuous motion, must feel anxiety akin to this.

Part 2. The Farmer, His Enterprise, and Society

"You have subordinated your life to money; money is the creature of the government; why be surprised to find yourself subordinated to the government? If in order to live you need somebody other than yourself, why be surprised if he becomes the master of your life?"

Jean Giono, *Lettre aux paysans sur la pauvreté et la paix,* 1937.

5. The Entrepreneur and His Decisions

Shaped in the mold of traditional society and accustomed to its slow and familiar functioning, the contemporary French peasant finds himself brutally plunged into continual technical and economic change, so that he lives simultaneously under two contradictory systems of logic.

Some remain fiercely attached to the traditional system in which they have been raised, which seems to them the only one that can justify their lives. They believe that to be free, to eat one's bread, and to respect nature are the three bases of moral and economic existence that cannot be ignored if one makes one's living from the land. And since traditional social structures remain essentially unchanged, they feel justified in remaining faithful to custom and in criticizing the wild schemes of young people and city dwellers.

In contrast to these there are others, especially members of the younger generation influenced by the Catholic Action movements, who have decided to play the modern economic game consciously. In meetings and conferences they learn how to become true entrepreneurs and to change the management of the family farm so as to make it into what they believe to be a genuine enterprise. Careful bookkeeping permits them to make investments in order to increase their profits, and they pay close attention to the economic situation and the state of the market. Unfortunately the enterprise is often too small to make these investments profitable, because they become obsolete before they are amortized and deficits show up in the accounts. So, what good is it to invest?

All these uncertainties probably account for the fundamental contradiction between a deep pessimism supported by a disparaging image of the farmer's occupation and condition and the remarkable efforts toward progress and modernization evinced by French agriculture as a whole. The great majority of farmers interviewed in our studies mentioned at least one improvement recently made on their farms. Only the oldest were not in the process of modernizing. Of course, these improvements were often minimal and reflected habits of maintenance rather than progress, yet they indicated that the pessimism did not go as far as defeatism or despair. The analysis of decision-making mechanisms and the economic mentality sheds light on these observations and above all opens perspectives for future research.

Aware of the collapse of the traditional world but still unschooled in the ways of conduct in the modern world, the great mass of farmers live astride both worlds, hemmed in by the old structures and yet continually attracted by the modern, by progress, by the city. One after another they try the new logic, then change back to the old, apply the new to areas where it has no application, and interpret the modern in terms of the old world, which is conceived as eternal. What is generally called agricultural extension or, in a broader sense, the diffusion of technical, economic, and social innovations, is commanded by this logical conflict in the mind of the family farmer and in his present situation.

Rural economists stress the "rationality" of the economic behavior that they would like to inculcate in the peasant. When held up to this rationality, all acts that do not conform to it seem irrational. We have shown how to a peasant a profitable investment can seem an extravagance, a luxury for the rich, whereas the purchase of an unprofitable tractor seems to him to be an unavoidable necessity. The rationality of traditional behavior in a traditional universe is obvious; its appropriateness is clear at first glance and is easily confirmed by analysis. But from the moment when the corresponding social systems themselves are in conflict, and certain elements of the old remain very much alive while others have yielded place to the new, it becomes hazardous to say what is "rational" and what is not, since the definition of the word depends on its context. The two rationalities are in conflict, and it is to be expected that the economic will eventually overcome the traditional. For the moment, the farmers are experiencing this conflict, and he would be a clever man indeed who could propose rational economic behavior here and now without the risk of reversing his opinion the next day.

There is an abundance of sociological literature devoted to the behavior and attitudes of farmers with regard to change. Essentially of North American origin and psychosociological inspiration,[1] it concentrates its analysis on the "good farmer," his qualities, his faults, his position, and his social role. As the good farmer is by hypothesis the one who conforms to economic rationality, he must have as his opposite number a "bad" farmer, that is to say a queer,

[1]See two presentations: Rogers, 1965; Lionberger, 1962.

incoherent, irrational person, a poor creature constructed *a contrario* of psychological dimensions that almost always bear a minus sign. Nobody takes the trouble to understand him; he is by definition incomprehensible. No study, to my knowledge, has been made of bad farmers that assigns a plus sign to their traits and seeks to contrast them with "good farmers" reconstructed in reverse, starting with the same traits pushed to the opposite extreme. Such a game would be instructive and well worth the effort.

In a study of the peasants of Winterswijk (Holland), Bruno Benvenuti posed the problem in terms of the conflicts between civilizations,[2] but at the same time he wanted to "study the influence exercised by an 'urban' type of civilization on the management of farm enterprises... and the process of urbanization to which, in every modern country, the farm population finds itself more or less subjected" (p. xxv). Starting from these premises he arrives quite naturally at the conclusion that the progressive farmer is characterized principally by his receptiveness to the external world. The tautology is obvious: since progress comes from the outside, one must face in that direction in order to welcome it. This simplistic conclusion does injury to the richness of the analysis in which Benvenuti stresses, in contrast to this openness, the "totalitarian" aspect of traditional peasant society. He demonstrates that in order to turn toward the modern system the peasant must completely master his own behavior as an individual; this presumes a clear awareness of his personal position in the traditional system he is thus challenging.

Seeking to sketch the portrait of the progressive farmer, Benvenuti contrasts him with the traditional farmer. Yet he emphasizes the idea that these portraits "are situated at two extremes of a continuum, and consequently it is perfectly logical that the differences should be sharply defined. This also explains...the impression of a strict and harmonious conformity between the activities and the attitudes of the two groups" (p. 225). Every continuum, unless it is the result of a precise technical construction, is a trick of analysis, enticing but deceiving.

Most American studies[3] do no more than enumerate the principal characteristics of those who are the first to adopt new techniques. In all cases the most progressive farmers have

[2]Benvenuti, 1961.
[3]For a bibliography see Rogers, 1962.

received better professional and general training; they are younger; and they work farms of acreages well above average for their regions, from which they draw higher yields. They read more newspapers and farm jounrals, go to town more often, participate more regularly in the work of various institutions, associations, and groups, professional and otherwise. All these studies bring out a close connection between participation and the spirit of progress. It is to be expected that the best farmers assume responsibility in unions, cooperatives, and other farm organizations; it is less predictable that they also participate most actively in social life in general. On the other hand, those Americans who are the most open to technical progress are also the most ready to accept changes in such different realms as the church or the school. In Europe, and particularly in France, the most modern farmers are often conservative in matters of politics and religion, and take no interest in village life. One must be careful not to generalize too hastily by transferring across the Atlantic conclusions that do not make sufficient allowance for the social context as a whole.

The few European studies that deal with peasants[4] stress the importance of the family situation and the system of values. Farmers who work lands they have inherited from their parents, and therefore have never moved about, are in general less inclined to innovate than tenant farmers who have changed farms or landholders who have acquired their land at one time or another. The younger a man is when he acquires direction of his farm (through inheritance, purchase, or rental) the readier he is to make changes. Extended families, in which several generations and occasionally several married brothers and sisters live together, are not favorable to change, especially if patriarchal authority remains undisputed and the education of the children is in the hands of grandparents. Depending on the circumstances, the wife may or may not contribute to innovation; everything is related to the family structure and the role she plays in it. In the area of good management, the most progressive farmers assign more importance to factors of an intellectual order (capa-

[4]Mendras, 1958; Benvenuti, 1961; Van den Ban, 1957–1960; Westermark, 1954; Harper, 1954; Jollivet, 1966; and Appendix 2, Nos. 18, 28, and 41.

city for organization, theoretical knowledge), while others insist
on emotional factors (harmony of everyday life, collaboration of
the wife and children in the work, and so on).

To study the qualities and the situation of the progressive
farmer and contrast them with those of the traditional farmer is
only the first step, and one that sheds very little light on the
mechanisms of the diffusion of innovations. The modern farmer is
the terminus of a number of communication networks originating
in the biologist's or the agronomist's laboratory, in committees
for economic study and observation, and in administrative offices
in which the great decisions of economic policy are made. As
the last link in these networks, the local agricultural adviser
serves the essential function of "translating" these scientific and
technical messages into the farmers' language and adapting
them to local conditions. But other sources of information are also
offered to farmers: the press and radio, advertising, salesmen of
agricultural equipment, conferences, and above all conversations
with neighbors and relatives.

Available studies show that 87 percent of French farmers listen
to the radio and 78 percent read a daily newspaper.[5] They look
to the radio chiefly for entertainment and general information
and to their newspapers for technical advice, and information
on market fluctuations, in addition to local news. On the other
hand, national farm weeklies and monthlies (e.g., *Journal de la
France agricole, Figaro agricole,* and others)[6] often seem to them
to be poorly adapted to the local situation. As one farmer said:
"They're a little beyond us; they're on the national level. There's
quite a study on sheep but it doesn't concern us." While he informs
himself through radio and the press, the farmer, more than anyone
else, needs to discuss, interpret, and evaluate the message
received by sharing it with his fellow farmers. Fairs and markets,
though they are gradually losing their economic function,
continue to be occasions for meeting and conversing. Generally,
the opinion of the big farmers carries weight; on the other hand,
it seems that the importance of the traditional notables
(squire, notary, teacher, and so on) is diminishing.

Almost half the farmers say that when considering a purchase

[5]*Sondages,* 1964.
[6]Labrusse, 1958.

of equipment they trust the salesman or the dealer completely
to guide their choices; only 15 percent mention their neighbors
and 5 percent the farm experts. On the other hand, 48 percent
have seen equipment on a neighbor's farm, and 40 percent have
discussed it with him. The farmers in this group say that they
learn from their neighbors but make their own decisions.
Finally, 75 percent have more confidence in what they are told
than in what they read. Our pilot studies confirmed these results,
which were taken from a national survey.

Studies now in progress will supply us with more details on
the mechanisms by which information is acquired and evaluated
and by which decisions are made.[7] It is necessary to make distinctions that take into account the type of technique proposed
and the type of social relations prevailing in the region under
consideration. One American study[8] shows that neighbors and
merchants are more often mentioned in connection with
techniques related to traditional market products, such as the
cultivation of corn; while agricultural advisers, radio, and the
press seem to have more influence in introducing completely new
techniques, such as the creation of permanent pasturage. In all
cases, well-to-do farmers depend more than others on agricultural advisers, radio, and the press.

Another American study[9] shows that in localities where there are
an intense neighborhood spirit and personal contacts that are
direct and frequent, conversations with neighbors are more
influential (mentioned in 48 percent of the responses) than the
press and radio (25 percent). In localities where the neighborhood
spirit is less pronounced, the results are the opposite: 28 percent
as against 42 percent. Moreover, in the latter places one speaks
as freely with the owners of relatively distant farms whom
one sees in the city or at meetings as with an immediate
neighbor, whereas in the former case conversations generally
take place between neighbors. There are thus two types of
communications systems: that of the face-to-face neighborhood in
which information and influence follow traditional channels,
whether personal or more general, and that of a more differentiated

[7] See Appendix 2, Nos. 18, 28, and 41.
[8] Wilkening, 1950.
[9] Lionberger and Hassinger, 1954.

society in which the means of mass communication play a larger part and in which organizations and institutions rather than proximity are the limiting factors. Agricultural advisers, who can work within either system of communication, are mentioned with equal frequency by respondents from both types of regions. Morever, Merton and Lazarsfeld have shown that these two systems of communication overlap as closely in a section of a city as in a town or rural district.[10] Information arrives through the press, radio, and television but must be discussed, interpreted, and evaluated in conversations in order to be truly understood and then put to use. It is by talking with her neighbors and friends, for example, that a young woman chooses among the different brands of underwear suggested to her in the advertising pages of the magazines she reads.

In this process of collective digestion influential people have a decisive role.[11] The more cosmopolitan are familiar with reliable sources of information, the best periodicals — those that are more difficult to read, more expensive, more technical, or more chic — and so their neighbors go to them particularly for information. Others, principally concerned with local problems, have a more personal and moral influence, and take special interest in family and neighborhood problems. Furthermore, everyone in each of these groups is generally held to be competent in one particular field, and one rarely asks advice of the same person on buying a tractor, finding a job for a daughter, or voting in the elections.

The diversity of influential people, their audience, and their sphere of influence form a fruitful and highly productive field of research for all those who are concerned with directing the course of a given region or the market for a consumer product. Innovators infatuated with progress and new ideas do not always find a following. On the other hand the traditionalist, to whom every change seems dangerous if not evil, generally has no difficulty in making himself heard. Everything depends on the dominant trend in the region. Where the farmers favor change they will seek the advice of progressive colleagues who are far ahead of them; on the other hand, where they distrust change

[10]Katz and Lazarsfeld, 1955.
[11]Merton, 1965, pp. 295–321.

they will associate especially with people who have prestige and influence in the community but who are not more qualified than themselves. That the influential people are more advanced than the majority is a sign and a source of dynamism in a region.

In backward regions, everybody being at almost the same point, the mechanism of interpersonal relations tends toward the status quo. The man who is conspicuous for his "progress" does not serve as a guide. In regions that are progressing, the advancement of some and the attempts of others to imitate them assure dynamism, and the larger the distance between them the more rapid the rhythm of change.

Daily observation and the few detailed studies that are available demonstrate that innovations are made by means of a collective process that resembles a phenomenon of fashion and imitation rather than an aggregate of reasoned calculations made by each farmer.[12] Any dealer in farm machinery can say in what year the purchase of tractors began and in what year (between five and ten years later) almost all the farmers had become mechanized; then came the period of binders, then harvester-threshers, and so on. The same was true of household equipment: in a few years butane stoves had spread to all the farms in one region; after this came the era of new bedroom furniture, followed by that of the refrigerator, and then the washing machine. Each region had its own sequence, rhythm, and chronology for the introduction of modern products and practices. Unfortunately, aside from one on Albenque in southern Finistère,[13] there are hardly any systematic studies on this subject in France.

In most cases the adoption of an innovation appears to proceed in three stages. First some pioneers try it out for a few years; then the mass follows their example, either because the advantages of the innovation command attention or because some sort of need arises; and finally the backward ones take the step.

The interviewer is always astonished, when he asks why someone has bought a binder or a butane stove, to hear the answer, "We needed it," without any more precise rational explanation. And still it is true: unsatisfied "needs" are innumerable in the country. Housing and household equipment were antiquated almost everywhere ten

[12]See Tarde, 1927.
[13]See Appendix 2, No. 35.

years ago and are so in some regions today. Besides, a farm is never completely equipped. The more machines one buys, the more one needs newer machines, more complex and costly than the old. From among these many needs some pioneers perhaps make a deliberate choice, but the mass of farmers, one after another, become aware of them as they see their neighbors satisfy them. There comes a moment when a particular purchase or practice becomes essential: "We couldn't do without it any more." As Jollivet remarks:

Peasants do not make a rational decision after appropriate documentary research in order to solve a problem of which they are consciously aware. On the contrary, it is by seeing in operation the machine which can be of help to them that they become aware of the possibility for improvement. The continuing demonstration given by the progressive farmer definitely guarantees the quality of the machine, the fertilizer, or the new seed, and permits judgment of the results. But more important, it is this demonstration that gives rise to the very idea of the possibility for improvement.[14]

To put it another way, the need is created at the same time that the means of satisfying it appears, and the distinction between the why and the how of an improvement is alien to a farmer. When he is asked where his idea came from, his numerous hesitations are more revealing than the answer he gives, for he is being asked a question he has never asked himself. A series of precise analyses would be needed to verify this schema; the process of collective acceptance is certainly different for a product of technology, such as a machine for the home or the farm, a biological advance that takes the form of a method, organization one must join, or a commercial, financial, or technical usage.

For a polycultivating region in Aude, Lanneau was able to construct a chronological chart (Table 8) in which the white portions of the bars indicate periods of an average rate of acceptance and the black portions indicate periods of accelerated acceptance.[15]

This chart shows clearly that the tractor is the first step, the one that precedes the use of credit and follows the process described above. Associations and cooperatives come later on and require more time to become accepted.

At Nay, in our sample of 100 farmers, 7 had tried hybrid corn in 1949 and 16 had not adopted it as late as 1957; a first group of 35 had decided for it between 1950 and 1953; the movement had

14Jollivet, 1962.
15See Appendix 2, No. 28.

Table 8. Rates of Acceptance in a Region of Aude

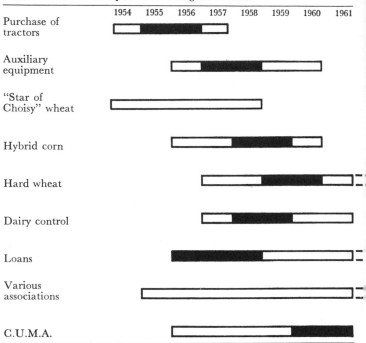

slowed down in 1954 and 1955, to accelerate again in 1956 and 1957. A period of 15 years will have passed before hybrid corn is cultivated on almost all farms.

Studies on the spread of agricultural progress and the traits of modern farmers furnish useful lessons for extension work and contribute to a sociological theory of communications and change, but they shed little light on the ambiguities and contradictions with which the peasant must struggle if he seeks to play the game of technological progress and economic rationality. One can see clearly enough what the expert and the economist propose, through what means of information they can make themselves heard, and which are the men most inclined to listen to them. In earlier chapters we have given some idea of the situation and the logic of the traditional peasant; can we pinpoint the way in which he understands what is being said to him and what meaning it can have for him?

Table 9. The Qualities of a Good Farmer

	Sundgau	Combrailles	Béarn	Léon
Has the means	30%	55%	36%	23%
Works hard	35		17	43
Modernizes	30	80	61	14
Other or no answer	20	50	31	48
Total answers per 100 interviewed	115	230	145	128

First, what idea does he have of the "good farmer," that mythical being whom he is called upon, even implored, to imitate? In four studies[16] we asked the question: "Do you know a good farmer? Why do you think he is a good farmer?" The answers we gathered (Table 9) can be summarized in three essential characteristics: the good farmer *possesses the means* to be one (land, livestock, machines, family manpower), he *works hard* and carefully, and he *aims for progress*. This last trait is only the affirmative form of the question; it was so strongly suggested at the beginning of the interviews that it would probably have been mentioned less often in a conversation less clearly directed. The distribution of responses should therefore be interpreted with caution.

Most of the "other" answers were simple descriptions: "He gets results" or "He's a good farmer because he has fine crops." If this distribution of responses were not in part a reflection of the questionnaire, it would testify to a fine spirit of modernization among farmers, particularly those of Combrailles. On the other hand, it is remarkable that in the opinion of approximately one-third of the farmers one cannot be a good farmer without having the means.

This apparently obvious fact is not a fact at all. It could be said that the farmer is all the more skillful if he has overcome more difficult conditions. In the thinking of the expert, the small farmer who draws a high gross income from eight or ten acres through very skillful cultivation and breeding is a better farmer than his neighbor who obtains the same income from about thirty acres while preserving the traditional system of cultivation. To the peasant, on the other hand, it is the latter who is the good farmer, and his neighbor is only an acrobat who has temporarily succeeded through a feat of strength that is doomed to failure, a small man who is straining every nerve to

[16]See Appendix 2, Nos. 1 to 5.

overcome his difficulties but will not succeed for long. To be a good farmer one must be capable of being one. If in our studies we had been able to learn the names of the "good" farmers mentioned, there is no doubt they would almost all have been "big" ones.

For their part, economists show that on farms of less than a certain acreage it is much more difficult to manage profitably. In the Châteaulin basin, in 1956, Chombart de Lauwe reported large variations in economic returns as related to size. If he was skillful, a small farmer could draw a good income from a small area, but on holdings of less than 37 acres the "average" farmer could not succeed in obtaining sufficient yields to support his family. In 1964 a student of Chombart de Lauwe, while redoing the same study in the same region by the same methods, concluded that this threshold had been raised to 52 acres, an increase of almost 50 percent in eight years.[17] After a statistical analysis of a large number of accounts, Louis Malassis reached similar conclusions: "As the surface area of the farm increases . . . the economic yield and the rate of profit increase (up to a certain limit), as well as the productivity, income, and standard of living of the worker."[18] Economists are in agreement, then, with the peasants: to be a good farmer one must have the means. In other words, those who are capable are good farmers; or, to be a good farmer is a luxury reserved for the rich.

Is it necessary to point out the importance of this idea in the farmer's rationalization? The conclusion is obvious: if I am not a good farmer, it is because I cannot be one. In fact, for most of the farmers questioned, the good farmer is the other person, or a simple stereotyped image, but it is never *myself*. The interview situation naturally induces this reaction, particularly insofar as the farmers seek to furnish the interviewer with the image they believe to be his: the implied expectation of the interviewer weighs heavily.[19] Deeper study would no doubt permit us to sketch the model that each farmer sets up for himself.

In the traditional image of the good farmer, possession of the means often goes hand in hand with courage and zeal for work. The factor analysis produced from the data common to the four studies[20]

[17]Chombart de Lauwe and Morvan, 1954, and verbal communication.
[18]Malassis, 1958, p. 287.
[19]See Appendix 1.
[20]See Appendix 2, No. 5. This factor analysis was conducted under the direction of R. Bassoul, whom the author thanks for his fruitful collaboration in this work as in others.

shows a significant connection between those two ideas. To say of a neighbor that "he spares no pains" is a great compliment. One of the men interviewed summed up his ideas on this point by saying: "There are some who don't work and others who work hard," and this closed the discussion for a substantial number of those who were questioned. If in addition the hard-working, well-to-do farmer has grown-up children who work for him, he is really a good farmer in the traditional sense; he has at his disposal sufficient amounts of land, livestock, and manpower.

When compared to this image, the "progressive" idea of the good farmer reveals a radically different viewpoint. It is no longer by his moral qualities that one judges the good farmer, but by the results he obtains and by his skill: he "gets good results, good yields," and besides he "goes along with progress," or he "uses fertilizer." All of this presupposes that he "does his homework," that he keeps himself informed, reads, goes to meetings: in brief, he "works intelligently" and "figures things out better than other people." According to the factor analysis, the connection between these traits is even stronger than between traditional traits. The modern image would consequently be more coherent but also perhaps more stereotyped, while the traditional image would more often be contaminated by modern traits.

The wine growers of Languedoc, who are monocultivators, are in a situation very different from that of other farmers.[21] Their product depends almost entirely on work and skill; thus it is not surprising that 67 percent describe the good wine grower as one who knows how to work hard, while only 9 percent say he is one who has good grapevines, and 5 percent one who makes good wine.

It goes without saying that in general small farmers insist above all on the necessity of having the means to be good farmers, while large operators attach more importance to personal qualities, both traditional and modern in type. In his study on southern Brittany, Maho asked his respondents not to describe the good farmer but to give an example of one. He found that small farmers readily cited somebody from the immediate neighborhood, somebody who did a little better than the others.[22] The average farmers chose their models within a larger perimeter. Among the large farmers, some referred to

[21]*Ibid,* No. 7.
[22]*Ibid,* No. 18.

well-managed farms in the region as a whole, while others stated that there was no good farm in Brittany and that it was necessary to go farther to find examples — to Beauce, for example. They obviously implied by this that they classified themselves among the best Breton farmers. Finally, to any farmer, no matter what size his holdings, a good farmer is almost always one whose farm is bigger than his own; one whose farm is smaller can only be a "little fellow who just manages to get by."

Under these conditions one would expect all farmers, and especially small ones, to stress the need for increasing the area they cultivate. But curiously enough, the responses to the question, "Do you think your farm is a good size, too small, or too large?" show that in three regions out of four the majority of farmers consider their farms large enough or too large (Table 10). Let us remember that in Combrailles, which is animal-breeding country, average farms measure between 37 and 50 acres, while in the other three regions they measure between 25 and 37 acres.

When farmers are asked, "How many acres must one have to support a family comfortably or to make it worthwhile to have a tractor?" the estimates are relatively low (Table 11).

The answers to the two questions are distributed in approximately the same way, which leads us to think that a tractor is normally a part of any farm capable of supporting a family. In fact, the factor analysis confirms the supposition that this link is very strong: family, farm, and tractor normally go together, and a farm without a tractor is not a real farm. Except in Combrailles, the majority of farmers are content with less than 37 acres, and in the four regions most would like to have several acres more than they now own. This confirms the preceding results. Similarly, close to half the winegrowers judge that in order to support a family one must produce between 11,000 and 15,500 gallons of wine, a figure that corresponds approximately to the median production declared in the answers.

If they are asked why their farms seem large enough or too large,

Table 10. Farmers' Opinions of the Size of Their Farms

	Sundgau	Combrailles	Béarn	Léon
Good size	55%	59%	46%	34%
Too small	29	30	46	65
Too large	6	8	6	1
Don't know	10	3	2	0

Table 11. Size of Farm Necessary to Support a Family or a Tractor

	Sundgau		Combrailles		Béarn		Léon	
	T	F	T	F	T	F	T	F
Less than 25 acres	2%	3%	0%	0%	13%	7%	21%	30%
25–37 acres	10	32	30	31	45	46	40	38
37–50 acres	25	31	30	31	16	23	24	21
50–75 acres	50	24	24	25	23	22	9	5
More than 75 acres	5	2	11	8	0	0	5	2
No answer	8	8	5	5	3	2	1	4

farmers simply say they have "enough work as it is," that one "can't find hired help any more" and that they could not work a larger area. For a portion of the answers this paradoxical result is explained by the age of the respondents: an older man is content with what he has and cannot increase his work load. The farmers feel caught in a contradiction for which they cannot imagine a solution: to be better farmers and hence earn a better living they would have to have more land, but to work more land they would have to have more manpower. This dilemma also explains the importance attached to the family work force in the traditional characterization of a good farmer.

To break this vicious circle and increase the acreage without increasing one's work force, one can either change the system of cultivation or buy machines that do the work faster. Or the yield from a given acreage can be increased through intensified cultivation or breeding, use of fertilizer, scientific feeding, and selected seeds or cattle. But one can clearly see that, except for the purchase of machines, these solutions are relatively foreign to the practice of the traditional peasant, for whom the system of cultivation is a fact, an imperative of nature inherited from his ancestors, one that it would be hazardous to change. As for "biological advances," they are difficult to learn of, to understand, and to handle, except for fertilizers now familiar to everybody; and even these are not always put to good use.

Marcel Jollivet's remark about the best farmers of Combrailles can be applied to all French farmers:

The most traditional still consider the system of cultivation a rigid fact.... What makes them unique is that they have mechanized, they use more fertilizer, and they get better yields....

One of them continues traditional polycultivation; he complains of it as a form of servitude inherent in the local agriculture, and the only improvement possible seems to him to be an improvement in yields .... The least traditional, on the contrary, not only consider it absurd to produce cereals; they understand as well that every crop, in order to be profitable, must be transformed into animal products .... Far from reducing their possibilities by bowing to narrowly-defined natural vocations, they multiply them by adopting flexible systems of cultivation that permit them to operate within a wide range of animal products, depending on price fluctuations.

Agriculture today is an art not only of producing but also of adapting to the demands of the market. From the moment that the farmer no longer thinks of himself only as a producer and begins to consider outlets for his produce, his entire universe is transformed. The peasant who farms to feed his family and the agricultural producer who responds to the needs of the consumer represent viewpoints that are totally opposed. Living as they do astride two contradictory systems of logic, farmers naturally tend to think that their role is to produce but not to sell. And so if they do not get good prices for their products the fault is others', not their own.

The winegrowers, of course, have a very different attitude. Half of them think that a good year is one in which wine sells at a high price; to 30 percent of them it is a year in which there is a large wine crop; and only 20 percent think of it as a year in which the wine is good. As a producer of wine, the wine grower thus is concerned chiefly with the income he derives from his product. Besides, he has the feeling that the produce is out of his hands once it is sold; he does not know "where it goes" and has little idea of the consumer, his needs, and his tastes.

According to a survey by the I.F.O.P., 71 percent of the farmers think that their farms are going well.[23] By local standards they judge themselves to be fairly good, and 9 percent of them to be very good, farmers. If they are asked what they could do to increase the income from their farms, half have no suggestions to make; 20 percent speak of increasing the selling prices of their products or simply of having more money to spend; and the 24 percent who are considering various technical improvements (land consolidation, purchase of equipment, use of fertilizer)

[23]Géraud and Spitzer, 1965; Jollivet, 1966. See Appendix 2, No. 23.

mention that they would need money to make them. Only a few think of changing their system of cultivation. As far as the great majority are concerned, they cannot modify their situation if they have no money to equip themselves, and they will have money only if the state intervenes in setting farm and industrial prices.

Thus the purchase of a tractor and other machinery is necessary for the farmer who wants to progress without calling into question the entire traditional system of farming. The tractor can be added to this system without changing it. Once acquired, it will permit the farmer to extend himself, to become bigger without modifying the system, and finally to raise himself on the professional and social scale of the village.

On the other hand, if additional land cannot be found, the underemployed tractor will be expensive. If it was not bought with savings it will have to be amortized, a process that could reduce the farmer at least to poverty, in some cases to ruin, often to leaving the land. The logic of investment in machinery, which should be profitable and amortizable, is introduced onto the farm with the tractor and forces the farmer to become an entrepreneur or disappear. Thus the recent policy of the administration and Farm Credit, which have made use of propaganda and loans to encourage farmers to mechanize, led simultaneously to the introduction of an economic rationale into farm management and the acceleration of the rural exodus.

Many peasants, more or less aware of the dramatic choice to which a tractor will push them in time, avoid it by not buying unless they have the money in hand. Before "treating themselves" they wait till they have enough savings, instead of calculating the profitability of the investment as a real entrepreneur would and as the economist advises them to do. The "rationality" of their extraeconomic motives has been demonstrated above, and we see here that their behavior in financial matters is also entirely rational. On the contrary, the ones who are "irrational" are those who borrow from Farm Credit in order to buy a tractor that does not pay. They are playing the investment game. They seem to count on an illusory increase in income to repay the debt and the interest, while logically they should look upon the expenditure as a consumer loan that will cost more than it returns; it will have to be paid back from income other than that produced by the false investment. It is with just cause that the peasant shakes his head skeptically at the "economic" reasoning of the experts and bankers; he is suspicious of a loan that could represent either an expenditure or an investment.

According to the I.F.O.P. survey, 28 percent of the farmers questioned declared that they kept written accounts. Granted that the entire questionnaire, and this question itself, invited a yes response, one can assume that about one–fifth or one–fourth of the farmers "do some bookkeeping." But what exactly is meant by this expression? About one farmer in ten keeps single entry accounts. Those who manage a farm know from their ledgers which products pay and which cost money; they know the remuneration for their work or their capital and the amount of their profit or deficit. They are the exceptions. Otherwise it should be said that the balance sheets for a family farm must not be taken literally, for how can it be explained that so many farms that are losing money, as they say, have continued for many years to be equipped and modernized and to support a family, sometimes very well? Jean Cuisenier's studies on traditional methods of management and their intellectual tools explain this paradox. One would have to elaborate the whole theory behind peasant economic usage and contrast it with that of the accountant.

It is obvious that when there is no budget, nothing about the management of the family farm is clear or certain. Observing the example of his neighbors, the farmer must decide on the basis of impressions, judgments, and evaluations. When he answers that one can make a living from 35 acres or that a tractor is profitable on a farm of that size, he is judging according to his personal situation, which he would like to improve a little, and according to what he knows about farmers in the neighborhood who seem to get along well. But to judge whether they are really getting along well, what criterion must he use? One man has a brand-new tractor, but his wife has no running water in the house and is working herself to death in the fields. Another lives well, his daughters are well dressed, and his house is in good repair; but it is said he is in debt up to his ears. In a third household, the son works at the factory, and the tractor must have been paid for with his salary. Who is rich and who is poor? Who lives meagerly and who lives well? Who has bought a great deal of land and equipment and who has not? Who sells at a good price and who too low? One could go on indefinitely with this list of criteria, each as imprecise and open to discussion as the next, and as impossible to weigh. Each case is a particular case, each man has his qualities and skills, each leads his life as he thinks proper.

On the other hand, it is an obvious fact that the big farmers are wealthier, live better, and seem to "get along well," all the while modernizing their farms and homes and putting their children through school. A man could follow their example with assurance. A false assurance, it is true, since by definition the big farmers are in a situation different from that of the average and small farmers. Their system of farming is not the same, and their methods of management meet other needs, since quantities sold and the monetary resources are more important, and self-consumption is negligible. And while the equilibrium of a small farm is easy for a neighbor to observe, that of a large one, being more complex, is less so. The neighbor sees the signs and interprets them from his own point of view. The small farmer, therefore, naturally tends to copy the signs and symbols of the big farmer's prestige, whereas he should try instead to understand the equilibrium of the large farm, and so be inspired to see his own total situation in a new light.

This fundamental mechanism of the diffusion of technological progress in rural areas — the imitation of farmers wealthier than oneself — leads to deplorable results for the small farmers. They emulate in big farmers the actions that best conform to the dominant image of progress (the purchase of a tractor, for example) and not those that are most effective (such as the use of chemical fertilizer and artificial insemination) and within their means. Farm extension agents are apt to be shocked when they see, in their own words, "mechanical improvements" spreading more rapidly than "biological improvements," though the second, which necessitate modest investments that can be financed by short-term farm credit, are more profitable for a small farmer. However, they are themselves partly responsible for this phenomenon, inasmuch as they contributed, particularly in the beginning, to the process by which progress came to be identified with the big farmers who were mechanizing.

They led people to believe that this constituted the only model for modernization, with the result that their efforts on behalf of biological improvements were less persuasive than they might have been. And since such improvements are difficult to handle, they are also difficult to explain and propose effectively.

Again the most striking example is the tractor, which the small farmer buys to exploit his twenty or twenty-five acres because, at the time, to be a real farmer he must have a tractor. It is the first mechanical implement that a peasant knows, and he utilizes it badly. Because it was expensive, it is "saved;" standing unused in its shed, it depreciates without being paid for. If there is not enough money to buy all the necessary fittings to go with it (plows, towlines, cutting bars and so on), it pulls the ancient cart, hand plow, or seeder. It replaces the team in its draft function, instead of pulling and activating powerful and improved implements and furnishing the energy necessary to their operation. In other words, it is used not according to its logic but according to the old preindustrial logic.

It is the same with running water. The installation of a faucet at which the usual pails and watering pots can be filled lessens the difficulty of transport; on the other hand, it does not take advantage of the new possibilities of running water, since they are based on waste and it is still necessary to economize. Conversely, the purchase of a washing machine on a farm where there are only cisterns that are dry every summer is even more paradoxical. Like every technical innovation, the tractor, running water, and the washing machine are not isolated objects that can be added to an old system; they belong to a group of objects and methods without which they are only symbols of modernism and not a genuine modernization. As Marie Moscovici writes:

Apparent change is thus only an appearance of change, an effort to maintain ties with surrounding reality without modifying it in its entirety. . . . While total modernization brings concrete progressive solutions to the problems posed by the necessity for change, symbolic modernization only reveals contradictions.[24]

Sometimes it happens also that the method precedes the corresponding equipment. By means of publications and meetings, Catholic Action organizations and home economics schools are increasing tenfold the influence of the feminist press, which has been widely read during the last decade in rural areas. Young countrywomen are

[24]Moscovici, 1960, p. 72; see also Appendix 2, No. 21.

discovering the virtues of personal and household cleanliness that were so lacking in some regions. One must wash, bathe the children, and have clean curtains at the windows. Who would not rejoice in such a movement? Unfortunately, on a farm that has only cisterns or a well half a mile away, it is necessary to economize on water or kill oneself carrying it. Besides, bathing and washing add to the innumerable domestic and farm tasks of the farmer's wife, who is killing herself in the attempt to do her share of the usual tasks (the milking, the pigs, and the poultry, not to mention work in the fields) while being a model mother and housewife according to the principles of such publications as the *Petit echo de la mode* or *Mon village*.

It would be easy to add to this list of "inconsistencies" in the behavior of peasants who want to modernize; and there would be no lack of amusing examples to illustrate each case, for farm experts and rural observers have a stock of tales both enjoyable and revealing. Behind their apparent incongruity, these inconsistencies often indicate a course that has its own consistency, one that is a response, sometimes clumsy but often well adapted, to a situation that is itself truly inconsistent and undecipherable. Alongside technoeconomic management and traditional routine there exist other measures less "pure" and well defined but more suitable to the present period of transition and uncertainty.

Let us discount from the start the kind of symbolic modernization described above. It is easily explained, but it has no logical basis other than social rivalry. Essentially conservative in spirit, it normally goes hand in hand with a scrupulous respect for routine dictated by custom; but it can also lead to progress and modernization, and thus play a role in the process of change. The traditional image of the good farmer has been contrasted above with the progressive image. This does not mean that the good farmer in the traditional sense does not introduce improvements in his farm. On the contrary, there is traditional progress and there is modern progress.

The traditional course consists of increasing one's means, in working hard, economizing, adapting production to price fluctuations without changing the system of cultivation, and managing in relation to money saved rather than future income. In this perspective, the improvements that seem the most desirable are those that increase means and capital: acquisition of land, equipment, and livestock;

repair of buildings; and incidentally, if one has the means for it, purchase of household equipment. The introduction of such improvements is as characteristic of big farmers as of small ones, of the young as of the old. The proportions vary, as we will see, but everyone follows the traditional course, small farmers who want to expand and big farmers who modernize without changing their habitual ways of doing things.

The modern course assumes from the start that the entire system of production and management must be called into question. It can lead to the same improvements as the traditional course, but these improvements are integrated into a more general "policy" and above all are coupled with control of management. Rudimentary bookkeeping, participation in farm organizations, and a desire to modify the system of cultivation by pushing a particular product further or by introducing a new product as a response to the demands of the market — these are the principal steps in this progressive course. The farmer becomes an entrepreneur, acquires the means of being one, and begins to manage his enterprise in relation to its outlets rather than simply to its means of production.

In the factor analysis based on our four studies we used various criteria suitable to each region in order to distinguish what we have called T modernism (traditional) and P modernism (progressive). It should be noted at the outset that there is a strong correlation between each of these forms of modernism and the circumstances of the farmers who exemplify each: young people and those who have large farms and families or who own tractors tend to be more modern in some respects. The existence of a son who will succeed the father encourages modernism, and particularly progressive modernism. On the other hand there is no connection between the mode of improving the land and either of the forms of modernism; in the four regions studied the majority of the farmers work lands they own as well as those they rent, and there is no real farmer who holds his entire farm on lease. As one would expect, the modernists are better informed than many; they are more likely to listen to the radio and read newspapers. Further, the progressives are clearly different from the traditionalists in two respects: they leave their farms more frequently to go into a neighboring city, and they are much more often on familiar terms with a farm expert. These contacts seem to be a decisive factor in their orientation with respect to change.

We have said above that farmers underestimate the acreage necessary to make a tractor profitable; the modernists do not differ from the others on this point. But the progressives are more likely to find their farms too small and to express optimism; they clearly have less tendency to fear a crisis for agriculture. Nevertheless, if such a crisis occurred and prices went down, they would fall in with the mass in seeing no solution, in thinking that they must tighten their belts or abandon their farms. Traditional modernists are pessimists; they fear a crisis, but they think, unlike the others, that they will be able to pull through, since they will be well prepared and the state will be obliged to intervene on their behalf.

In other words, those who play the economic game are aware that their gamble cannot succeed if there is a crisis, while the others think that the farmer can always survive by applying the principle: "Help yourself and the state will help you." Some of them rely on mass demonstrations to force the state to apply this principle. If they are asked what must be done in the country to improve agriculture, the traditional modernists consistently say that without state aid nothing is possible. The progressives have less confidence in the state and think that technology and individual effort will be decisive. Finally, as explained above, in their image of the good farmer the traditional modernists stress moral qualities while progressives stress professional qualities.

A study done in Léon makes it possible to outline the relationship between the farmer's attitudes and the economic results he obtains. In this study (conducted by Madec under the direction of Louis Malassis with the cooperation of the Rural Economy Laboratory of the I.N.R.A. at Rennes and of the Division of Rural Sociology), a financial analysis of each farm was combined with a brief socio-psychological questionnaire.[25] This analysis made it possible to distinguish five categories of farms based on economic yield:

(1) *Category A* comprises profitable farms (18 percent of the sample). They bring a profit to the farmer after work and capital are remunerated according to accounting standards.

(2) Farms in *Category B* (11 percent) are in equilibrium but do not make a profit; the income of the farm consists of the equivalent of the farmer's salary and the income from the land he owns.

[25]See Appendix 2, No. 4.

(3) *Category C* (14 percent) comprises the farmers who do intensive farming. They obtain large yields per acre but small yields per worker. In other words, they work hard to make their land yield its maximum, but their work is poorly recompensed. In terms of rural economics, RP/PL>RP/MH: the proportion of the raw product to productive land is high in relation to the raw product per man hour.[26]

(4) Conversely the farmers of *Category D* (10 percent) do extensive farming. The product per worker is high but the product per acre is low: RP/PL<RP/MH.

Categories *C* and *D* are not "profitable" in the accountant's terms; one factor is unproductive, either the land or the manpower.

(5) In *Category E* are the farms that produce very low yields both per acre and per worker. This category comprises almost half the farms (47 percent).

It should be pointed out that the ages of the farmers who obtain good yields (*A* and *B*) are neither above nor below average. On the other hand, there is a close connection between acreage and yield. Almost half the farmers who make profits (*A*) farm between 22 and 28 acres (42 percent as opposed to 25 percent for the whole sample); one-third of the farms in economic equilibrium (*B*) measure 30 to 35 acres (35 percent as opposed to 15 percent of the sample); intensive agriculture (*C*) is characteristic chiefly of small farms (15 to 20 acres) and extensive agriculture (*D*) of large farms (37 to 80 acres); the bulk of category *E* is distributed among farms of all sizes. The last result is striking; it shows that in this category young people and big farmers do no better than others, contrary to the frequent claim.

The big farmers easily obtain better returns per worker as a result of extensive farming. They profit from their situation. But the most skillful management is in evidence on farms of average, even mediocre, size. The farmer who wants to survive on thirty acres must be an excellent manager. It is not among the big farmers that one is most likely to find those desirous of progress, but among the lesser ones, as all our studies and those of Bruno Benvenuti confirm. As an oversimplification it might be said that the big farmers do not need to exert themselves and that such efforts

[26]For an explanation of the definitions of farm accounting, see Chombart de Lauwe and Poitevin, 1957.

are impossible for the owners of small farms and useless for owners of the next-to-smallest farms, but that they permit the owners of the next-to-largest farms to move out of that category and join the ranks of the big farmers. In view of what we have already said, that innovations spread first among the big farmers, it is clear that what is good for them is or will be good for owners of the next-to-largest farms but could destroy those who are below the critical threshold and should seek special solutions. It should be repeated that unfortunately no one helps this last group, and that with few exceptions they do not have the means to invent their own solutions and put them into effect.

As might be expected, the farmers who adhere to the old routine (E) are not as well informed as the others. They are less likely to listen to the radio, read farm journals, make frequent visits to the small towns in the vicinity (Landernau, Landivisiau, and Morlaix), or associate with farm experts; on the other hand, they read the newspapers as regularly as do the others. For their part, the "best" farmers (A) are clearly better informed than the others, go out more often, listen more to the radio, and, most important, two-thirds have contacts with farm experts as compared with one-third for the group as a whole.

The "good" farmers $(A$ and $B)$ think that their most important problems are land reform (consolidation, road construction, abolition of slopes and hedgerows) and the alteration of the system of cultivation. Land, they say, is in shorter supply than equipment, buildings, and manpower. On the other hand, the best farmers (A) say that if they had money available they would continue to buy equipment. This apparent contradiction is not a real one; for them, the extent and arrangement of their holdings is the most pressing problem and the most difficult to solve, for there is hardly any land to sell. Land consolidation is by no means imminent, and with the available money it is always possible to buy equipment. Naturally the farmers who work their lands intensively (C) usually find their farms too small (80 percent), followed closely by the best farmers $(A, 72$ percent; average for the sample, 65 percent).

Almost half the farmers estimate that with 38 acres it is possible to buy a tractor and still support a family. The good farmers do not differ from the others on this point. Once again it should be stated that, in making this judgment, farmers take into consideration the average situation in the region and not their personal wishes. A man can have high ambitions for himself, but when he is making a general judgment, the situation slightly above the average seems a satisfying ideal.

Curiously enough, the good farmers are those who most often look to government to solve the problems of local agriculture; as previously stated, they probably think that they have done everything in their power and that someone else must do the rest. As might be expected, they describe the good farmer in terms of professional capacities rather than traditional values. Otherwise they are as pessimistic as the others, if not more so (particularly the farmers in B), and are just as likely to consider abandoning their farms in the event of a crisis. In contrast with the general pessimism, a larger proportion of the A farmers than of others want their sons to remain on the land (44 percent as opposed to 31 percent) and want them to continue their studies until they reach the age of eighteen (20 percent as opposed to 8 percent).

Various authors (notably Jollivet and Benvenuti) have set up character types for routine-bound, modernizing, and progressive farmers, seeking thus to make their analysis more varied, more subtle, and more precise. Unfortunately, a typology built on particular cases does not lend itself well to the systematization that factor analysis permits. Since they were not conceived with this end in mind, our studies do not furnish sufficient data to construct a typology. They permit us only to distinguish some traits that could ultimately be combined with the results of new studies aimed in this direction, to form a genuine typology.

(1) A first factor permits us to distinguish the principal traits of the routine-bound small farmer, who has undertaken symbolic modernization, although he could be ruined by it and is aware of the fact. He proclaims that his farm is too small to support a family and a tractor, knowledge that has not prevented him from buying one. He is poorly informed, does not read a newspaper, does not know any farm experts. He sees no solution to the crisis that he fears will occur. His son will leave school when he is sixteen. There is no connection whatever between this factor and traditional modernism, since our questionnaire did not make it possible to distinguish traditional modernism and symbolic modernization; on

the other hand, there is a clear connection between this factor and the absence of progressive modernism.

(2) If we invert this factor and eliminate a few inconsistencies, we can describe the progressive big farmer who is well informed and wants to put his children through school. The size of his enterprise (land and equipment) and his managerial ability make him confident that he will pull through even should a crisis occur.

(3) A second factor defines the profile of the discontented big farmer. His farm is well above average size, but he finds it too small. His system of cultivation, therefore, is probably extensive. He thinks that to support a family and own a tractor one must own a farm far larger than most. Curiously enough, this factor is unconnected with modernism, pessimism, and level of information. The big farmer may thus be discontented because he is routine-bound; he may or may not attempt symbolic or traditional modernization, and he realizes that, in order to follow either path, he must have large holdings. If he is progressive, his methods of management demonstrate that progress is an endless process; the more he becomes involved in it, the more likely he is to see new possibilities, demanding more land and greater financial means — the process that gives rise to his dissatisfaction.

(4) By inverting this factor, it is possible to describe the small farmer who considers himself too wealthy. He has less than twenty-five acres at his disposal, but he finds his farm too large and thinks that one can own a tractor even on a farm smaller than his. He is probably advanced in age.

(5) The third factor enables us to describe a similar type: the contented and routine-bound small farmer.

(6) The inverse of this third factor is the mass of average farmers who display anxiety about the future, who realize that they need more land than they own in order to support a tractor and make a living. Feeling themselves helpless under the new conditions imposed on them, they expect everything of the state and very little of individual or collective effort.

It would have been possible to add to these six types if each of the studies had furnished facts on the economic yield of the farms, extra-agricultural income of the family, participation in farm organizations, and so on.

The existence of other sources of income for the family distorts all the principles of accounting on a family farm: autarchy becomes a prime objective, amortization of investments ceases to be necessary, and so on. The extreme case of double identity is that of the fortunate city dweller who annually makes up the deficit of his farm in order to have the pleasure of owning and managing it and spending his vacations there. His management logic is no different from that of the small farmer who sends his daughter to the nearby factory to bring home a little money. In various forms, instances of a combination of farming and nonfarming activities are increasing in response to certain present needs. An economist's analysis of the management of such farms would prove useful. For our purposes here a separate study would be necessary, for one can find all types of farmers in this economic situation, from the most routine-bound peasant to the entrepreneur who knows the exact amount of his deficit or profit.

Participation in farm organizations and confidence in the effectiveness of collective action in its various forms are certainly traits of progressivism in French agriculture today. Still, appeal to state intervention, confidence in organized action, efforts toward technical modernization, and skillful management are not necessarily connected or contradictory. Some farmers, who are capable technicians and managers and depend on all sorts of organizations to sell their products and give them advice, think that without state aid all their individual and collective efforts would be in vain, and that this aid can be obtained only by collective action. Others expect everything of the state, look to it to solve all their problems. The individualists believe that the shrewdest will survive and that the government and the organizations are more harmful than useful. And there are also those who, having no confidence in the state, expect organizations to provide solutions and collective action to defend their interests against those of the government. Finally, a general feeling of pessimism about agriculture and the farmer's condition is quite compatible, as we shall see, with efforts at modernization and participation in organized group action.

Let us assume that improvements made or planned, the characteristics of the good farmer, and a certain type of management are the criteria for the modernist and that they can be classified along a line between the traditionalist and the progressive poles. Let us exclude from our analysis routine-bound farmers, whether or not they are involved in symbolic modernization. We have seen that age is not a determining factor and that extra-agricultural income belongs to a different logic and analysis. Let us assume, finally, that we have at our disposal sound criteria for evaluating optimism and pessimism. In sum, then, six coordinates would suffice for constructing a typology:

(1) Size of the enterprise (not simply area of the land)
(2) Economic yield
(3) Traditional or progressive modernism
(4) Optimism or pessimism
(5) Participation in organizations and collective action
(6) Dependence on the state

This effort to classify the situations, attitudes, and behavior of farmers leads to the conclusion that there is, in the final analysis, little connection between the individual situation of the farmers and their attitudes. Age has much less influence than is thought on disposition to change; "bad" farmers are distributed over all categories of farming; and if traditional modernists usually own the largest farms and progressive modernists the next-to-largest it is because there exists a direct relation between available resources and types of change possible. Otherwise certain attitudes and judgments are shared by almost all farmers: they are pessimists and they agree in thinking that acreage slightly larger than the regional average is enough to support a family and a tractor. Whether they have fifteen acres or seventy-five, whether they are thirty years old or seventy, whether they are proprietors or tenant farmers, the diversity of their situations does not prevent their sharing the same view of things, nor does it lead to specific attitudes or behavior. One man makes a profit, modernizes, and plans ahead; another barely survives. Though the situations are many and varied, the "mentality" is collective and shared by all, and the individual can act as he thinks proper. In other words, these three areas of life are relatively independent of each other; it would be worthwhile if we could measure the degree of freedom in their relationship in each social context.

This conclusion is surprising. Experts and students of the peasantry tend to accuse farmers in general of being hidebound and stubborn and of failing to see the possibilities offered them by technology and adaptation to consumers' needs. But they admire the imagination, initiative, and courage of the modernists, who, according to them, are almost always young and often large-scale farmers. Right or wrong, the sociologist refuses to believe this and to accept such a neat conclusion.

It is entirely true that there exist in the country, within face-to-face communities, collective stereotyped attitudes shared by everybody and expressed in the same manner; we have been advancing this hypothesis since the Introduction. That the technoeconomic situation is less restrictive than the farmers and economists maintain is natural in the present period of upheaval, when the most diverse attempts can succeed or fail, according to the circumstances. On the other hand, the idea that the diversity of attitudes and individual behavior cannot be explained by the abilities of each farmer contradicts all the experience of the social sciences and moves us to pursue our research further.

What we have understood here by "situation" was limited to some information about the farm itself, but we would have to describe in detail the social position of each farmer in his community before drawing any conclusions. We should know the traditional position of the family in the village and in the social hierarchy and with relation to politics, religion, and the local sociopolitical authority. We should also study the communication networks at the heart of the community and the position of the farmer and his family in these networks. Finally, the personal history of the individual should be studied and viewed in the context of local history. Have the village or the region known significant changes in the areas of politics or agriculture? Have farm organizations sprung up? Have political or religious movements had an important influence on youth? Have there been individuals who have left their mark on the village or the district?

An analysis that bears solely on individual farmers completely distorts the perspective. Even when it is largely inoperative, a face-to-face society imposes itself so strongly on individuals that it is impossible to isolate them by analysis. Indeed, our results prove that the individual maintains considerable freedom in our present-day society, but that this freedom can be understood only in relation to institutions, customs, and restrictions with which it must be consistent in one way or another. Unfortunately there exists no detailed study on channels of information and influence and on the interpersonal dynamics at work at the heart of the village. And yet this seething mass of individuals and groups supports the entire recent history of the French country-side. We would need to undertake a series of detailed studies on the social history of agricultural progress in French villages in order to understand the influence of war and occupation, the work of Catholic movements, the role of strong personalities, and so on.

Natural conditions, customary techniques, and existing institutions condition the farmer's entire point of view. It is in relation to these that he judges himself and the situation and decides whether to remain faithful to routine or to question it. His classification as a big or small farmer, that of his holdings as large or insignificant, is essentially relative; everything depends on his neighbors. The "profitability" or the "necessity" of the tractor is also a relative matter, as we have said. Hence, while the agricultural structures impose fewer restrictions on individuals than is maintained — since some farmers know how to use them to advantage — they nevertheless act as a tight curb on the actions of farmers over an entire region. If one farmer or one particular group of farmers invents a successful solution, it will not do much to solve the problems of the region as a whole.

By its very nature the collective solution is different from the individual solution. Need we give an example? Since land area is the decisive factor, the success of some farmers is necessarily based on the disappearance of many other farmers. Sometimes collective and individual solutions coincide approximately, especially if the producers accept a common discipline in order to achieve mass marketing of a standardized product. But recent events show that this theoretical coincidence is not evident to the farmers, each of whom is in a peculiar position. The story of the artichokes of St. Pol de Léon is a relevant example.[27] As he views himself in relation to others, each farmer is particularly sensitive to the peculiarities of each case. It is with reference to his own case, unique by definition, that he makes his plans, whether he is routine-bound, traditionalist, or progressive. And each plan, having thus its particular conditions and its own rationality, cannot be joined or integrated into others, although all the farmers live within the same agrarian structures and share the same general attitudes. In fact, it is within this common system that each one does his planning, while the system must impose its logic in order for individual designs to be united.

And finally, who is right in the long run? The man who is bound by routine, faithful to the traditional model of the peasant, has

[27]Tavernier and Mendras, 1961.

the feeling that he is going to his ruin; he assigns responsibility to the adversity of the times and the treachery of those in power, and he urges his son to learn another trade. The traditional modernist invests, "feathers his nest," and thus prepares to weather the blow if hard times come, knowing well that his politicians will never allow times to become too hard. The progressive has grasped the functioning of an economic system he does not control. He takes chances, creates new institutions, adapts to variations in the demand for his product; but he risks being ruined if he makes a misstep or if the game turns against him without his realizing it. Of these three "policies," which is the best for any farmer?[28]

Considering the present state of the system of distribution, and taking into account the uncertainties of any agricultural policy in a national or international context, who can know if the skillful manager will not some day be in a situation more uncertain than the traditionalist big farmer who maintains a semiautarchic system of production — less refined, less modern, but also less fragile? Clever managers, it is true, are usually average farmers who do not have a choice between two courses and can only survive by their skill.

Each has taken a chance without knowing the future course of agriculture or what chances have been taken by other farmers of the region and the nation, and hence without knowing whether there is any harmony among these actions. The whole problem of agricultural planning thus comes to be posed from the farmers' point of view. They must make their decisions, each for himself, without having the great national options clearly presented to them and without intermediary organisms to make choices that could guide their own. In the absence of a more radical overall solution to the farm problem, we must hope that the organization of agricultural markets, farm contracts, and the strengthening of cooperative institutions will all aid farmers in the future. Under difficult conditions and with very little guidance, they have shown courage, imagination, a spirit of enterprise, and an economic sense as remarkable as they are admirable.

---

[28]For similiar problems in average industrial enterpises, see Benoit-Guilbot, 1966.

6. The Farmer's Life and Occupation

"I would have done better to learn a trade than remain a peasant."
This regretful statement, which came from many of the peasants
we interviewed,[1] summarizes the contrast between the peasant's
state and other occupational situations, a contrast that all
observers of the peasantry have long stressed,[2] and one that
was discussed in a preceding chapter in connection with the
confusion of roles. A man is born a peasant and remains one;
he does not become one. And if he is a peasant, he has no trade.
"Peasant" is a complete and static definition of self, whereas
every other occupation is something that one "has," that one
acquires and owns. What the peasant has or possesses is the
field he has inherited, just as another person has a trade,
possesses a skill. A man can be a good or mediocre peasant and
have a good or bad farm. The farm, like the occupation, permits
him to exercise his abilities, both natural and acquired. A clever
man, a strong personality, may have a "good" trade in which
he finds self-fulfillment, or he may bemoan a situation that
hems him in on all sides. A "good peasant" may have a farm
large enough to allow him to exercise his *savoir faire,* or, on the
contrary, he may be forced to struggle with a small parcel of
unproductive land. And of course the farm may make a good or
bad farmer; it is easier to be a good farmer on a good farm.

Furthermore, as we have said, face-to-face society impels its
members to be true to themselves and to respect the rules of conduct
imposed on them by their position. Consequently, to be himself is the
first imperative for the peasant; while to become something or somebody is contrary to custom, dangerous, and even morally repre-
hensible. Bernot and Blancard found this attitude in Nouville:

> The conscious idea of *becoming* does not exist. What exists is the
> idea of *being*. One does not say, for example, 'So-and-so is educated
> because he has worked hard' but 'he is educated because he has
> degrees.' In some cases criticism will be directed more toward those
> who *acquire* than those who *already have*. It is normal for the mayor
> to have a car with front-axle drive, but when the teacher got his car
> some found him 'too rich.'[3]

At the other extreme, one pessimistic small farmer stated: "I've

[1]Mendras, 1958, p. 75.
[2]Maspétiol, 1946.
[3]Bernot and Blancard, 1953, p. 480.

gotten into the muck, I'm stuck in it, and I'll never get out." Already
mentioned in connection with change, these observations explain why
the farmer cannot have a set of attitudes about his professional
activity similar to those of other workers.

From this fundamental contrast spring several others. An occupation
is learned in an organized, rational fashion, and this knowledge can
be continually supplemented and perfected. But the peasant, not
having learned his occupation (since it is in some way "consubstan-
tial" with him), feels every failure as a personal injury. Every
effort to become a better peasant is an effort from within and not a
new knowledge or *savoir faire* that he acquires. Since the peasant
knows his land and how to cultivate it, imperfection can come only
from a lack of application, from slowness, inattentiveness, insufficient or shoddy work — in short, a failure of personal discipline.

All of this is summarized in one word: courage. The good peasant
is courageous. Courage is here a synonym for devotion to work and
for self-control, a concept that has nothing to do with the courage of
the soldier (*virtus*). Traditional peasant civilization was founded on
the former, while modern agriculture, the work of engineers, is
essentially based on ingenuity. In the past, technical competence
counted for little alongside moral qualities. Today, on the contrary,
intelligence and skill are more important than energy. The good
peasant does not complain of his hardships; the modern farmer
spares himself hardship by the use of intelligence and machinery.

The absence of choice that characterizes the whole of the peasant's
existence is particularly obvious in early life, since the occupation of
farmer is never chosen. It is true that some farmers say they were
free to quit the land and chose to remain voluntarily, but it almost
never happens that a real possibility of taking up a trade appears
and is rejected in favor of remaining a peasant. The son stays in his
father's household because a child must live in his parents' home.
Among the farmers we interviewed, many were shocked because we
asked questions on the reasons that led them to stay on the land. The
problem had never in their lives been openly stated and there seemed
to them to be something unwholesome about doing so. In a survey
by the I.F.O.P., 61 percent of the farmers said they had never thought
about leaving the land, and those who had thought about it almost
invariably did so before they were twenty years old. However, this
question was obviously asked only of those who did remain; to be

accurate we would need to know also if many of those who left the farm would have liked to remain peasants.

In a period of such rapid rural exodus as recent years have witnessed, those who leave have rarely learned a trade. They abandon a farm that is hardly large enough to assure their parents a livelihood and that offers them no hope whatever of survival; they seize whatever occasion presents itself or simply leave on impulse. The sons of farmers who learn a trade are as rare as those who go to agricultural schools; according to the I.F.O.P., almost two-thirds of the farmers think that they would find it very difficult to change occupations.[4] Their situation has been "given" to them and it seems to them to be so restrictive that they can hardly imagine leaving it.

In his study of migrations, André Levesque has shown that those who are the most attached to their farms and their communities are the small farmers.[5] Their means are the most limited and hence they should, it seems, be the most inclined to leave the land, where they have very little to hold them; but that little imposes on them worrisome burdens that interfere with their freedom to think of another solution. Nor does their situation serve them as a basis of departure; it permits them to survive from day to day and represents a security beyond which they see only the unknown.

The restrictions imposed by forms and customs weigh less heavily on the others, yet they have less reason to leave the land, where their families have made a mediocre but secure living for generations. A man stays because he has no choice; because his parents are there, and he must remain near them and take over when they are gone. Once he has reached his thirties, departure becomes more difficult. He is more and more "tied" to the farm materially and sentimentally. As one farmer said: "To get to know your land, to improve it, takes a long time; and the more you know it, the more you become attached to it." Another summed up his viewpoint by saying: "I was raised there, I earned my living there, I'm happy there, and besides, what else could I do? ... Anyhow, it would be too much trouble to leave."

Micheline Fairé makes the following comment on the results of her study on this subject:

[4]Jollivet, 1966.
[5]Levesque, 1958.

Table 12. Liking for the Land

One must have a liking for it	69
Do not know	7
One must be born to it	69
Do not know	7
One becomes attached to the land as one grows older	54
Do not know	22
Number of Responses	76

When a farmer is asked why he has stayed, and why his neighbors have stayed on the land, in his judgment of the others
the emphasis is on inevitability. It is usually inertia and
incompetence that obliges the others to stay; he conceives of
them as less dynamic and less capable of choice than he is. One
wonders if it is not when he is speaking of others that the farmer
analyzes his own situation best and most freely.[6]

In other words, he maintains and makes use of an illusion of
choice, which he doggedly affirms for the benefit of the interviewer
in order to make it convincing to both of them.

Moreover, as in every profession, whether one has chosen it
or not, after a period of anxiety, which in industry is expressed
by professional instability, and which in agriculture is seen in
the desire to leave or in the desire for technical change, a man
accepts his occupation, adjusts to it, and develops a liking for it.
Almost all the farmers who have thought about leaving the land
thought about it before they were twenty. The mechanism
is indeed ambivalent, for in order to have a liking for the land
one must be born to it, and yet this predilection also comes with
age (Table 12).

The absence of choice at the outset is compensated for by
the fact that the farmer is his own master. But here again the
"freedom" of the farmer conceals contradictions.[7] He may flatter
himself that he is his own master and has no boss, yet he
also complains of his servitude to a profession in which he is
never free. In fact, the possibilities of choice are not the same
in agriculture as in most other activities. The contrast with factory
workers and office employees is particularly striking; it can be
said of them that they have "chosen" their profession, but,

[6]See Appendix 2, No. 6.
[7]Milhau, 1962.

once the choice is made, they no longer have autonomy in their working life.

Provided that he respects the exigencies of nature, the peasant is free to organize his work as he thinks proper, as we have shown above. Some of these exigencies are as restrictive as the workday of the factory or office, if not more so; for example, the cows must be milked morning and evening. But this demand is imposed by nature, and the farm worker who attends to it himself can always, in organizing his time, take his personal needs into account. By contrast, neither factory workers nor office employees feel directly the fundamental restrictions of their work; these are mediated for them by the hierarchy. At most, the rules may seem to them to be dictated by the employer's pleasure. Beyond this, it is difficult for them to perceive the limitations imposed on the employer and carried down to them by the hierarchy, for these are usually commanded by the economic and social system, which, in the last analysis, can also seem artificial and a creation of those in power. The regulations of a factory or office have an aspect of contingency that does not exist on the farm, where the worker determines his conduct according to the immediate demands of nature. On the other hand, as we will see later, the contingencies of the economic and social system are felt by the farmer as head of the farm when he rebels against "the state," "politics," or "prices."

To "call nobody his boss" or to "have nobody on his back" is the pride of the farmer, who is quick to compare the factory worker to a farmhand. The factory worker's servile condition convinces the peasant that such a worker cannot "be a man." Having no father to succeed, he has no hope of one day becoming his own master. But at the same time farmers envy the worker's freedom when he leaves the factory after a day's work, and also the regularity of his salary. "Animals mean slavery, never a vacation, never a Sunday off." Or again: "How nice it must be to get your pay at the end of the week and be free!"

Farmers rarely see the connection between lack of freedom at work and freedom outside of work. They do not see that one is the condition of the other. For them one is evil, contemptible, and unacceptable, whereas the other is enviable. They would like to have their cake and eat it too, to remain their own masters and yet have a fixed work schedule and an assured salary, a combination that is obviously unattainable in our social system. To be fixed, a work schedule must be set by somebody. Only a few monocultivators — wine growers from Languedoc or cereal growers from the Paris basin, for example — have succeeded in limiting their working hours. But the small family polycultivator, who is the subject of this analysis, cannot escape the contradictions of his situation as a nonspecialized producer; though he may be master of his time and free to use it as it suits him, his time is never free. As we will see later, only other structures of production would enable him to escape this paradox.

A fixed salary is the other cause of the peasant's envy of the "salaried worker." But unless he renounces his position as head of the enterprise, can one imagine his receiving a fixed salary in our social system? Here the contradiction is so obvious that most farmers are aware of it. Their salaries consist of the prices of their farm products, notably those fixed by the government. In this case they can protect their salaries by demanding that the state raise, for example, the price of wheat or milk. But the small polycultivator who consumes more wheat himself than he sells cannot play the same game with his meat or fruits, the prices of which are not controlled by the government. In this debate today the two sides are represented by traditional farm unionists, who defend high prices to protect the farmer's income, and young people who want to play the capitalist game and demand that the government give agriculture the means to invest and rebuild its structures. The former present the farmer as a worker who deserves pay equal to his work. The latter see the head of the enterprise as wanting not only to make a living from his work but also to repay his investment and be successful — that is, to make a profit and expand his enterprise.

To treat agricultural problems by analogy with those of industry leads to insoluble contradictions or to solutions largely outmoded by social evolution. It is the structures themselves that must be rebuilt in order for agriculture to pass directly from its present precapitalist stage to a new form, bypassing a capitalist transition if possible. In the meantime, farmers think of their problems in the terms proposed by their leaders, even if they feel that these apply imperfectly to their situation, and this state of affairs deeply affects their morale with respect to their occupation.

For the farmer, the land is at the same time his field, his occupation, and all other farmers, yet he rarely makes a judgment about his occupation insofar as it is his job. If he is asked to analyze in detail his so-called occupation, he tends to speak of the conditions of its exercise (the land, his family, and so on) rather than of the activity itself, the work, and the qualities necessary to a worker.

Conversely, the occupation is above all the land, and the outdoor life of the country, close to nature. "Fresh air" is a stereotype that recurs in almost all conversations on this subject: "Here the air is healthful," while in the city "you suffocate and the air is bad." Need we point out the moral flavor of this theme? The city is dangerous to moral life. The air one breathes there is foul both morally and physically. Children grow up to be stronger when they eat nutritious food and live with a closely-knit family. They have less occasion for dissipation and meet fewer dangers. In the city you do not feel at home, and everything seems to threaten you.

On the other hand, life in the country has its obvious inconveniences. True, one breathes fresh air, but by the same token one has to suffer inclement weather as well. Generally life is too isolated on a farm or in a hamlet lost at the end of a pitted road. Some, on the contrary, never have a chance to be alone but live with no real independence in the narrow society of the village. Usually isolation and the absence of autonomy are just as evident on the dispersed farms of the Bocage in Brittany as in a village in Beauce. One is alone, hemmed in on all sides by a face-to-face society.[8]

Despite this disadvantage, nothing seems worse than the crowded city, where one knows nobody. Peasants see urban society as anonymous, and they rarely perceive that this anonymity is the condition of a certain form of independence and freedom of choice with respect to others. They complain about being alone or too much exposed to others. Eighty-seven percent of the wine growers of Languedoc whom we interviewed said they would not like to live in the city. At Péage-de-Roussillon, their preferences

[8] See Appendix 2, No. 16.

Table 13. City versus Country Living

Would like to live in the city	5
Would like to live in isolation	26
Would like to live in the country without isolation	45
Number of responses	76

were distributed as in Table 13: almost two-thirds would like
to live a little way from a market-town in order to take advantage
of its city life and thus not suffer the material and moral
disadvantages of isolation. The five who chose the city were
less than forty years old.

A desire to be near their fields is the principal argument of those
who want to preserve their isolation: "A peasant of real peasant
stock likes to live on his own land." But this isolation is still felt by
most of the farmers to be one of the major inconveniences of country
life and the farmer's occupation; and, according to Géraud and
Spitzer, it has very deep psychological and emotional repercussions:

A whole series of petty dissatisfactions is somehow wrapped up in a
vague sense of psychic isolation, of desolation; the water supply is
slow, the communal sewer needs repair ... This psychic solitude,
this feeling of sadness that the farmer so often evokes as he
laments depopulation, the exodus of the young people, the abandoned houses, and so on, is particularly painful during the long
winter days, when he vegetates in a state of inactivity and boredom.

Love of one's work, the countryside, and the land is one of the
major themes of rustic literature and traditional peasant ideology.[9]
It is not our place to analyze this ideology, nor to ask to what extent
peasants participate in it or how it is being modified in the course of
present-day transformations. Our studies and that of the i.f.o.p.
stress the deep satisfaction that many farmers draw from their
occupation. To see fine crops grow, to take care of handsome animals,
to live close to nature, to be one's own master, to divide one's time
among varied tasks, to be responsible for the entire cycle of
production from sowing to harvest or from pasture to milking —
these are all sources of keen satisfaction to a farmer. It is well
known, for example, that some like to tend crops, while others
have a feeling for animals and prefer to take care of them.
When a farmer of the Paris basin or elsewhere leaves animal
breeding to devote himself solely to growing cereals, or when a

[9]Arland, 1941; Barjon, 1945.

small farmer replaces his team of horses or oxen with a tractor, the whole organization of his work, all his tasks, may be modified; normally they are lightened. But what are his emotional reactions? No study has yet dealt with these problems.

There are few occupations in which the diversity of the tasks is as great as this while the job is treated as a single entity.[10] There are no studies similar to those done in industry on occupational analysis, the worker's satisfaction, job evaluation, and so on. Peasants, it is true, have little desire to express themselves on these subjects. They have the feeling that they "must do everything." To their way of thinking, the system of cultivation cannot be modified in relation to price changes and market demands, as we have seen. It must not, therefore, be open to question because of the tastes and preferences of individuals.

Work is the realm of enforced duty, discipline, and courage. The peasant seems to fear that by questioning this imperative he would be calling into question the very essence of his life. To an interviewer who asked him, "If you had six months to do nothing, what would you do?" one shocked farmer answered, "In this business we work, we can't rest!" It would be immoral to rest. Similarly, to say "I like" or "I don't like" a particular task would be confusing the realm of pleasure and consumption with that of obligation and production. Moreover, since the farmer imposes his discipline of work on himself, all its fundamental logic would be disturbed if he took his tastes into account. The factory worker, for whom the professional role is clearly separate from others and whose discipline is imposed by the hierarchy, can ask himself if he "enjoys" what he does without danger to his work or his morale. But not the peasant, since for him the job is so dependent on morality and his personal discipline that it is unwise to ask himself such questions.

If farmers want to judge and evaluate their work, then, they must resort to some standard other than morality. Economics furnishes them with one by saying what is profitable and what is not. Before accounting determines the net cost, farmers know that a particular crop pays well while another does not. This does not eliminate the necessity of producing both because, the system of cultivation being, as we have said, an intangible whole, the farmer must do everything without stopping to ask questions. As soon as a sufficiently refined

[10]Artaud, 1944.

accounting system permits him to measure the salary appropriate to each task, the farmer will be able to rid himself of the feeling that all work is an imperative and ask himself which jobs please him and which are distasteful, for he will then be imposing the latter on himself only in order to earn money. One can balance pleasure against salary; the scale will move in relation to the weight given to each. One cannot do the same with pleasure and moral imperatives; the latter, being absolute, cannot be weighed.

This puritanical attitude toward the job rests on an analogous conception of the occupation. "The land is the hardest," say the farmers readily, thus flattering themselves that if they have not chosen, they have at least accepted "the hardest." Only courageous men who do not complain of their hardships can make such a choice. From this point of view, those who have left their farms have chosen the easy way; in military terms they are the "slackers," or at worst, deserters. It is said of them that they have "deserted" the land for the pleasures and conveniences of the city, as well as its dangers. One of this group, on the other hand, spoke of how he had "overcome his poverty" by dint of courage and perseverance.[11]

From our studies and those of the I.F.O.P,. there emerge the constrasting traits of the peasant and the city dweller as farmers see them. On one side lack of education, awkwardness of words and gestures, wretched clothing, the "entrenched peasant" (*paysan empaysanné*) described by Bourdieu;[12] on the other, the educated, elegant, well-spoken city dweller, always at his ease. As superficial and stereotyped as it may be, this contrast has its influence on the attitudes of the peasant and feeds his social "inferiority complex."

To compensate for this, there is a strong feeling of moral superiority. The city dweller is too shallow, too superficial to inspire confidence. He is even dishonest, for he lives in an entirely man-made environment in which one succeeds through cleverness and trickery, while farmers, "confronted by natural forces like the weather, the seasons, the land, plants and animals, cannot cheat."[13] To cheat men and governments is normal; it is part of the rules of the game as much in modern society as in peasant society. In matters of social security and taxes, fraud is customary and creates no risk of reproach.

[11]Norre, 1944.
[12]Bourdieu, 1962.
[13]Appendix 1, No. 23.

Similarly, on the fairgrounds the honest man makes a fool of himself; it is the shrewd one, who knows how to cheat his customers, who comes out on top and thus wins esteem and admiration. But neither the peasant knave nor the city cheat can fool nature; hence the city dweller, who lives outside nature in a universe entirely fabricated by man, can only be a cheat, like the horse trader, who lives on the fairgrounds and is never faced with the inflexibilities of nature.

In the final analysis, does a farmer wish for his children this difficult occupation that he loves, that demands and instills a superior morality? When we ask farmers about their intentions and desires for their children, we get contradictory answers. Almost all are agreed that it is better to have a trade than to be on the land, but many nevertheless hope that at least one son will take over the farm. It is very rare that a peasant willingly faces the disappearance of his farm and says: "My son can do whatever he wants, but he won't be a peasant; he'll have a trade." The conditions and reactions vary with the region. In Brittany, overpopulation makes migration necessary; in Alsace, it is possible to be a factory worker and maintain a farm; in Combrailles, the standard of living is poor but there is no lack of land; in Béarn, agriculture has new possibilities, but the farms are very small, and urban life is making inroads in the villages. But in the four regions, as elsewhere, the great majority of farmers wish their daughters to leave the land, although they often hope to keep one boy there. (Table 14).

These results are confirmed by the i.f.o.p. survey: 40 percent of the fathers want their sons to become farmers, and only 13 percent of the mothers would like their daughters to marry farmers. As head of the farm, the farmer desires to see his work perpetuated, while as father and mother he and his wife

Table 14. Farmers' Ambitions for Their Children

	Léon		Béarn		Combrailles
	Boys	Girls	Boys	Girls	Boys
Want them to stay on the land	33%	13%	47%	13%	30%
Do not want them to stay on the land	24	29	11	28	17
Children already settled	43	58	42	59	53

(This question was omitted in Sundgau)

wish their daughter to leave the land. This paradox is singularly indicative of the ambivalence of the farmer's feelings about his situation. Moreover, a man may deplore the exodus that is taking away the young people and depleting the work force, and yet wish his son to take up another occupation.

The occupation of farmer seems suitable for a man, but the peasant condition is rejected strongly where women are concerned. Behavior conforms to these attitudes, since the daughters are made to continue their schooling more often than the sons. The few daughters destined for the land must usually serve to attract a son-in-law to replace an absent son. In many farm regions, demographic statistics confirm these facts by showing that men are more numerous there than women.

Only a very extensive study on this subject could enable us to determine how often those who want to have a successor condemn their sons to the peasant condition in order to maintain the family line, or consider farming to be satisfying for a man but farm life unbearable for the farmer's wife. In other words, do farmers project their personal desires onto their daughters, for whom they can dream, while they forbid such dreams for themselves or their sons, feeling that it is unsound to contemplate suicide even if it is only professional suicide through an intermediary person?

These observations suggest a study of the role of women in the process of rural exodus. Most of those interviewed in our studies have been men, but perhaps women would more easily face the departure of their sons or young daughters the departure of their eventual spouses. It is frequently said that fiancées demand that their husbands-to-be promise to leave the family farm. Also, mothers probably have a stronger influence than fathers in guiding boys toward occupations other than farming when this turn is taken early and prepared for by an apprenticeship. In fact, as we have stated, the mother tends more and more to take responsibility for contacts with the outside world while the father limits his role to farm work properly so called.

Farmers do not generally have academic ambitions for the sons destined to succeed them. After receiving his diploma, the boy will stay at home and take correspondence courses (a condition of eligibility for government allotments) but no more than this. In our four studies, less than one-fourth of the farmers considered leaving their sons in school after the elementary level or making them take professional training such as that provided by an adult education course, a winter school, or a School of Rural Apprenticeship. If young people remained too close to their parents, each generation would be exactly like the previous one. Like the notables of the last century, farmers continue to fear that "too much studying turns one away from farming." They are aware of the present upheaval, but, according to them, school is not the place where one learns to face this new situation. In short, farmers do not believe that agriculture can become an occupation one chooses and learns, but that it will always be a state handed down from father to son.

The fundamental pessimism of peasants is so well known that it is the subject of much humor. It is often said that nobody has ever seen a farmer satisfied with his crop. Daniel Halévy says that one of the fundamental traits of peasant character is anxiety or insecurity. He recalls Guillaumin's remark: "The peasants of the past were always afraid."[14] The fear of tomorrow and the expression of this pessimism were coupled, however, with a fundamental optimism that made them go through the same movements over and over again in order to assure the continuity of life and the fertility of the land. Today the same contradiction exists between anxiety about the future of agriculture and the desire for a son who will assure the succession.

Besides, farmers have a strong feeling that their condition is deteriorating from generation to generation by comparison with the increasing prosperity and the *embourgeoisement* of other social categories. Not all of them become poor and proletarianized, obviously, especially not those who have been able to modernize and make investments in step with the times. But even these farmers share the common feeling that they are lagging behind other social categories. "I learned to work hard from my father, I succeeded him, and I cultivate the farm the way he did. Well, I don't live as well as he did; he was able to send me to school till the tenth grade, but I don't know if I could do the same for my son. You know, sir, I find that unfair." In these words a polycultivator from Aude summarized the feelings of many farmers.

Seventy-one percent of the farmers think that their farms are

[14]Guillaumin, 1942, 1953; Halévy, 1935; and verbal communication.

Table 15. Unfairness of the Peasant's Life

	Cited First	Cited Second	Total
Farmers do not earn enough money in relation to the work done	62%	19%	81%
They can be ruined financially	13	45	58
They are obliged to work until they die	6	41	47
They can never take vacations	3	33	36
They are not accorded their rightful place in the nation	6	25	31
If they wanted to change their occupation, many could only be unskilled laborers	2	25	27
Country life provides no pleasure	1	12	13

going well, and 84 percent declare that they like their occupation, but 61 percent think agriculture is declining. On the scale of prestige and income for various occupations, almost all the farmers classify farming at the next-to-lowest level, one grade above unskilled industrial labor. Moreover, they feel they are at a disadvantage in the nation: 45 percent think that farmers face greater problems than other Frenchmen, 38 percent that they pay more than their fair share of taxes and do not profit from such benefits as public utilities, social security, and so on, as do other social categories.

In short, they are, like the polycultivator from Aude, satisfied with their agriculture but dissatisfied with "Agriculture" in general; they strongly feel that their lives are unfair, as shown in Table 15.

This table can be summarized in one sentence: peasants work until they die without taking vacations, and they risk being ruined and reduced to the status of manual laborers, but neither their hardships nor their risks are rewarded or recognized.

If farmers are asked the cause of their dissastisfaction, the reasons cited are those given in Table 16. In short, all the misfortunes of agriculture come from the economic policy of the government and the poor organization of domestic and international markets. Inclement weather and the demands of agriculture also share responsibility for making life difficult for farmers who are doing their best.

The farmers, in fact, have learned to do things "the right way," and they continue to be faithful to the rules of work that assured

Table 16. Cause of Farmers' Unrest

	Cited First	Cited Second	Total
Inadequate prices for their products	41%	30%	71%
High prices for industrial products necessary to agriculture	13	47	60
Lack of government interest	9	30	39
Poor organization of markets	8	26	34
Competition from foreign products	4	21	25
Recent poor crops	9	13	22
Poor organization of production	2	17	19
Too many small farmers	4	12	16

their parents security and even prestige. They feel therefore that they should be rewarded as their parents were, and consider themselves morally justified because they are doing the right thing. But they do not receive a just reward, and so "the world" is unfair to them; in other words, immoral. This analysis of the situation in terms of morality is perfectly coherent by their logic; it sufficiently explains their present troubles, suggests a remedy in state intervention, and, if this fails, permits them to place the blame on scapegoats. If the world and people are unfair and immoral, and we are faithful to our duties, all the troubles can be created only by Them (*ils*) and not by Us. This attitude is easily super-imposed on what is called nowadays the peasant's social inferiority complex. Not feeling himself sufficiently "recognized" by society, he compensates with a moral superiority complex, investing himself with moral qualities he judges fundamental and denying them in others.

In concluding his admirable study of a village in Provence, Laurence Wylie asks why "there is a bit of madness in the relationship of the Peyranais with the rest of the world."[15] He suggests that it is possibly the steadiness and *savoir vivre* that characterize the life of the village. Bernot and Blancard earlier pointed out the relationship between Us and Them (*ils*) in the thinking of the people of Nouville, which was summarized in the exclamation: "Let Them leave us alone with Their ideas!"[16] Wylie notes this fundamental contrast:

[15]Wylie, 1957, p. 339.
[16]Bernot and Blancard, 1953, p. 107.

The outside *ils* are like the weather; they are the necessities which one must accept because 'that's the way it is.' It makes a person feel better to curse the weather and to curse the outside *ils*.[17]

Technical and economic change fall somehow midway between the weather and the *ils*, since one can do nothing about them. They are necessarily responsible since We are suffering. But in the definition of Bernot and Blancard, *ils* means the city, the factory workers, the middlemen, and above that the whole government; in a word, those who "made things go badly for Us." Thus the circle is completed: the technical and economic imperatives can be seen as the work of others.

Farmers are rarely content with such self-justification. They are all aware that technical, economic and social changes are facts they must recognize and take into account. But as they lack a means of economic analysis to help them understand the new imperatives imposed on them, they tend to see this new adaptation as an evil — necessary, no doubt, but an evil. Thus they reconcile the preceding moral analysis with their realistic but vague analysis of the course of the world. Among the youngest, some see possibilities in the new conditions that warrant great hopes for anyone who is ready to assume new responsibilities. Wylie remarks that "one does not have to be naive to the point of taking all these curses too seriously, but it would be just as naive to ignore them.

The peasant cannot have confidence in a government that is supposed to protect him from harm and render him justice, since it is this same government that serves him as a scapegoat, the embodiment of "the others" and of evil. "The absence of farm policy" is the stereotype the great majority resort to in order to explain the farmers' difficulties. Politics are usually scorned and politicians looked upon with suspicion; they think of their personal interests rather than those of the peasants, and they make grandiose speeches to hide their inactivity. We found in the course of a study made in the autumn of 1957 that peasants were quick to link their local farm crisis with the political crisis of the Fourth Republic. They expressed themselves in particularly aggressive terms in communes where Communist influence was strong. "This is a funny kind of politics . . . . It's always

[17]Wylie, 1957, p. 209.

the same people!" Or: "Things are bad in France now; I don't know how we'll end up." Or: "With all that money they're spending on the war in Algeria, they could build us a road." Or: "The government's going to take everything; they'll take over land and sell it like they sold Algeria." "The Germans are lending us money. It's a disgrace! What a mess!" In other words, if agriculture is going poorly it is because everything is going poorly in France; it is a sign and an example of the evil and immorality of the society and those in power.[18]

Paradoxically, this defiance does not exclude dependence on governmental aid, the solution most frequently advanced for the problems of local agriculture. In Alsace and Combrailles almost all the farmers (90 to 95 percent) demanded state intervention in one form or another: farm policy, price support, social legislation, loans and subsidies, and so on. In Béarn and Léon less than half the farmers (39 percent and 42 percent) answered the same way, but they usually mentioned improvements that depended in fact on the initiative and aid of the administration: public water supply, roads, land consolidation. In Combrailles these last improvements were also demanded by almost half the persons interviewed.

In describing the "political mentality" of the French, political scientists have often referred to this image of a government that does not inspire confidence but is expected to remedy all evils. What concerns us here are the effects of these contradictory attitudes on the professional morale of the farmers. These two attitudes are complementary and reinforce each other: the more one expects from the state, the greater the chance of being disappointed and the tendency to consider the government an "unworthy father" who does not do what he should for his children. Should the situation become critical, it will be a handy scapegoat, assuming all blame and thus relieving the farmer's conscience. Meanwhile he is sure he cannot "pull through alone," for there is "nothing to be done if the state doesn't support us."

While he can expect only to be deceived by the government, can the farmer have more confidence in his brothers — other farmers and the various farm organizations? Here again, not only are the fundamental attitudes contradictory, but they are also

[18]Appendix 2, No. 2.

undergoing a transformation at the present time, differently in each region. Traditionally the peasant bewails the fact that "the peasants aren't united enough." When one asks if farmers might go on strike like factory workers, the response is usually one of disillusionment. At the idea of a milk deliverers' strike, for example: "And what if I don't carry milk and my neighbor does?" — implying that I will be swindled. It is well known that this fear is fundamental in the thinking of the French.[19]

Until recently individualism governed the farmer's life. By being a more skillful producer and cleverer in the marketplace, he pulled through better than his neighbor. These small differences between the clever farmer and his friends assured him prestige and economic success; his glory was in what distinguished him from others, as small as it might be. When a man has been brought up to play this game, it is difficult for him to believe that his neighbor will not try to be shrewder than he is and that collective action is the best way, in the present situation, to improve the condition of each and every one. The mass demonstrations in the spring of 1961[20] show that this last attitude, very new to rural areas, is making progress in the west and south of France. Today it is always possible for farmers to band together in self-defense. But this does not mean that they are ready to sacrifice an immediate personal advantage in the long-term collective interest. Gourvenec was obliged to recognize this fact and had to resort to coercion at St. Pol-de-Léon to discipline the produce growers, even though they were more advanced that the mass of farmers in other regions.

The various farm organizations (unions, cooperatives, farm credit agencies, mutual insurance societies) have a dark political past, and the peasants hesitate to trust them. Of course, they admit in general that they need them, and they do not fail to draw all the benefits they can from them. At the beginning of the century, unions had to turn themselves into shops and sell a little of everything in order to attract their clientele. As long as it distributed rubber boots and various other benefits, the C.G.A. (General Agricultural Federation) had a large number of followers after the Liberation. And a study done in connection with the creation of the Societies for Land Management (S.A.F.E.R.) shows that even today the first reaction

[19] Gulliver 1958 and undated.
[20] Tavernier and Mendras, 1962.

of the farmers is to wonder who is going to manipulate and exploit them.[21] Even an organization as dynamic as the National Center for Young Farmers (c.n.j.a.) is not above suspicion. Every leader who works for a cause or an organization is presumed to have personal or political ambitions and motives.

As producers of a mass product whose sale depends almost entirely on governmental decisions and cooperative outlets, wine growers are not likely to belong to unions and cooperatives: 53 percent declare they belong to a union, 58 percent to a cooperative. The big wine growers who make their wine and sell it themselves are less often members of cooperatives, but almost three-quarters belong to unions. The small wine growers, who leave the wine making and marketing to the cooperative, do not find it necessary to look to the union as well for protection; more than one-third of those questioned display interest in organizations for the protection of wine growing and almost one-quarter show none; respectively half and 10 percent of the first group give these responses.

In a modernized region like Béarn, where hybrid corn has spread by way of the unions and where the cooperatives assure the storage and sale of the entire crop under excellent conditions, a question as weighted as "Who best protects the farmers' interests?" received answers as in Table 17.

The vague and often complacent response, "the union," is surprising in view of the dynamism and effectiveness of certain institutions and leaders, in the category of cooperatives. According to the studies of the i.f.o.p., which are more recent and apply to all of France, 39 percent of the farmers say they are satisfied with the unions' activity, but 33 percent are not members and only 33 percent consider the unions active in their regions.

In addition, 32 percent declare they have participated in mass demonstrations. This figure seems substantial. Indeed, for the past ten years roadblocks, meetings, mass demonstrations in front of prefectures, assemblies, and similar measures have become increasingly popular. That one-third of the farmers have participated in these at one time or another shows that mass politics have entered into the customs of the peasantry. On the other hand, feelings about leaders and the farm organizations still seem to be mixed. If two-thirds of the farmers do not consider their unions active, although

[21]Appendix 2, No. 24.

Table 17. Protection of the Farmer's Interests

Nobody	14%
The union	43
The farmers themselves	11
No answer or Don't know	26
Miscellaneous	6

they have manifestly been so for ten years, it is obvious that their activity is not in the farmers' interest. Should we conclude that the farm organizations and their leaders are ranked with the *ils* one must beware of, even if they are sometimes useful?

In case things should go from bad to worse, what solution does the farmer see as a way out? The majority can see only a choice between "tightening their belts" and leaving a profession that has become so difficult and unrewarding. To the question, "If prices went down how could you manage?" we obtained very diverse answers, which can be distributed among several categories (Table 18).

About one-third or one-half of the farmers (an average of one-half if we include those who do not answer) see no solution other than to meet such additional misfortune with resignation and courage: "It will mean ruin," or "I'll just have to go begging," or "I'll have to get by, live poorly, buy less," or "hold on as well as I can." About one-third consider clearing out, selling their holdings, and seeking work elsewhere. And it is only a feeble minority who see the possibility of increasing yields or changing the system of cultivation. Some simply refuse to face such a possibility; they think that prices are already too low to go any further, and in any case they hope the government will give them support.

The age and size of the farm and the economic yield have little influence on the distribution of answers. In Léon, where it was

Table 18. Plan in Case of a Drop in Prices

	Sundgau	Combrailles	Béarn	Léon
Passive reaction; no solution	37%	30%	30%	54%
Quit farming	33	40	26	16
Improve productivity	12	7	17	4
Miscellaneous, including state intervention	8	16	20	19
No answer	10	7	7	7

possible to measure yields, the farmers who were making money spoke of limiting themselves more often than did the others; with a margin of profit at their disposal, they do not expect unfavorable circumstances to have economic or technological repercussions. They have something to fall back on, and they count on it to help them survive better than their less well-to-do neighbors in lean times. In other words, their economic success does not lead them to modify the traditional view of their occupation. On the other hand, we find that the Béarnais are less pessimistic than the people of Combrailles and Brittany in the sense that they are more self-reliant and more confident that help from outside can prevent a drop in their standard of living.

Since they cannot trust other farmers, political representatives, or the authorities and are convinced that they cannot help themselves, the peasants are naturally inclined toward a general pessimism and see the future in a sad light. To the question, "Is agriculture moving towards crisis or prosperity, or will it remain stationary?" we obtained the answers in Table 19.

As could be expected, the Béarnais farmer who introduced hybrid corn into his system of cultivation and was selling it at a good price at the time of the study is less pessimistic than the farmer from Combrailles, who cannot see a way out of the crisis his region is passing through.

Within a region, those who rely on cattle and hogs to protect them financially and those who have prosperous farms should show higher morale than others, yet this is not the case. In Léon those farmers who are making a profit fear a crisis as much as the others, and the minority that believes in prosperity is hardly larger in this category than in the others (16 percent instead of 9 percent). It is generally believed that young people are more hopeful than their elders and that the big farmers should reasonably feel better armed for the future than small farmers. In the four regions, our results disprove this

Table 19. The Future of Agriculture

	Sundgau	Combrailles	Béarn	Léon
Moving toward crisis	70%	78%	51%	70%
Will remain stationary	15	12	18	14
Moving toward prosperity	5	5	22	9
No answer	10	5	9	7

hypothesis: the responses vary little in relation to age and size of farm. On the other hand, in the study on feeling for the land among peasants of the Rhône valley, arboriculturists show markedly higher morale than polycultivators.

These observations reinforce the preceding ones and lead to two hypotheses. First, the pessimism that is voiced for the benefit of an interviewer who comes from the outside is a general and collective stereotype accepted and expressed by "everybody" but relatively superficial, and possibly in contradiction with behavior.[22] Moreover, this pessimism, being collective in nature, is not affected by individual economic success but only by the overhauling of the system of cultivation and the opening up of new market opportunities. If this second hypothesis could be verified, it would strongly support the contention that the "peasant mentality" (not to say the "peasant soul") cannot long survive changes in the farm economy, and that farmers will become more and more like everyone else.

In the meantime, how do farmers envisage this crisis that they are undergoing or fear they will have to undergo? Lack of money is certainly the most immediate sign of it in their minds; our studies and the I.F.O.P. surveys demonstrate this fact. In the past one did not spend money; one earned it and saved it, since it was "good for nothing" in everyday life. Today, on the contrary, "you always have your hand in your pocket," although it is hardly refilled any faster than before. Shall I modernize? be a good farmer? improve the agriculture of the region? send my children to school? To all these questions the answer could always be the same: "Yes, but where shall I find the money?" To resort to borrowing only makes this fiscal crisis more difficult, because borrowing is not yet free of all moral stigma, because debt is a sure sign of poverty, and finally because one becomes "a servant to the loan." A slogan comparing agricultural and industrial prices that was recently coined by the farm organizations in response to this anxiety has enjoyed a lively success. The farmers so quickly adopted it that less than three months after the start of the campaign it emerged in our interviews.

The new attitude towards money contributes to making its absence all the more irritating. If the parents were happy without money, their children tell themselves there is something evil about being unhappy because they have none. As everybody knows, "money

[22]See Appendix 1, and Appendix 2, No. 38.

doesn't buy happiness," so why aren't we happier, as our parents were? Have we become bad, or is it the times that are bad? Moreover, people are beginning to need money just at the moment when inflation and devaluation are depriving it of its value. Isn't it unhealthy to be so preoccupied with money when it is "worthless?"

Finally, farmers are all the more sensitive to the crisis because they feel that they are the only members of the population who suffer from it. To feed their famous inferiority complex they have been abundantly provided with arguments showing the ingratitude of the cities they are nourishing and enriching at their own expense. They are the "outcasts of the nation," the "forgotten proletarians,"[23] and agriculture is just as underdeveloped here as in North Africa or India. The members of the other social categories, who do not have to finance their enterprises on personal income, are spending more and more money, and the stores in town and city bear witness that "the others don't lack money." Why do farmers alone suffer this lack?

Among expenditures it is impossible to distinguish those that are investments from those that go to consumption. The farmer who buys a tractor does not feel that he is enriching himself; he knows only that he has bills to pay and that his wife does not have enough money for daily living expenses. For his part, the neighbor who does not seek to modernize and continues to live self-sufficiently does not have all these worries; the price of fuel and fertilizer hardly concerns him, and he has no debts. While in the long run his farm may be doomed, today he does not live any the worse, and he can afford the luxury of mocking the pretentions and burdens of the farmer who has chosen progress.

The departure of the young people is a second sure sign of crisis. All farmers complain that they cannot find workers anymore and that the younger generation is abandoning the land. On the one hand they understand and approve, as we have said, since they advise their daughters, and to some extent their sons, to learn a trade. On the other hand they bemoan this departure as an exodus, a desertion, and hence a result and symptom of crisis. Where the economist sees a condition necessary to an increase in productivity and standard of living, they see the death of their countryside. In their minds agriculture is primarily farmers and their families; to distinguish one from the other seems meaningless. The land, the men who live off it,

[23]Dumont, 1955.

and the products they derive from it form an inseparable whole. One cannot imagine farm production without land or men. Technicians are now studying a mode of cultivation without soil that will probably require very little manpower, but for the traditional peasant this is an apocalyptic vision.

The best sign of farm prosperity is obviously the prosperity of large numbers of farmers. If agriculture were prosperous, the young people would not be abandoning it. The spectacle of a deserted farm, even where the surrounding fields are being cultivated by neighbors, immediately gives rise to a feeling of destitution. It is difficult to accept the fact that its abandonment is a necessary condition to the neighbors' prosperity. The image is singularly more convincing than reason, no matter how well argued. This is all the more true because it evokes the drama and anxiety of the farmer himself; despite his unrelenting labors, despite his efforts to follow "progress," won't he be obliged in his turn — he or his son — to abandon his ancestral home? And if so, what good are so much work, effort, and misery? These are the searching questions that the farmer of Combrailles asks himself. They betray the repressed but fundamental anxiety of peasants in all regions, even those that have begun well, such as Béarn and the Rhône Valley.

Only young people who believe in the future of modernized agriculture base their hope on the despair of others; it is because a neighbor deserts his home that they are able to cultivate his abandoned field. They do not linger sentimentally over the old stones that illustrate a past they are struggling against with all their resources. Their own success blinds them to a drama they are confident they themselves will escape.

Any farmer, young or old, traditionalist or modernist, considers production his occupation and vocation. The peasant has always striven to increase the fertility of the land; to multiply, discipline, and improve upon the gifts of nature. An abundant harvest repays him for his pains. Recent technical, biological, and mechanical advances have in a few years increased tenfold the productive power of man and his land, yet the unlimited abundance that results has been transformed into a calamity, an occurrence unknown and unimaginable to the peasant of the past. The source of anxiety for the peasant, as for the prince, is no longer scarcity, but the superabundance of necessities.

The farmer is discovering that it is no longer enough to produce; he must sell, and his produce, the hope and reward of all his efforts, cannot have any value in a wasteful society. The paradox seems all the more incomprehensible to him when he sees cities increasing in size and population at the same time that the number of farmers is decreasing and overproduction is becoming more and more a threat. The economist serenely explains that maintenance needs have little elasticity, that farm productivity has multiplied prodigiously and international markets are distorted. This does not lessen the peasant's dismay.

American studies teach us that every agricultural producer, even if he is not a traditional farmer, shares this dismay. Under the farm program of the New Deal, provisions for soil conservation were well received because they found an echo in the ideology of Midwestern farmers; a good cultivator must do everything to conserve the fertility of his land. On the other hand, measures intended to regulate production, notably subsidies to encourage cutbacks in wheat, were accepted (who would refuse subsidies?), but only reluctantly. To limit production, to interfere with the fertility of the land, is considered a sacrilege.[24] In France, 76 percent of the wine growers of Languedoc declare that it is detrimental to tear out vines (as regulations urge them to do), and only 20 percent concede that it sometimes serves a purpose. Because it is a sort of negation of the finished product, distillation is felt to be a wrong by 60 percent of the wine growers, who wish to avoid it at all costs, while 37 percent admit that it is an evil that is sometimes very useful.

Agriculture remains an artisanal occupation in which the producer can identify with the product he fashions himself, from the seed to the harvest or from the newborn lamb to the fine animal that earns him the compliments of neighbors and customers. Moreover, it is by fertilizing his land and caring for his flock over long years that he attains such perfection. Each of his products is thus literally the result of a whole lifetime of effort and the proof of his experience, his *savoir faire,* and his toil.

Furthermore, the farmer's products are not ordinary. They are of noble essence. Bread, wine, and lamb have been sanctified

[24]Miner, 1949.

by the entire Judeo-Christian tradition. A fine ox or a good ear of corn, like a journeyman's masterpiece, is unique. Of course, as far as the consumer is concerned, they are lost in the mass, but for the producer they have their own personalities. To feed humanity is the justifiable pride of the peasant, who sees in it a sort of vocation in which man extends the work of the Creator by maintaining life. The symbolic and sacred character of the principal farm products was one of the bases of peasant civilization, and the ideology of farm organizations, notably those that are of Catholic sponsorship, has adopted and modernized these themes in order to convince young farmers of the nobility of the land as a profession. Finally, the recent war has shown that factories could stop production but that the land had to continue under any circumstances to feed man, for better or worse.

But the market and mass consumption are transforming the unique and sacred product of the peasant into an unimportant object whose whole value can be snatched away by a whim of circumstance. Are there too many peaches or tomatoes? They rot without finding takers. Is the harvest abundant, as every peasant wishes it to be? The government must seek ways to dispose of it. Thus society can destroy these products that the farmer brings to life. To destroy his work is to murder the worker.

This demoralizing contradiction can best be illustrated by wine growing. Wine, as refined and sacred a product as it is, is one of the great mass alimentary products. The bottle of rare vintage and exceptional year does honor to the wine grower, while "watery wine" (*vinasse*), destined for doubtful mixtures or distillation, crowds the market. The winegrowers of Languedoc are proud of their job; they think that wine growing is an art. They rejoice too in the great freedom and leisure it allows; they are aware of this privilege and everything that distinguishes them from small polycultivators and breeders, who are slaves to their animals. They greet without enthusiasm the idea of irrigating their land to transform it into meadows and produce milk and meat. Finally, they live well and have scarcely anything to envy in urban comfort: 82 percent have automobiles, 27 percent washing machines, and 33 percent refrigerators. Eighty-seven percent have no desire to go to the city; compared with both city dwellers and peasants, they feel themselves privileged.

This situation they owe to the solicitude of the government, and they know it. All the rules and regulations applying to wine are certainly shackles difficult to bear, but they are also a protection (Table 20).

Finally, 42 percent of the winegrowers admit that "without the government we would never manage." It does not seem exaggerated, then, to conclude that, whether explicitly or not, the winegrowers feel themselves protected.

This protection is essential in order to assure their security in a market where an arbitrary principle operates brutally and where the pressure of imports is making itself felt. If the crop is large, the wine finds no buyers and prices collapse. On the contrary, if it is small, the wine is expensive. Finally, the winegrower often draws a higher monetary income from a bad crop than a good one. The previously cited definition of a "good year," as seen by winegrowers, is therefore not surprising.

Winegrowers have the feeling that their wine, once sold, is out of their hands. If they are asked what the consumer thinks of it, one-third refuse to answer, saying that their wine is "mixed with others" or that they "don't know where it goes." Their wine is not treated as a particular product that deserves a particular evalution; most farmers think that prices cannot be discussed, "they're already set." And when they bring their grapes to the cooperative their product is out of their hands even before it exists; they furnish only the raw material.

The winegrower of Languedoc, as we see, being a small producer of a product for mass consumption, cannot maintain for his crop any of the feelings of identification and pride that moved the traditional artisan and peasant. He does not give it its final form but sends it off to be mixed and lost in the mass, a drop in the ocean. No longer being able to rely on his product to justify and protect him; he must, like the industrial worker, fall

Table 20. The Regulation of Wine

Is an unqualified evil	36%
Is a necessary evil	14
Is desirable but involves inconvenience	33
Is desirable	12
No answer	5

back on pride in his *savoir faire* and collective defense of his acquired rights. According to 67 percent of the answers, the good winegrower is the good worker. The winegrower sees himself above all as a worker, while the farmer, as we have said, sees himself as the head of a farm who succeeds if he has the means to do so. And this worker knows that his income and his relatively satisfactory standard of living are assured only by government intervention, while the farmer feels strongly he is the object of a deep injustice.

Hence it does not seem exaggerated to say that the winegrower who preserves his legal position as an independent entrepreneur is in fact in a social situation that more closely approaches that of the factory worker than that of the polycultivating farmer. He owns the means of production (his vines, his implements, and machines); but since his product vanishes before his eyes, it is his work itself that justifies him in his own thinking, and it is by collective action that he assures his place in society. Though the wine grower and the polycultivator appear to be alike, there is actually a radical contrast; and it is certainly not bold to think that in many ways the wine grower prefigures the farm producer of tomorrow.

A very difficult occupation but one that is loved and nourishes deep feelings of moral superiority; a deplorable social and economic condition, whose future seems dark and that finds no defenders worthy of confidence; produce that may rot or be destroyed when it has scarcely left the farm; government subsidies that reduce the worker to beggary since his work does not earn a fair salary but an arbitrary handout — all this is enough to explain, and even justify, the feeling of persecution and the curious mixture of optimism and pessimism that characterize the attitude of farmers in contemporary France.

This attitude varies much from region to region, probably more than from individual to individual within the same region. We have spoken several times of the relative homogeneity of collective opinion in rural society. During the brutal transformation that the French countryside has undergone for ten years, certain regions have remained relatively unaffected, and others have essentially completed their transition; but most are presently in the process. A number of studies have shown clearly that the morale of farmers and their wives is distinctly higher in the first and second cases than in the third.

As long as the traditional system preserves its coherence, daily life and work can be painful, but they continue to have meaning. Moreover, farmers know they must adapt, and they look to technology for relief from their hardships. Traditional logic dominates and orders each act and each choice. In her study, Marie-Thérèse de la Rivière states that women have a much harder life than men in the *département* of Manche.[25] Since the farms are very small and only slightly modernized, the wives participate in all the farm work and take care of the cows. Despite this fact they are relatively satisfied with their lot. Similarly, the I.F.O.P. interviewers were surprised to find in peasants of the Margeride area, isolated on their arid, high plateaus in a harsh climate, a much better morale than elsewhere.

But, when farmers have taken a chance on modernization and decided to play the economic game by entering the market, they have in some way "embarked." They are creating aspirations and needs for themselves and putting forth all their efforts to satisfy them. Armed with his knowledge of bookkeeping and the financial and technical advice he receives from his adviser and from various organizations, the farmer is endlessly seeing the machine that will facilitate his work, the technique that will improve his yield, the product that will pay him best. This does not happen without strain and reverses; the road is rough, but it leads somewhere. Moreover, he is traveling with his neighbors; he is part of a group and can feel that he is in the forefront of his profession. His wife, for her part, devotes herself entirely to her roles of housewife and mother. Like her city counterpart, she equips her kitchen, makes her house sparkle, takes care of her children, and sews cheerful aprons. Money may always be lacking and she may have to help with the man's work from time to time, but the model is clear, and it is with a deep sense of satisfaction that she seeks to conform to it. Marie-Thérèse de la Rivière and the I.F.O.P. interviewers met this situation on the plateaus of Lozère and the region of Auge.[26]

By contrast, in other regions where they have conducted

[25]De la Rivière, 1961.
[26]Géraud and Spitzer, 1965, p. 13; and Appendix 2, No. 27.

their studies, these researchers have encountered a lower morale and a more marked dissatisfaction — just as often, let us note, in countries slowing down as in those which are rapidly modernizing. This effort to adjust, which has not yet found its strength and meaning, excites doubt and anxiety and leads to a desire for scapegoats on whom to place responsibility for the uncertainties and vexations. In the traditional village we must protect ourselves against the *ils*, against *them*, whom we simply ask to "leave us alone." In the modern village we try to know these people and gain their good will. Everywhere else *they* are ill-disposed; they wish us evil and are responsible for all our misfortunes. In a word, it is the effort to adapt and the change now in process that arouse anxiety and aggressive reactions, and not the situation itself. Thus the whole range of standards of evaluation, comparison, and judgment is in fact called into question. One does not know any longer who is successful, or how, or why, since the models and criteria of success are fluid, uncertain, and contradictory. In the end we ask ourselves if success itself has a meaning and whether it is not better to abandon everything.

It is obvious that traditional categories and criteria are becoming inadequate. But what is most troubling is that those proposed by the broader society are just as much so. The farmer is certainly not an employer, since he does not generally employ any work force but his own family. Neither is he a worker, since he is not salaried and owns the means of production. He is not head of an enterprise, since his farm is not truly an enterprise and can eternally show a bookkeeping deficit without ever being in bankruptcy. He does not even have a trade which would permit him to find a job elsewhere. It is impossible for him to find a place for himself in modern society, which was constructed on principles totally foreign to him; it classifies him as an "independent worker," together with the liberal professions, artisans, small merchants, and even — why not? — vagrants (a residual category defined by the negative and always treated separately because one never knows how to handle it). And nevertheless everybody delights in recognizing in the peasant the archetype of the independent free man who is his own master and whom the world proposes as the model for the alienated man, the "stranger," of modern technological civilization. Can we hope that new political and professional institutions will be able to reconcile these opposites and permit the farmer to enter into industrial society without losing the uniqueness of his condition, sad though it may sometimes be?

7. The Farmer in the National Context

Stendhal tells how Lucien Leuwen went to Calvados to take part in the elections; Balzac portrays the political life of the peasants of Morvan, particularly the discussions at the Cabaret du Grand I Vert; and Tocqueville tells in his memoirs that in 1848, having decided to run for office, he traveled to his native Normandy to appear before the voters. Here is how they voted in his village:

The morning of the election, all the voters . . . met in front of the church. All the men got into line two by two, in alphabetical order. . . . When they got to the top of the hill overlooking Tocqueville, they stopped a moment. I realized they wished me to speak. So I climbed onto the side of a ditch, they all made a circle around me, and I spoke a few words inspired by the occasion. I reminded these good people of the grave importance of the act they were about to perform. I advised them not to let themselves be accosted or turned back by those who might seek to mislead them as we entered the town, but to walk without becoming disunited, staying together each in his line until we had voted. . . . They cried out that they would do this, and so they did. All the votes were cast at one time, and I have reason to think they were all for the same candidate. As soon as I had voted myself, I said goodbye to them; and, getting back into my carriage, I left for Paris.[1]

This anecdote illustrates quite accurately the role assigned to peasants in the politics of the last century. They held the bulk of the votes obtained or needed in support of a candidate, votes that he undertook to win by "concerning himself" with the peasants, in his village as well as in Paris.

Each new regime, each new political party, has sought to establish itself in rural areas by doing something for the peasants.[2] In the hope of forming a republican elite among the peasantry, the government of the Second Republic organized for the first time a complete system of agricultural schools on three levels, comprising seventy farm schools, four regional schools, and the *Institut agronomique*. The government of the Second Empire, which had other means of keeping its hold on the farming community, soon abandoned this program and did away with the *Institut agronomique*. The Third Republic took up the projects begun by the Second. The "Republic of Dukes" reopened the *Institut agronomique* and built technical schools for farmers' sons, who had to be educated if they were to be persuaded to stay on the land. Soon the republicans did their share, in 1879, by instituting professorships of agriculture, first by *département,*

[1]Tocqueville, 1856.
[2]Leveau, 1958.

and then by *arrondissement* — forerunners of future farm service agencies, whose history, according to one biased view, is only a reflection of the electoral history of the Third Republic. Likewise the Ministry of Agriculture, founded by Gambetta in 1881, was to become a "ministry of peasants."[3]

We have explained elsewhere that the history of farm organizations can be summed up as a long rivalry between the squire and the Radical Socialist deputy.[4] In order to preserve their social, hence political, influence, the conservative nobles who had retired from political life and gone back to their villages after 1876 founded and kept alive the right-wing farm organizations with offices on the Rue d'Athènes in Paris. Their success moved the republicans, who wanted to extend politics into the villages, to create a similar network of cooperatives, farm credit agencies, and mutual insurance societies, based in offices on the Boulevard St. Germain and supported by subsidies from the Ministry of Agriculture, which the opposing party rejected as a shameful and wanton compromise.

By studying a few biographies it is possible to define the different types of *cursus honorum* that, depending on the ideological tendencies, the region, or the personalities involved, once made it possible to use farm organizations to further a career in politics. Participation in a national organization (such as the director-ship of a national federation, cooperative, or union) enables a politician to rely on "professional" connections and to gain the confidence of his rural constituency. At the other extreme is the farmer who has been active in different professional organizations: beginning as president of a local union, he becomes director, then president, of a cooperative, takes on responsibilities in his *département* and finally at a national conference is elected to the board of directors of a national federation. Generally a career so strictly professional does not lead to politics, but if a man has been elected county councillor and is attracted to the idea of a national political job, he may take a chance on the legislative elections. This was the case in the "civic action" movement that swept thirty-eight farmers into the *Parlement* in 1951.

Professional leaders and political representatives were until recently almost all notables, middle class men from small towns, or large

[3]Cépède, 1964; see also Fauvet and Mendras, 1958, pp. 261–268.
[4]Fauvet and Mendras, 1958, pp. 231–252; Augé-Laribé, 1926 and 1950; Wright, 1964.

landholders. It is very difficult for a small peasant to leave his farm, even for a day, to go to a conference or a board meeting. If the meeting is held in the village, or in the district headquarters, or even if necessary in the capital city of the *département,* he can milk cows before leaving and when he returns; but if he has to go overnight by train to Paris, all the work falls to his wife.

Furthermore, faced with the problems that arise at the level of the commune, the district, or even the *département,* the small peasant feels at his ease. The problems are similar to those of a farm enterprise and he has enough daily experience to enter these circles with interest and without awkwardness. At the national level, on the other hand, the problems are abstract, and the forces at work are difficult to evaluate. The rules of the political game, the methods of action, and the code of conduct are strange to the peasant. Whether consciously or not, he feels himself in an unknown world — that of the city, of power, economics, and international affairs — whereas he is a country boy suspicious of power, a farm specialist for whom the outside world is narrowly limited. He finds that in national politics even words themselves do not always have the same meaning.

Supported ably by their wives or sons or specialized farmers, some particularly gifted men adapt to this new situation and become national leaders. They spend several days a week in Paris and preside each Sunday at a conference or meeting somewhere in France. They may be even elected to a European or international organization. The same man can be simultaneously a working farmer, mayor of his commune, president of a local cooperative, president of the chamber of agriculture, or director of several federations in his *département,* president or vice-president of five national federations, director of several national associations, member of numerous committees, of the Chief Planning Commission on Modernization and Equipment, of the Economic Council, and can finally be elected president of an international organization. It is enough just to read this list, incomplete as it is, to imagine what his life must be like.

On the other hand, a man who has gone to an agricultural school, who directs an enterprise of eight hundred acres fifty miles from Paris, can, if he has a good foreman, devote some time to activities in the city. He does not share the manual labor, and managing his enterprise has already demanded of him a certain understanding of the social and economic mechanisms of our civilization; hence there is a smaller discrepancy between his occupation and his activities in the union. This is all the more true because the union is often devoted to the protection of two or three products of his enterprise (wheat, beetroot, oleaginous products, for example).

Finally, there is the squire who spends his winters in Paris; he can, while managing or even farming his lands, busy himself with the affairs of regional and national organizations. His name, his family and social connections, and his education make this task easier. But he is becoming more and more rare.

The latter two types of men are in need of the first, for one must have "calloused hands" and "peasant guts" if one is to be a spokesman of the French peasantry. From the moment that he arrives on the Parisian scene, the small peasant risks being drawn into the play of powerful forces and becoming driven away little by little from his base. When he returns to the village, he thinks in terms of the Parisian game and no longer in terms of his neighbors' problems. In short, though he is ill at ease in Paris, he no longer belongs to the village. Aware that this may happen, the best men often refuse to leave their villages and take on responsibilities that extend beyond the *département,* a fact that explains why the peasantry has not always sent its best-qualified men to Paris.

In former days, the farm organizations of the Rue d'Athènes claimed to be apolitical in denying the Republic and following the current rightist ideological trend. But this position did not prevent close contacts in the provinces and in Paris between "peasant" leaders and politicians, almost all of whom belonged to the world of the high *bourgeoisie* and conservative nobility. They relied on the same men and the same connections. Among those who met on the Boulevard St. Germain, politics was explicitly accepted, and the combining of political and professional roles was more frequent. On one side there were dukes and *marquis,* on the other ministers and future ministers, as Augé-Laribé facetiously points out.

Each side comprised a small world: a few families, a few regions. The Vogüé, Guébriant, Roquigny, Duport families, and others depended on two strongholds: Brittany with the bureau at Landerneau, and the powerful Southeast Federation of Lyon. "Radical"*

*Note that radical in France means center left, or membership in the Radical Socialist party. (Trans.)

Beauce was represented by the large Benoist family;[5] from the Charente *départements* and the southwest came militant republicans. In certain regions, such as the north, the two tendencies were almost equal in strength, both in Paris and the provinces. The right-wing unions performed the function of cooperatives and the left-wing cooperatives that of protection; until 1930 each had its own network of farm credit associations.

To distinguish among themselves and hide the political cleavages that exist, farm associations assume various labels that do not correspond to their structures, their membership, or their functions. The words union, federation, and confederation are used interchangeably, as are general, national, and central; rural, peasant, farmer, and cultivator. For a long time the unions were real cooperatives (the most striking case being that of the threshing unions). Cooperatives devoted a large part of their activity to the defense of professional interests. Specialized trusts, simple associations under the law of 1901, are in truth employers' associations. And farm credit associations take care of everything, even the technical aspects of rural housing. On the other hand, the boards of directors of various organizations following the same "tendency" bring together the same people, with few exceptions, since the choice is made by coopting rather than electing. This confusion of terms, functions, and roles testifies to the contradictions and rivalries that divide the peasantry.

Curiously, certain traits of village society are found also in this Parisian society of farm leaders. The overlapping of roles permits choosing responsible leaders according to their family ties and their ideological orientation rather than their competence. In this way federations are formed, and their salaried "permanent" directors and secretaries are chosen. The son or the son-in-law succeeds the father or reinforces his power by occupying a supporting position. These ties of ideological, personal, and family affinity, extending to the administration, explain and underlie the complicity and rivalry between the "Ministry" and the farm services of the *départements* and professional organizations in Paris and in the provinces. Behind the institutions and the services there are always families, regions, or parties, particularly because, institutions being very numerous and members being scarce, each man occupies several chairs. When an elected official has to be replaced, there is often only one name to

[5]Rémy Leveau, 1958; See Appendix 2, No. 20.

propose to the members for election; just as in a small commune, where the municipal council necessarily remains stable because of the small number of candidates.

The older men tend to keep their seats on boards of directors until they die, just as they maintain the direction of their farms. So the young people, not feeling at home in the "paternal" organizations, create new ones. Hence, each organization has been the work of a generation: the country squires of 1880 formed unions, the Radicals of 1900 cooperatives and mutual insurance societies. In 1930 the young Catholic farmers, influenced by Dorgères, corporatist doctrines,[6] and the beginnings of Catholic Action, created and established new unions on the Rue des Pyramides, which were more concerned than their predecessors with the protection of products and prices. It was trade unionism by conference and by mass action, from which came the leaders of the Peasant Corporation of the Vichy government and the present National Federation of Farmers' Unions (f.n.s.e.a.). Following the Liberation, as we shall see, a new generation created a whole range of institutions directed toward technical and economic aid to farmers.

It is true that the generations succeed each other, always influenced by the Church but with profoundly different doctrinal tendencies, social origins, and ambitions. It is also true that this succession is sometimes accomplished with difficulty; the young people who had founded the organizations of the Boulevard St. Germain at the beginning of the century resumed their places after the Liberation or yielded them to their own sons, but the new generation did not establish itself. The Socialists and the Communists occupied some positions without either creating new institutions or renewing the old ones.

The "young" farm organizations are opposed to the "old" ones, and these rivalries often cut across political lines. In a region where the old Catholic organizations are predominant, the young people of the j.a.c. naturally tend to assert themselves by opposing their elders, sometimes brutally, even to the point of joining with Radical or anticlerical organizations. Elsewhere the same young people, confronted only by left-wing organizations, find themselves thrown back toward the right. Active members of the same movement, directed by the same ideas and ambitions, thus find themselves prisoners of

[6]Salleron, 1937.

contradictory positions as defined by regional political chessboards. In this way there has grown up in Paris a sort of farm village with its whites and its blues, to whom are joined reds, then young people, and others, who play on the national chessboard the game they are familiar with on the local level.

In the village the peasants, equally inured to the political game of the notables, uncover the slightest political affinities, sometimes overestimate them, often play on them; and by thus making themselves accomplices they accentuate them. But as soon as we pass from the national level to that of the *département* or village, political conflicts take on very different meanings in each region, in relation to the type of stratification and social life one finds there.

It is enough to recall the differences among communes in Brittany, Alsace, Provence, or Gascony, to see that one cannot generalize. Bedel explains that in his Limousine village "there are a rightist and a leftist blacksmith. One shoes pious horses, the other unbelievers. It is good," he concludes, "that right-wing plows do not think like left-wing plows. This is what saves the village from boredom, what preserves this minimal activity. . ."[7] Thus do not town and village politics seem to be only a distraction, a social game, maintained for no other reason than to enliven the dullness of pastoral life? The intensity of political rivalries at the turn of the century in the county seats of the southwestern districts is perhaps largely explained in this way. Small, languishing factories, meager tenant farms, and a few public offices left much leisure time to a rustic *bourgeoisie* quick to become embroiled in a political quarrel and revile their adversaries. The "idealist from the provinces" was in some way the harbinger of this contest, which had its deep springs in conflicts of economic interests and struggles for social influence.

We need not seek to determine exactly how much this was due to "sublimation" or to the ideological "superstructure." Yet the style, the rules of conduct, and the vocabulary definitely took on an ideological and gamelike character, at least in the southwest and the Midi. In Brittany and the Vendée, the rigidity of the social hierarchy imposed a more restrictive framework and made the struggle harsher and less entertaining. Jean Yole has described the seizing of municipal power by those he called "the newcomers," who led the peasants

[7]Bedel, 1937, p. 114.

against the squires; the latter, bitter at such ingratitude, reacted brutally.[8] Similarly, Thabault has told of the battles engaged at Mazières-en-Gâtine between the dairy cooperative of the Marquis de Maussabré and that of M. Proust, who was "resolutely conservative and passionately anticlerical, and who dreamed of progress . . ."[9] In certain mountainous regions of an egalitarian tradition, struggles for influence between family cliques gave a more subtle and personal flavor to the rivalry of political labels, and a few reminiscences were sometimes enough to set up the political chessboard. Everywhere the Church furnished a battle flag and a set of symbols, to its partisans and adversaries alike.

The autarchic stability of the traditional rural economy was a necessary condition to this relative autonomy of political life. One could take politics as a game, involving no grave consequences for the material life of the peasants, which was subject more to the hazards of nature than to those of the market. This was not the case, however, for predominantly monocultivating regions. Wheat-selling country since the end of the Second Empire, Beauce fashioned its electoral behavior to the economic policy of the candidates; thus Zola's farmer Hourdequin voted for the man who promised him the best price.[10] Nevertheless a careful observer can still today analyze the political life of a village in Beauce in terms of families and cliques.[11] Similarly, we have only to recall the political crises generated by the winegrowers of Hérault and Aude in pointing out that certain types of political life are tied to certain types of rural economy.[12] We would have to gather a large number of systematic descriptions before trying to draw up a theory of politics in limited, face-to-face communities such as villages, to discover how certain characteristics of this political life have been modified over the past half-century.

This theory would also permit us to analyze the political game better at the national level, for in fact there is an obvious connection between certain rules of the game in the village and in Paris. By the same token, it would be fruitful to study the refraction in Paris of the many local and regional games. If we recall that the Peasant Corporation of the Vichy government was animated by Guébriant, and that

[8]Yole, 1909.
[9]Thabault, 1945.
[10]Zola, *La Terre.*
[11]Appendix 2, No. 16.
[12]Warner, 1960.

Tanguy-Prigent was the founder of the c.g.a. (General Confederation of Agriculture) in 1954, we are obviously led to analyze the
politico-agricultural rivalries of northern Finistère, from which both
men derived. Similarly, the law on tenant farming and *métayage*
cannot be interpreted entirely without reference to the particular
problems of Landes, nor the Pisani Law without reference to those of
Maine-et-Loire. Each movement, each party, each trend has a
regional origin that gives it its particular tonality in relation to the
political traditions of a region or regions. Hence it is natural that the
representatives of agriculture in Paris tend not only to recreate
among themselves the schema of political life in an "ideal French
village" but also to transpose to Paris the rivalries and problems of
their native villages.

Deep ideological agreement on the essential values of the peasantry
has existed, however, among all the parties, from the extreme Left to
the extreme Right. This agreement has probably even been the condition of the competition among these friendly rivals who have
quarreled among themselves but know each other well — "like two
old lovers," according to one observer. Reading professional journals
and reports of conferences leaves no doubt of the community of
thought among farm officials and representatives of all political
tendencies. While the tone is sometimes different, the themes are
similar, and it would be easy to amuse ourselves by putting into the
mouth of a militant Communist the words of a professional leader
with Maurrassian leanings.* There is a true French peasant ideology,
the basic elements of which could be quickly outlined.[13] Griswold's
international comparison shows, furthermore, that this ideology is
common to the entire West, even the United States, which one
would have thought far removed from any peasantry.[14] In fact, the
peasant remains the archetype of man for our entire civilization;
farm leaders know this well and frequently remind us of the fact.

We need not insist on the Virgilian theme of rustic happiness. Even
now in the twentieth century, while peasants are crowding the gates
of the cities, in flight from the land, which no longer feeds them

*Refers to Charles Maurras, a French theoretician who advocated
monarchy. (Trans.)
[13]The quotations that follow have all been extracted from professional
journals and reports of conferences, mostly from the years 1954
and 1955.
[14]Griswold, 1948.

adequately, one still finds, even in literature intended for these peasants, passages praising the healthful country life, the equilibrium and harmony that characterize it — in a word, the happiness that only a peasant can know. When specific problems arise, farm journalists evoke this theme as something self-explanatory and generally accepted. For example, in connection with a national plowing contest, it was written: "From time immemorial plowing has always symbolized best the love that the peasant bears for his land." Happiness comes also to the peasant through a warm family life with his parents and his children:

The flames rise quick and clear. The children do their homework. The housewife cuts up the thick bread for soup. The weary father is seated. . . . His expression as he looks at the children tells us his heart is at peace and all is well on earth. His eyes have that tenderness with which fathers regard their sons.

Happiness comes to him, finally, from his experience in the village; he is "a complete and healthy creature" who enjoys "a jovial harmony of heart and mind, a gay robustness of the spirit."

From this union of man with nature and from this life among traditional social structures is born a deep sobriety "handed down through the centuries." "The French peasant, in the calm of his fields, keeps a clear, cool head; his foremost quality is common sense." He keeps his serenity in the midst of the turbulence of modern life. Some people reproach him for his "slowness," but this is the fruit of the "ancient knowledge" of the biological rhythm of nature, the "eternal order of the fields," which will never submit to the rational order of the planners.

The peasant, being a man of eternal nature, is necessarily a man of the past:

This is the whole value of the landed condition, which was the basis of strong civilizations and great institutions. Today we have only to think about it to wish to preserve its essence . . . .In order for the modern farmer to remain a worthwhile man, he must continue to think and to regulate his work, to rule his farm freely, participate in local communities where closeness and solidarity still figure . . . Rapid change must not destroy the inestimable fund of human riches accumulated over the centuries by man and the land.

The future is always uncertain and even worrisome, while the past is reassuring. A study of word usage would probably show that "the past," "slowness," "continue," "preserve," and so on, always have a favorable meaning, and that by contrast "future," "rapid," "new" generally have a pejorative value. The use of words like "centuries," "accumulation," "tradition," "still," is also revealing in this respect. While the industrial worker places his golden age in the future, the peasant places his in the past. Young peasants who want to build it tomorrow are still the exception.

This idealization of nature, farm work, and peasant life involves an idealization of the peasant, and particularly of the small peasant who works his land by himself. The theme of "calloused hands," of the "peasant's rough handshake" returns frequently as a symbol of hard farm labor, as well as a summation of direct experience whose value is vastly superior to all theoretical knowledge: "These rough hands, accustomed to the handle of the plow, are not skillful in holding the pen." To be the son of a peasant and a peasant oneself is a sort of mark of initiation that alone permits "thinking like a peasant" and speaking of matters of the land. Sharing this conviction, those who have "white hands" have a feeling of inferiority and feel obliged to apologize; high officials and politicians never fail to remind us of their "peasant ties" in order to show that "my whole past links me to you." The title of "small peasant" has a quasi-mystical value for everyone.

There exists, in fact, a sort of peasant messianism comparable to the worker's but with a very different meaning; the working class constructs the world of tomorrow, whereas the peasantry are the chosen people who preserve the eternal values on which this world will necessarily be built.

Whatever a writer's philosophy, he invariably considers the peasant the healthiest political basis of the nation. If he is right-wing he thinks that the peasant "has the respect of the hierarchy, being a prince himself among his family and on his farm." If the author is left-wing he may write:

A farm in our country is a community enterprise .... The conduct of this social microcosm poses the same problems as that of a more far-flung republic. The peasant man and woman are the administrators of this community; they must put to work all the qualities of a citizen. We can understand better why the men of antiquity saw in agriculture the most laudable activity for a free man.

In addition, the peasant gave proof of his patriotism in the trenches. Casting about for arguments, his defenders do not find it irrelevant to recall the sacrifices and deaths at Verdun to justify an increase in the price of wheat. The great adventure that the war of 1914 represented to the peasants inculcated our countryside with a Barresian* ideology, kept alive for a long time by veterans' movements that have left their mark. From chauvinism to xenophobia there is but one easy step. If one holds foreign agriculture up as an example one gets the prompt reply:

We do not accept that, because it is absolutely contrary to the truth to claim that foreign farmers do better, produce more cheaply than we do. What must be said again and again is that our peasants are capable of doing as well as the peasants of other countries, if not better.

Every attempt to introduce Dutch immigrants into swampy regions, or Italians into underpopulated regions, comes up against the fierce hostility of every group: farm services, "professionals" of the right and left, political defenders of our agriculture, from Communists to the extreme Right.

The peasant is a "good Frenchman," and yet this elite citizen "has not been given his rightful place in the nation." Doesn't he represent a third of the population? Isn't it his hard toil that feeds the entire nation? But alas! The nation hardly recognizes him for this. The farmer's income is half that of other producers, though he is "neither less nor more intelligent than the others." It must be that there is some defect in the system or something lacking in farm policy.

In the first place, agriculture is a separate and unique world to which it is useless to try to apply the same rules and frameworks as to other sectors. Why do the decrees and reforms serve for naught?

Because they try to ignore the peasantry, to ignore agriculture as a particular economic family having its limitations, risks, working conditions, and requirements distinct from those of other professions. Because they persist in likening the peasant to an unskilled laborer, an anonymous citizen, a second-class man-of-all-work. Because they refuse to recognize the individuality of the farmer's profession.

The peasants feel that they have been deceived:

In 1944–45 a near-famine reigned in France. Our leaders, distraught and powerless to buy abroad, addressed themselves to French agriculture to assure the country's supply of food. To these exhortations the peasants answered 'present' as they knew

*Refers to Maurice Barrès, French nationalist author. (Trans.)

well how to do. They rolled up their shirtsleeves a little higher and production increased. The tragedy, as our peasants sadly testify, is that while they were doing their duty, our leaders folded their arms and did nothing.

There is a striking contrast between the happiness of the eternal peasant and the "tragedy" of the French peasant today, who understandably has a feeling of deep injustice: he is the "outcast" of the nation, the "forgotten proletarian" of the modern world.

What can he do to obtain his rightful place in the nation? First, unite. There is a myth of peasant unity similar to the myth of the unity of labor. This unity has never been realized except superficially, on the occasion of the two wars, in the national Confederation of Farm Associations of the 1920s, in the Peasant Corporation of Vichy and the General Agricultural Federation at the time of the Liberation. Nevertheless there persists the dream of uniting all the peasants in a professional movement or a political party that would represent a third of the nation and would thus be in a position to impose its will. The f.n.s.e.a. is justly proud of having realized some unity among unions, even though the majority of the peasants still are not included in its membership.

How can we unite the winegrowers with the producers of hops and apples if not in order to claim a prerogative? How can we reconcile the interests of a potato producer of Haute Loire with his competitor in Morbihan? Around what, finally, can we rally the small autarchic polycultivator of the southwest, the breeder of Charolles, the winegrower of Languedoc, and the tenant farmer of the Paris basin? It is clear, on the other hand, that the inequality of farming conditions creates a profit on paper for the big farmer of the Paris basin if the price of wheat is fixed by law to enable the small polycultivator to survive; the former thus has an obvious interest in maintaining the latter in as anachronistic a situation as possible.

Under these conditions, discussions about rural exodus, safeguarding the small family farm, and even the beauties of traditional peasant life are not always disinterested. It is especially true that to speak of "French agriculture" as a homogeneous block with common interests, proclaiming oneself its only spokesman, is obviously nonsense, the proof of which is the great number of such spokesmen and the disagreement that reigns among them.

The most striking common characteristic of all the examples given above is a stubborn moralism that obscures any objective analysis of the situation. All discussion of the future of agriculture is charged with emotionalism, burdened with myths, and distorted by emotional reactions. Can it be said, as we have suggested in preceding chapters, that the moral criterion is the first by which a peasant judges any situation? This would explain why he is always justifying his technological and economic inflexibility on a moral basis; and why, by continually asserting his own good conscience, he projects the ills he suffers onto others, not on himself or society as such. This deep feeling of being the object of an undeserved injustice also explains the appeal to the protective, paternalistic intervention of *Monsieur l'Etat* [Mr. Government] to solve the crisis, an appeal by turns filial and supplicating, then arrogant and threatening.

The extraordinary discrepancy between the dream of peasant happiness and the actual tragedy, which seems impossible to solve, would also reveal to a psychopathologist a marked social maladjustment. We have shown to what extent the peasant's situation in our urban capitalist civilization is ambiguous and contradictory. The behavior and the sentiments that the peasant displays with respect to this civilization are always ambivalent and waver between rejection and acceptance. The constant assertion of moral superiority could be interpreted as a compensation for a feeling of inferiority.

This maladjustment is also expressed on the political level, where the peasants do not know with whom to ally themselves. They reject the industrial worker's condition but try to borrow his methods of action and defense. They assert themselves as heads of enterprise but battle against the interests of industrial leaders. They share in large part the ideology of employers and small merchants but hurl insults at those parasites of society who live at the peasants' expense.

The farmers who were between fifteen and twenty years of age during the Occupation developed some scorn for the kind of politics that had impassioned their elders but seemed no longer to respond to their problems. The fathers thought

"politics first," the sons proclaimed "economics first." It is
easy to find motives for this sharp reversal of attitude among
farm leaders.

Since 1930 Catholic action movements, notably the J.A.C., have
had unique success in accomplishing a program of popular
education that began to bear fruit in 1944. Oriented from the
start toward spiritual and doctrinal questions, this program
broadened progressively to include all the economic, social, and
human problems of the rural environment, thus responding
to its leaders' desire to create militant members fit to "deal
with the problems of their environment" and take on responsibilities in farm institutions.

Moreover, the Occupation gave the peasantry an entirely new
position. Peasant values were exalted by the government and
embodied in the "peasant Marshal." It is generally agreed that the
Peasant Corporation "represented an important theoretical effort
whose consequences are still being felt." In fact, it realized the
old myth of the unity of the peasantry: membership being
practically obligatory by force of circumstances, all the farmers
participated in it to a greater or lesser degree. A good number
of local and national leaders who are still active today served
their apprenticeship there.

For their part, prisoners of war had the occasion to observe
German agriculture and compare it with their own, and from
this opportunity they drew conclusions that they put to use
when they returned to their farms. Finally, scarcities gave a
relative affluence to country people, since they were better fed
than city dwellers, and it moved farmers to improve their living
standards, particularly their homes. Some observers of these
changes for the better began to worry about the consequences:
"Not being able to buy farm equipment, the peasants are setting
themselves up in lives of ease and giving in to useless expenditures." Thus new needs arose from the deprivations.

At the time of the Liberation, all conditions worked toward a
complete transformation of the rural regions. The mass of farmers
awoke to the "modern world" and demanded to enter it forthwith.
And the young people, who wanted to build their futures themselves,
showed a particular eagerness for change and modernism, not only
in technology but also in daily and social life. They wanted "to know

in order to act" and they impatiently rejected all the old political quarrels as "unprofitable." Let us note that this economic vocabulary, applied to politics, is itself revealing. This reaction was in part motivated by the feeling that politics had often been used by the notables to manipulate and dupe the peasants, but it also had deeper causes.

In most institutions the positions of responsibility are occupied generally by older people. At the time of the Liberation, the average age of the town councillors in rural communes was quite high, and most of those who had founded farm organizations (cooperatives, credit associations, and so on) in the fervor of their youth still held their seats in administrative councils more than a half-century later. Above all, becoming acquainted with new techniques and learning how economic mechanisms function required all the energies of the young people and held all their attention. Their fathers had inherited their professional skill from their families; if the sons wanted to be modern farmers they had to learn everything from courses, seminars, and reading. And it was to respond to this need that the J.A.C. and the M.F.R. (Rural Family Movement) developed a whole system of education and a wide range of publications.

For the past fifteen years, two new institutions have known success among the farmers: the Centers for Technical Farm Studies (C.E.T.A.) and the Schools of Rural Apprenticeship. A sort of bureau for group research comprised of about fifteen farmers and one farm engineer, the C.E.T.A. divorces itself from any religious or political activity. Its conferences, dedicated to discussions of technical or management problems, are real study sessions. The ten to fifteen thousand members of the C.E.T.A. are peasant leaders. Quite young on the average, they have in many cases received their training in Catholic action movements; indeed, more than half of the centers are Catholic, about ten are Protestant, and another ten or so, founded at the instigation of teachers, are Communist or Socialist. As for the rest, they are for most purposes under the control of the older Catholic militant membership.

The Schools of Rural Apprenticeship are centers of apprenticeship managed by associations of farmers who meet with their pupils one week in every three for a theoretical course. The other two weeks the students spend with their parents, working on their farms and doing their "homework." The 300 or so centers (*maisons familiales*), consisting of 30,000 boys and girls, are located in very religious regions, where they are often a form of parochial education, and in less devout regions, where they are usually created through the initiative of Catholic action militants.

These two new institutions are not the only ones. More recent than the c.e.t.a., the Centers for Management and Farm Economy are of similar inspiration and often recruit the same members. For its part, the Ministry of Agriculture has created experimental stations and centers for research. Some cynical observers have interpreted this policy as a reflection of the political situation. But the proportion of technology and economics to political concerns has usually been the inverse of that which characterized the farm organizations of the past, and curiously similar, *mutatis mutandis*, to that of the j.a.c.

Finally, in the past several years some farmers have come to question the traditional structure of the family farm and are combining their lands with others to constitute larger cooperative farms that permit a certain specialization of tasks, and in the use of land and men. These are the Farmers' Organization for Communal Land Use (g.a.e.c.), whose legal status has recently been codified.

It is remarkable that these new institutions, so deliberately different from their predecessors, draw their support from young farmers and not from notables or officials (teachers or engineers from the farm services). A real shift in traditional rural leadership is being engineered entirely by farm leadership. Furthermore, these young farmers have received almost all their training from Catholic movements. They have almost no competitors today; radicalism is quickly becoming obsolete and neither the Socialists nor the Communists have been able to find leadership among progressive farmers. As one j.a.c. priest said: "In the *département* all the successful young people are with us — the others, those who are dying, vote Communist."

The *départements* in which the Communist votes are the most numerous — Creuse, for instance — are also those where the modernization of agriculture is the slowest. We have hinted at this in discussing the diffusion of hybrid corn; it seems that technical conservatism lives happily with political progressivism and that technical revolution does not incite to political revolution. This is easily explained. The small farmer who has lost all hope of keeping up with progress and who refuses to leave his land can only hope for his salvation by political intervention. This no doubt explains why, despite the great number of regions where farmers vote Socialist or Communist, very few organizations are directed by militants of these two parties. The spread of the newspaper *La Terre* and the growing influence of the M.O.D.E.F. (Movement for the Organization and Protection of Family Farms) mark a renewal of extreme left-wing activity in agriculture, but five years ago a good foreign observer like Gordon Wright had some difficulty in recognizing the "Red villages" he had studied ten years earlier.[15]

The alliance of the Church with technology and economic success entails risks and cannot help but present several theological and political problems to the Church. In fact, if the first generation of Catholic farm action, that of the period between the two wars, was especially concerned with progress and spiritual influence, that of the postwar period is above all seeking solutions to economic and social problems. One of its most brilliant representatives does not hesitate to state that he was active in the J.A.C. because he had to "find a way out," and not because of his religious conviction. Many are militant country people with a religious affiliation rather than militant Catholics concerned with the problems of their environment. One wonders if this is not a consequence of their initial rejection of politics and ideology.

In the meetings, seminars, courses, and conferences of the J.A.C., the work is done in a realistic and rational atmosphere. Participants almost never resort to ideological or sentimental arguments, but speak in terms of figures, facts, and yields, possibilities of expansion and outlets, competition within the Common Market, and so on. For the observer there is a striking contrast with traditional farm meetings and banquets where emotional and moral argument took precedence over rational argument, even in economic discussions.

This analysis seems to lead to the conclusion that the peasants will increasingly lose interest in politics and ideology as the young generation takes on new responsibilities. Paradoxically this is not the case. In fact, this young generation was quick to perceive that technical progress clashed with agrarian and legal structures and that economic success was conditioned by the mechanisms of the market and the decisions of those who wield economic influence. Moreover, the most brilliant

[15]Wright, 1964.

technical successes of a research center can be illusory if a cooperative does not manage to sell at a good price what has been well produced. But the cooperative has usually, as we have said, been in the hands of the bearded radicals or country squires who owned large properties. Should the young give into the temptation to organize new cooperatives or try to take over power in the old ones? Here is a problem of economic tactics that is also a political problem, and one that also has implications for farm credit, since new farm management demands investment credit.

Besides, what sense is there in buying tractors and trailers with pneumatic tires if the rural roads are still impassable bogs? Some leaders have undertaken to create cooperatives to buy steamrollers, bulldozers, and other equipment necessary for the improvement of roads. Is it not simpler to obtain a ruling from the town council and a subsidy from the county council? But this method presumes that the farmers are represented in these councils and, if possible, have a majority. In the purely farm communes it may seem normal that the town council is occupied with collective solutions to certain problems common to the farmers that do not involve new cooperatives; and in communes dominated by an administrative market-town it is hard to see why farmers should be in the minority in the town council when they are in the majority in the population. Until now, elections were based on political or personal rivalries; why should they not henceforth be based on a program of concrete action? Thus by a curious twist in the logic of their position, those most fervently for apoliticism and "technology above all" are found at the top of the electoral lists before they have grown old; in the municipal elections of 1959 many mayoralties passed into the hands of young people.

This logic is no less operative in Paris than in the village. For a dozen years the young Catholic leaders devoted themselves to understanding world events, such things as economic processes, power conflicts, and so on, and explaining them to their active members. This long education led them to develop a doctrine that would take too long to explain here but whose basic points we can summarize.

Even if they sometimes state the contrary, these leaders are convinced that they must play the capitalist game and succeed on an economic basis, in other words that agriculture must be profitable, as they have been taught by the economists, Dominican monks, and law school professors. On the other hand, because of their social origin, they naturally maintain great respect for the family farm. These two premises being accepted, the whole doctrine is deduced logically from them: (1) profitability requires an increase in surface area of the farms, whence comes the acceptance of rural exodus; (2) economic success presumes profitable investments impossible in agriculture without state aid; (3) consequently farm policy should no longer seek to sustain farm prices but, on the contrary, should permit "good" farmers to make investments; (4) finally, modern techniques demand large units of cultivation that can only be created by breaking down agrarian structures and especially the principle of private ownership of the land, for neither tenant farming nor land consolidation permits both the stability and the growth of the farm.

The conflict between this attitude and the peasant ideology outlined above is so fundamental and total that no compromise is possible. It is in fact a conflict of world views. For one group, moral and philosophic principles must determine action, and the reality must be subordinated to the idea. For the others, it is the situation that conditions the action, and one must "know in order to act." Two philosophies, two ways of viewing the world, are implicit in these attitudes. They belong to two generations, but it would be simple to specify the social groups and economic interests to which they are ultimately linked.

One is tempted to state that in the last analysis this conflict of generations is a conflict of civilizations. In fact the traditional doctrine, details apart, has been sustained by the Right, the Center, and the Left; and who can say if the new doctrine is rightist or leftist? The "new Left" believes it has found a popular base in the rural regions because it discusses the abolition of the right of property with some Parisian farm leaders. The M.R.P. (Popular Republican Movement, or Christian Democrats) probably gains most of these people's electoral votes and hopes to recruit valuable cadres among them. A person who analyzes ideologies tends to see in this doctrine of economic success an ideology of new kulaks, sons of small farmers who want to become big ones by letting those who are not modernizing die off. But has anyone ever seen left-wing kulaks?

A curious comparison could be made among the ideology of the J.A.C., that of the radicals of Beauce in 1900, and the "Franklinian" ideology described by René Rémond.[16] If it were conclusive it would lead us to think that the passage from a precapitalist to a capitalist economy raises similar ideological reactions in different historical, economic, and philosophic contexts.

While this ideological conflict is not a conflict in political tendencies, it is nonetheless political in all the meanings of the word, since it is ideological and poses essentially political problems. Rural exodus challenges the equilibrium of French society and causes certain electoral cliques to crumble. The removal of price supports would lessen the differential profits of certain big modernized producers and alter the balance of power in farm organizations. Finally, the right of property (need we remind the reader?) is "one of the foundations of Christian civilization."

Having created new institutions with a technical bias and being themselves influenced by the Catholic action movements, the young generation has remained outside the traditional organizations. We must remember, in fact, that sons of farmers have no independent social existence as long as their fathers are alive. Since they are not salaried workers, they have no place in the farmers' union or in cooperatives or farm credit associations. They are in fact, if not by law, *alieni juris.*

To remedy this deplorable condition, the former national leaders of the J.A.C. acquired control of the National Circle of Young Farmers (C.N.J.A.), which they transformed into a genuine union of young farmers and farmers' sons.[17] They set up federations within the *départements,* and in 1957 a reform of the regulations of the National Federation of Farmers' Union assigned them a conspicuous place in the leading circles of that organization. Thus the conflict became in some way institutionalized and officially recognized by the entrance of two leaders of the C.N.J.A. into the Economic and Social Council.* In a similar way, more and more

---

[16]Rémond, 1960; Appendix 2 , No. 20.
[17]Tavernier, 1962; and Appendix 2, No. 32.
*Advisory body of the National Assembly. (Trans.)

young people were elected to the administrative councils of various departmental and national organizations, and to the Parlement, in the elections of 1958. They thus became initiated into the mysteries of the professional and political game, and wisely observed the behavior of their elders before throwing their hats into the ring.

The f.n.s.e.a. greeted the Fifth Republic with favor,[18] although Gaullism held for many people unpleasant associations with the Liberation and the c.g.a.. But soon, in the face of the government's Algerian and farm policies, this support was transformed into outright opposition. After the events of January, 1960, and the disorders at Amiens, the f.n.s.e.a. campaigned for a premature convening of the Parlement, which was met by the refusal of the President of the Republic. To the informed observer it was clear that the justifiable discontent of the farmers was being used for purely political ends by leaders faithful to the old quarrels and closely allied with the Algerian farmers.

Faced with this opposition, the government sought new farm "interlocutors" and found them quite naturally in the c.n.j.a., all the more easily since these young people spoke the same language as the ministry attachés at the Hôtel Matignon or the Rue de Rivoli and the specialists of the Planning Commission. Curiously, the result was that the Ministry of Agriculture met the same fate as the f.n.s.e.a.; both were left out of the decision-making process, a turn of events that shows to what extent an age-old battle had made them complementary and hence interdependent. From the moment the rules of the game were changed, these brotherly enemies or friendly rivals could no longer remain in the forefront; they had to yield to new protagonists. But this substitution, while apparently in progress, is still far from being accomplished; it will not be fully so until the Ministry of Agriculture itself is staffed with officials from the new generation.

Then the young people, who profess such great scorn for politics, will have completely won the battle. They will hold political power in Paris as in their villages. Meantime the farmers should be particularly well protected: the f.n.s.e.a. obtains the best possible prices each year, the c.n.j.a. is preparing the basis of a long-range policy that should eliminate in the future

[18]Tavernier, 1962.

the uncertainties of the past, and the exigencies of a European farm policy are operating in their favor.

Intrigue, negotiation, and pressure in the high councils of the nation and in directorial or ministerial offices, whether conducted by young or old people, must be extended and carried on through mass demonstrations. The older people preferred to rely on rhetoric rather than arouse the peasants. Before the war Dorgères had organized demonstrations,[19] and the Catholic unions of the Rue des Pyramides increased the number of their conferences. Farmers would like to borrow the idea of the strike from labor, but it places the head of an enterprise in an ambiguous position. If he does not sell his product he risks considerable losses. Moreover, the peasant always fears that his neighbor will not join in the movement to strike, for he is convinced that "there is too much individualism among the peasants."

The roadblocks and violent demonstrations of 1961[20] are very new phenomena which testify to the revolution accomplished in the rural regions; they show the mentality of the young people and the new form that tensions between national and local leaders can take. In appearance these demonstrations might seem to be only a new form of *jacquerie*. It was possible to see in the Brittany peasants who occupied the subprefecture of Morlaix and burned the ballot boxes of Pont-l'Abbé the direct heirs of the fourteenth-century rebels or those who burned castles in 1789. The roadblocks of 1954 were in many respects a *jacquerie* if one understands by that a brutal revolt against a political and social authority too long accepted passively but with reluctance, a revolt that decries an intolerable situation but which does not have any substitute solution to propose to those in power. In 1954, in the words of their representatives, the peasants wanted to give a "warning" to the government and draw the attention of the French people to their problems.

In 1961 the peasants of Brittany began in this way. But they were faced with a specific situation, and if they had no complete solution, they did not expect to be given one by the very authority against which they were demonstrating. They knew, more or

[19]Royer, 1958.
[20]Tavernier and Mendras, 1958.

less clearly, what they wanted and did not want, and their most sensible leaders even had some concrete proposals to present. The best proof of this is that, at the time of the artichoke crisis in 1960, they had called to their aid "technical advisers" such as Daniel Barrère and Edouard Leclerc. Did *jacquerie* ever surround itself with technical advisers? Furthermore, these movements very widely extended the limits of the region where they were born and involved farmers whose situation and problems were very different from those of the peasants of Finistère. And above all, these demonstrations did not express the anxiety of small peasants condemned to pauperization and proletarianization. They resulted, on the contrary, from the anxiety of progressive farmers who had made investments that they feared would suffer: a crisis of growth, not of decline.

The remarkable "checkerboard" organized by the local unions of Finistère made it possible to mobilize all the farmers of one region in a few hours. The long education provided by the farm unions of the Comte de Guébriant and the tenant farmers' unions of Tanguy-Prigent was put to good use by young leaders who had learned "revolutionary warfare" methods during their military service in Algeria — a remarkable combination of circumstances! Born spontaneously in Finistère as a result of the artichoke and potato crisis, this movement spread rapidly in Brittany, then to almost all the regions of France, notably the center, the southwest, the Midi, and the Rhône valley. For once peasant unity seemed to be on the right path.

The national leaders, both young and old, who for almost a year had been carrying on a courteous dialogue with the government repeatedly interrupted by false breakdowns, considered these "spontaneous" demonstrations singularly untimely and disturbing to the conduct of their negotiations. Until then they had been able to forestall and restrain the discontent of the farmers in order to use it as a weapon against the government. But, as far as the young leaders of Finistère were concerned, all this Parisian palaver put off their problem without bringing a solution, and to them violence seemed more profitable; by taking over the subprefecture, burning the ballot boxes, barricading the roads, destroying the factories of participating manufacturers, they could force the "Parisians" to react.

The peasants feel humiliated, as we have said, by their social situation and their mediocre living standards, their work without respite, and their great efforts to adjust economically and technically. In recent years it has become usual in circles that study farm problems to speak of the underdevelopment of French agriculture, and this kind of "scientific" analysis (at least in the form of verbal discussion) has spread with astonishing rapidity among all the militant peasants, throughout the press, and in political, professional, and religious circles. Thus one fine day the French peasant woke up to the fact that he was backward, which led him to resort to rebellion.

The young leaders of Finistère, like other leaders, had received some instruction in political economy, which had taught them in a simplified way about the functioning of a complex society. The experience with artichokes confirmed their ideas and their confidence in direct intervention. Solely concerned with their problems of production and marketing, they did not have a clear awareness of their position in relation to the national market. Also, they tended not to go beyond the frontiers of their own region and consider the problems of other French regions or other countries. Their scorn for politics led them to work out a socioeconomic view of society that was based on ideas curiously similar to those that move leaders of certain Parisian pressure groups, whether agricultural or industrial. For example, a study of innumerable debates that took place on the subject of landowning would certainly show that the land is always treated solely as a factor of production and never as a space with several uses or even as an object of speculation and investment.

In order not to be taken in by politics, the young generation has refused to support traditional political trends. But it has not yet found a spokesman able to express its interests and problems in the context of the national policy. Moreover, this generation embraces varied political and ideological tendencies, sometimes contradictory, often poorly defined. When someone asks himself the exact position of a particular leader, he is obliged to put off judgment; the most revolutionary is not always the one who seems to others or to himself to be so. Let us hope that the best of them, coming at a young age to represent their *départements* in the Parlement or to bring new life to a national organization, will be able to acquire a political education, and will not simply be the spokesmen of one professional group or one region, a new leader setting out to seek power.

The peasant, the majority voter of the past century, counted on his elected leaders to protect him. Each deputy and senator had farm voters, and rural regions were clearly overrepresented in the Parlement, particularly in the Senate. Each year the budget discussions of the Ministry of Agriculture allowed every political party, indeed almost every deputy, to show solicitude for a peasant constituency. The essential choices concerning agriculture were political choices made in relation to general electoral, moral, and political considerations. Consequently the peasants could with good reason consider themselves well protected in Paris. The historian and the economist can retrospectively condemn without appeal the farm policy of the Third Republic embodied in Méline,[21] yet it is nonetheless true that all of France, from the depths of the rural villages to the "Parisian farm village" and to the Parlement, were practically unanimous in supporting this policy.

This fact probably explains why there has never been in France a large agrarian party of national dimensions. The parties that called themselves agrarian or peasant have always been rooted in only one or two regions and have had a very special political orientation. In fact, all the parties have had peasant voters and have represented the peasantry. Electoral studies show that the votes of farmers are distributed over the whole political spectrum with, however, a strong attraction for the Center and the Right (Table 21).

In the present situation, it is extremely difficult to know if changes in agriculture can lead to a regrouping of the farm electorate or if it will remain dispersed over the whole political spectrum and exercise its influence only by the roundabout means of professional organizations acting more or less as pressure groups. It is certain that all these upheavals are making farmers, especially farm leaders, an available group that most political parties try to attract.

Furthermore, the percentage of farmers in rural societies is

[21]Augé-Laribé, 1950; Gervais, Servolin and Weil, 1965.

Table 21. Distribution of Peasant Votes, Election of January 2, 1954

	Percentage of Votes Cast	
	Farmers	Electorate as a Whole
Communist Party (P.C.)	17.5%	26.0%
Socialist Party (S.F.I.O.)	14.0	15.5
Left (Radical, etc.)	14.0	15.0
Christian Democrats (M.R.P.)	12.5	11.0
Moderate	24.0	19.5
Union for the Defense of Merchants and Craftsmen (U.D.C.A.)	14.5	11.5
Extreme Right and Miscellaneous	3.5	1.5
Total	100.0%	100.0%

constantly diminishing, and other social categories tend to set the tone for the countryside. What will be the effects of this change on the political attitudes of the rural population? Inasmuch as the farmer does not seem to have a political attitude radically different from those of other groups, one could advance the hypothesis that there will be little change. On the other hand, insofar as all of rural society will be transformed, all of political life, not simply attitudes, will take on new forms. For example, the introduction of factories into rural regions poses the problem of the direct influence of a group of new factory workers arriving in a region, and of the peasant who becomes a factory worker though he remains in his village. Finally, those who leave their villages to go to work in the city can also have an influence on their new environment. It would be interesting to follow the evolution of their political behavior.

One can advance the hypothesis that there is no peasant "class," and so no party to represent one. Nevertheless, impressed by the successes of industrial workers' representatives, some farm representatives speak of a peasant class that they wishfully invent and endeavor to bring to reality. Curiously, Catholics are among the most ready to do this, although it is contrary to Church doctrine. But the Marxist idea of classes is becoming more and more inadequate to account for a society characterized by a multiple stratification, a marked social mobility, and many group conflicts. It is singularly anachronistic to want to build a peasant class at this time, with no regard for cost.

Indeed, social distinctions are becoming blurred, and the uniqueness of the farmer's condition more and more clear, but at the same time economic conflicts are also becoming sharper. A region that is half peasant is entirely different in nature from one where farmers account for only 10 percent of the population. In the former case the whole society is dominated by the weight of rural strata and its problems and political representation are "rural" — although generally not "peasant," as we have said. In the latter case the farmers are only one group of producers among others, and they naturally tend to organize their political activity in the image of other groups: various pressures on politicians, influence on public opinion, more or less violent mass movements. It is of the greatest importance that the public and the leadership be informed about farm problems, and if possible that they consider these with a favorable eye.

There is certainly good reason why young leaders attach fundamental importance to the influence of professional pressure groups on the Parlement and the administration and concern themselves less with direct political representation. Under the Fifth Republic, the functioning of institutions pushes them to this view as much as does their natural ideological leaning. They plan reforms and bills on which they reach agreement with the Ministry of Agriculture, and the minister becomes their best spokesman in the government and in the Parlement. A detailed analysis of the debate and vote on the supplementary farm law and of legislation on the s.a.f.e.r. (Society for Land Management) illustrates this process.[22]

In this game of influence, farmers have some advantages over other groups. Being dispersed over the whole national territory weakens their position in decisions and economic bargaining but considerably increases the possibilities of their influence, since almost all political representatives count farmers among their supporters. Moreover, it frequently happens that in one constituency their votes may represent for each candidate the margin necessary to his success; hence they are particularly pampered and can accept higher bids, to their profit. In other cases, on the contrary, this marginal situation can decrease their importance.

[22]Rimareix and Tavernier, 1963.

International comparisons on this point would be illuminating. Besides, the peasant remains the embodiment of certain essential moral values, the family farm corresponds to the ideal of free enterprise and economic independence, and the idea of working close to nature exerts a great emotional pull on city dwellers. Thus the farmers have important weapons and arguments in ideological debate, and they can always mobilize certain deep and widespread sentiments to support their case. The economic protection that they enjoy in countries as different as the United States, France, and Switzerland is justified by closely-related doctrines. Furthermore, many people think they owe assistance to the peasant as they do to elderly parents: isn't every city dweller more or less a son of the country and "the city a daughter of the village?" Economists expound a new version of this doctrine when they explain that the logic of the industrial system dominates the modern economy and is detrimental to farm production; hence it is only fair to protect and support agriculture, notably under the famous principle of "parity."

Farm policy used to have essentially social objectives and imperatives. The price of grain worried governments solicitous of the less well-to-do people, who were consumers rather than producers. Today farm prices are the object of pressures that work against each other: producers consider them unjustly devaluated and manufacturers (employers and workers) would like to bring them back to the level of the world market. Only government subsidies of all kinds make it possible to resolve this conflict. In the regions where there is planning (authoritarian or not) and in those that reject it, the problems are posed in approximately the same terms. Everywhere the government intervenes, and yet, when it engages in planning, it does not do so in the same manner for agriculture as for other sectors. In all cases, social, moral, and political arguments continue for the most part to be more decisive than economic rationality in the development of farm policy. Perhaps it is fair that this should be so on a national level; on the other hand, in international relations economic conflicts cannot be divorced from higher values, and those who lament malnutrition and famine are looked upon as idealists with no grasp of reality.

Henceforth decisions on farm policy will doubtless be thought out in economic terms rather than political or moral terms. If this trend continues, it will be a genuine revolution fraught with consequences not only for the political and economic life of farmers but for the country as a whole. The industrialization of agriculture is becoming the only conceivable objective for high officials and farm leaders brought up on liberal economics and Marxism. The old political and moral language was, everything considered, less inadequate than the economic language for understanding the rural economy and the regulations necessary for agriculture. And until an adequate language is developed, the resistance to reform in the face of the realities of life will create continual problems for those who govern all countries.

In conclusion, we can ask ourselves if the logic of the development of agriculture does not apply equally in all countries, whatever their level of economic development and their socio-political characteristics. The replacement of traditional society by industrial society is not accomplished by way of the same paths, but the fundamental facts of the problem are the same everywhere.

Conclusion: Perspectives on the Future

The limitations imposed by technology and nature, which seemed so determinant to the agronomists of the nineteenth century, are becoming more and more malleable today. On the other hand, it will be impossible to deny much longer the obvious contradiction between the polyproducing enterprise and the growing technical complexity of agriculture. Agriculture can no longer escape some form of division of labor. Whether it is of peasant and family ownership or "capitalistic" and "industrialized," the polyproducing enterprise is essentially the social reflection of the technical demands of the last century's agronomy; but these demands are not as rigorous as they once were.[1]

The agricultural revolution of the eighteenth century involved the use of certain new techniques and crops, but its most important innovation was to combine into one single system of production both crop cultivation and stockbreeding. Abolishing fallow land and replacing it by artificial forage crops made it possible to "complete" crop rotation without considering the herd an enemy of the crops. Before, the cattle had to seek their food on untillable land given over to pasturage, on brushwood, and on fallow ground. The new cultivation furnished more fodder, permitting larger herds, which in turn furnished more manure to fertilize the fields and increase their yield. Chemical fertilizers, introduced more recently, have strengthened the system.

The main concern of the good farmer was to find a judicious equilibrium between animal and vegetable production and maintain the maximum fertility of his land, by giving it in fertilizer and humus everything it in turn gives to the harvest. The fruit of long and skillful patience, this fertility was formerly valued and esteemed without being precisely measured. In regulating the lengths of rural leases, the legislator had no other concern than to avoid wearing out the land.

Once the guardian of the fertility of the land through the vigilant maintenance of equilibrium among the various products of breeding and cultivation, the peasant farm is no longer necessary to the

---

[1]The reflections that follow owe much to discussion with D. R. Bergmann, L. Malassis, G. Sévérac and S. Wickham. Economists have made similar conjectures; see Gervais, Servolin, and Weil, 1965.

agrarian system. Already agronomical and accounting techniques are taking the place of experience and *savoir faire*. The improvement in fertilizers makes it possible to isolate one product: it is possible to cultivate corn on top of corn in the same soil, without any crop rotation and without cattle. Thus technological progress, which in the last century led to a refined and integrated system of cultivation, today makes it possible to break up this system in order to profit from the advantages of specialization and mass production. Complex crop rotation has dispensed with fallow land; soil chemistry and biology are making crop rotation unnecessary. Curiously enough, this progress appears to the peasant as a regression, since all his skill and learning were oriented toward the knowledge and conservation of the soil and its fertility. Skillful monocultivation is for him a return to the simplistic agriculture of his ancestors.

Specialists are divided on the question of what we can expect from progress in biology and agronomy. There are two opposing schools of thought. One eminent agronomist foresees an agriculture without land and proposes that France be fed on several thousand acres under glass. He points out that photosynthesis, an essential mechanism in the growth of plants, can produce a yield of 50 percent in the laboratory, while its yield is on the order of 1 percent in outdoor cultivation, and 1 percent for France as a whole. Spectacular progress can also be expected in genetics and molecular biology. Others think that natural mechanisms will not allow themselves to be so easily and completely domesticated, and that respect for the land will remain the foremost element of agriculture.

In some cases, agronomy and accounting provide means of measurement that make it possible to reconcile these needs by isolating each plot while preserving the rotation. For example, if it is to be cultivated scientifically on a large scale, corn requires large-scale mechanical equipment and high skill. Aware of the necessity for this specialization, one farmer has combined all the necessary equipment: seeder, anticryptogam outfit, sprinkler system, corn picker, stripper, dryer, and so on; and every year he rents the lands that have been cultivated in cereals the previous year. A soil analysis allows him to fix the rental price exactly, to know which fertilizer he should use, and to forecast scientifically the yield he will obtain under "normal" meteorological conditions. Thus he has at his disposal all the information for making an advance estimate of the cost price. And each year he abandons the lands he has farmed in order to rent new ones. This form of enterprise respects both the advantages of traditional crop rotation and the exigencies of the division of labor necessary to scientific, economical cultivation.

This example suggests that land is no longer the necessary foundation of every farm. In fact, economic development gives less and less value to the land, which is becoming less important as a means of production than mechanical equipment and the farmer's skill. Agronomists frequently say that there is no longer any bad land; there are only bad farmers who do not know how to make proper use of it. And farmers know that land, which used to represent the essential capital of a farm, now normally represents less than half.

In the fertile wheatlands of the north and Paris basin, it often happens that the farmer does not know the proprietors of the land he cultivates. They are known only to the notary; he unites into a single tenant's farm the land of a substantial number of persons descended from old local peasant stock, who have emigrated to the city, Paris or elsewhere. He points out on the map the area he is leasing to the farmer and takes care of allocating the rent among the proprietors. Which area he cultivates matters little to the farmer. For him, skill, machines, livestock, and bank account are the essential components of a farm.

To the traditional peasant, ownership of the soil was a sign of prestige and above all an assurance of survival for his property and thus his family. The tenant, whether farmer or *métayer*, lived in fear that his lease might not be renewed. Recent legislative measures assure him some guarantees, and an option in case the proprietor wants to sell. But these laws are of no avail against the major risk that weighs so heavily today on the farmer: that is, the economic risk.

The major problem of every farmer is no longer to preserve his property or the right to farm a particular plot, but rather to know whether his enterprise is condemned to disappear with him or will survive. The small tenant farmer who has bled himself white to buy back his farm may see his son abandon it, having given up all hope of modernization. If he had lost the farm, the same small farmer would have been able to invest his savings in machinery and livestock, which would have permitted him to rent a larger piece of land elsewhere, where his son might have stayed. Thus his enterprise, if not his farm itself, would have survived; and his son, who could no longer be a peasant like his father, would at least have remained a farmer. Today the security and survival of the farm enterprise are already commanded by market outlets, and they will be to an even greater extent in the future. Consequently the forward-looking father who wants to establish his son should be able to buy him a clientèle rather than a piece of land. From this point of view agriculture, if it is to remain in the hands of independent producers, will come more and more to resemble small business and the liberal professions; the farmer who has acquired a market outlet and has capital at his disposal will have no trouble establishing himself in one of the regions where there is plenty of land. For the farmer's purposes as for the merchant's, working capital is the enterprise, rather than real estate.

In the long run, as techniques are improved, the land will lose its privileged productive role and will again become a plot of ground, a space, man's environment and habitat. Agriculture will be concentrated on the best soil and in the regions best situated economically. Hence, according to good economic logic, the price of land should go down, especially in regions where the present population density maintains an anachronistic competition for the smallest strip of land. A massive farm exodus should restore some balance.

In the short run, on the other hand, the present rise in prices is likely to be prolonged. The dominant ideology continues to assign preeminent value to the land. For the Frenchman it is the best form of capital, the surest "investment" and the one that provides greatest emotional satisfaction. The land thus remains valuable as a retreat. Moreover, it is an object of speculation, and in certain urbanized regions arouses competition among builders, vacationers and rustic suburbanites. In the future as in the past, the farmer risks paying much more for his field than it is worth as a means of production.

Thus on all levels the complex and refined structure of the polyproducing family farm is breaking up, and will no longer be able to resist the division of labor that is being imposed on all sectors of production. There is an obvious contradiction between the small polyproducing enterprise, where one man must do everything and know everything, and a form of agriculture that is increasingly specialized and informed. Aware of this contradiction, farmers have delegated their buying and selling functions to cooperatives; they have confided the care of their security to mutual insurance societies; when mechanical equipment became too burdensome they set up

Cooperative for the Collective Ownership of Farm Equipment
(C.U.M.A.); to master techniques they formed Centers for Technical
Farm Studies (C.E.T.A.); finally, when accounting became the condition of good management, management centers where born.
Today some farmers are taking the last step by forming farm trusts
(G.A.E.C.); they join their lands, regroup their fields into larger
units, and organize around each product a workshop under the
direction of one of the farmers. Thus, division of labor and specialization shatter "peasant individualism" and make new progress
possible.

Today it is the harvester-thresher or the electric milking machine
that determines the form of the enterprise. Armed with such equipment and indifferent to his land, specialized in one market product
whose demands he knows well, the producer of the future will no
longer have anything in common with his peasant grandfather, who
was bound to the soil as to a tyrannical wife, and who had learned
from his ancestors a system of cultivation and a delicate, refined
savoir faire. In the past he had to be born on the land in order to
know and treat it properly; tomorrow he will need only some education and some capital in order to take up farming as a trade.

The reconstitution of a group of traditional farms into workshops
specializing in one stage of production can be quickly outlined.
Suppose there are ten dairy farms, each with forty acres and fifteen
cows; they can be reorganized into a workshop for the production
of fodder four hundred acres in size, plus a workshop for the production of milk with two hundred or two hundred fifty cows, the optimal number for the use of present-day milking machines. The twenty
nonspecialized workers of the old farms will be replaced by six specialized workers (two for the fodder and four for the milk) assisted
by technical and commercial services equivalent to one or two experts.
Dairy production would probably be doubled and its cost considerably lowered; all the food production necessary for feeding fifteen
peasant families and their unproductive draft or breeding livestock
would disappear — no more cereals, poultry, or vegetables.

It is possible to imagine similar reorganization for different farm
products in each of the stages of production. The harvester-thresher
determines the size of the workshop for the production of cereals,
the anticryptogam machine that of the orchard, and so on. The agronomist and the economist could devise a national plan that would in-

dicate what the workshops should be and their mutual relationship, their distribution, production, manpower, and so on. The multitude of current attempts and experiments along these lines can furnish useful illustrations and estimates.

If each agricultural phase of production were accomplished in a specialized workshop, one could imagine assigning the nonagricultural phases of processing, packaging, and transport to other shops of the same type. Thus the entire cycle of production would be accomplished in a chain of workshops linked to each other by contracts for disposal and supply.

It will become very difficult to distinguish between agricultural and nonagricultural production, since certain workshops typically agricultural will no longer need land. The dairy farm, for example, will resemble a factory for transforming fodder into milk rather than a stable. Perhaps it will be better off for having moved away from the source of supply (pasture) and closer to its market outlet (city dairies and stores), and we will see dairy cows installed in the suburbs. Then it will be necessary to distinguish between "landed" farm workshops, for which land will be an important factor of production, and others. Except for this distinction, there will no longer be agriculture as opposed to industry. As in primitive societies, there will be an alimentary cycle of production, from nature to the finished product.

It is indeed regrettable that peasant farming should be doomed to extinction at the very moment when the peasant has just realized his supreme ambition: to be master of his own property. But how could we justify refusing farmers the benefits of the division of labor and thus forcing them to survive without anachronistic structures of production that condemn them to poverty? Only an unacknowledged sentimentalism, acting in response to powerful demagogic appeals, can explain the prevailing conformism on this subject.

Moreover, the freedom and power of decision of the traditional peasant must not be overestimated. They are more apparent than real. Indeed the peasant is in principle free to direct his farm as he likes, but traditional technological and social structures left him almost no choice to make. He conformed to custom on almost all points. And now that custom no longer furnishes him

with models of thought and behavior adapted to constantly new
situations, his ignorance of technology and economic mechanisms obliged him at the moment of decision to rely on
the influence of neighbors as incompetent as he. Aware of the
opinions of irresponsible technicians, the lure of fashion, or
the influences of neighbors as incompetent as he. Aware of the
dangers of this new adventure for which he has no guide, he
prefers in many cases not to leave the rut that is leading inevitably
to the disappearance of his kind. Nevertheless, while he is
not as free as he appears, he is subjectively and potentially so.

Finally, the peasant's uniqueness in our society rests on the
lack of differentiation of his roles of producer, owner of the means
of production, and entrepreneur. To maintain this lack of
differentiation, insofar as it is possible, seems desirable to many
who see in it a condition of equilibrium and a prerequisite of
freedom and self-realization for man; particularly all farm leaders,
young or old, powerful or insignificant, rightist or leftist, Catholic
or secular, are agreed on this point. It is for this reason that
traditional organizations defend the family farm.

The family farm is also what the young people want to preserve
at all costs; and the admirably strong enthusiasm and energy
of the new peasant generations are easily mobilized in its
defense. It would be regrettable if this strength were spent in
vain in defending a cause doomed to failure. In fact, one can
imagine legal and social structures other than the family farm
that would preserve the farm producer's ownership of his means
of production and a part of his prerogatives as an entrepreneur,
especially his power of decision.

In the last century, the industrialization of factories was accomplished with the help of the manufacturer's capital and the work
of a proletariat with no resources but its hands. Today in
agriculture the situation is reversed: the worker holds the
capital, an essential trump card he must be able to put to use so as
to be the master and not the slave of tomorrow's socioeconomic
structures.

It is up to the legislator to prepare new legal structures that
will make it possible to utilize this exceptional situation so
that the mass of farmers is not reduced to the proletarian
condition. In fact, the schema that has just been outlined, while it

seems to be commanded by technological and economic imperatives, can be embodied in radically different legal and social structures. The role of the sociologist is to point out the exigencies of scientific progress and the mass market, and at the same time to mark as clearly as possible the dividing line where the freedom of the individual man, the judgment of the moralist, and the will of the body politic can all be exercised. He must also outline alternative solutions, even the most utopian, for their benefit.

Just as in industry, a capitalist entrepreneur can buy peasant farms and combine in one single enterprise several workshops more or less important in scale. If the land is not excessively overvalued, and if the prices of food products are high enough, the enterprise will be profitable. It is particularly the gifted farmers who have knowingly taken a chance on planned modernization who will be able to follow such a path. Their success will mean the decline of the majority of their neighbors. Some formerly independent peasants will become salaried workers; others will move into other professions. The new farm enterprise that many hope for is sure to pose social problems similar to those of industry, and all the structures of production in industry and agriculture will be constructed on the same model.

Conversely, each workshop specializing in one product, whether it be landed or not, can constitute a small, independent enterprise that will employ seldom more than ten workers. This enterprise can be of an artisanal type, consisting of an employer and his workmen, or on the contrary it can be a cooperative set up by several former peasants, each of whom contributes his farm. In both cases these units of production will be too small to enjoy real independence and should be linked to others in a larger "horizontal" or "vertical" organization. To refer again to the example outlined above, the workshop for the production of fodder will be able to sign a contract to supply a workshop for the production of milk, which in turn will have a similar contract with the workshop down the line: processing of cheese or milk, production of powdered milk, and so on. But the workshop for the production of fodder would also be associated with others to form a federation for the production of fodder, or again it might prove to be more profitable to link the production of fodder to other vegetable production.

Depending upon the economic imperatives, legal frameworks, and ideology of the society as a whole, different legal and social institutions can be conceived and brought into being, such as the "family" farm of the American Middle West, the "group farming" of Breton villages, the great cereal enterprises of the Paris basin, the *podere* of Italian agrarian reform woven into a cooperative network, the integration of poultry farming into industry, the Ukrainian *kolkhoze*, the Israeli *moshav* or *kibbutz,* the Chinese commune, the Iranian cooperative, the Tunisian unit of production, etc. Again, neither the sociologist nor the economist can make a choice among these solutions. It is up to the politician and the moralist to say what social form they judge best, to the jurist to adapt it to the society by fitting, just, and foresighted laws, and to the administrator to supervise the application of these laws.

As soon as we pass from their legal status to the links between these workshops, we must be careful to regulate the power relationships between unequal contracting parties. All of the old legislation on rural leases and the recent statute on tenant farming were concerned only with this point. If the economic and social forces of our "capitalist" society operate freely, manufacturers and big farmers who possess capital and technical skill can impose their law and drive small farmers to a choice among exodus from the farm, a salaried position, or the condition of a pieceworker. In this case, the investments and the efforts at modernization undertaken over several years will have been a sheer waste and will only have delayed the outcome, instead of serving as the instrument of a revolutionary social creativity.

The contract system and the various forms of "integration" already well-established in the United States are beginning to spread into France. The industrial hatchery or cooperative that raises chicks makes an agreement with the farmer, to whom it furnishes one-day-old chicks, the necessary food, and sometimes even the equipment for raising them, and it "buys" the chickens from him at the end of several weeks. The contracting parties are reviving a very old form of domestic labor that became widespread during the Middle Ages in the weaving trade and was perpetuated in many rural regions until the end of the nineteenth century, when almost every farm included a loom in its household equipment. In this system, despite appearances, the farmer is losing all his autonomy and becoming a true salaried worker doing piecework. He furnishes only his work; the price paid for his chickens is only a salary in disguise, and even the hours of work are implicitly fixed by the contract.

To avoid such a situation, the producers could unite into unions that would discuss the terms of collective agreements with their buyers, both manufacturers and cooperatives. Canadian farmers have already tried this system with success. If there are cooperatives among the contracting parties, it will be advantageous if the producers belonging to the two sides can see the bargaining from the two points of view.

In such a system, chains of farm workshops connected by reciprocal contracts would constitute a form of organization of production, product by product. It would no longer be necessary to think in terms of farm production, even less of agriculture as opposed to industry, but rather in terms of food products and branches of production. Each branch would be organized into a hierarchy of institutions from the national or European level, where general objectives would be fixed, to the rank and file workshops, by way of regional or local federations of workshops for production and processing. Thus one could speak of milk production from the fodder to the package of powdered milk, the barn and the dairy being only intermediary phases that we cannot clearly designate as belonging to agriculture or industry.

In the French planning system, agriculture is the only important sector in which there is no intermediary decision-making agency between the government, the ministry, and the Planning Commission on one hand, and the two million entrepreneurs who are at the same time rank and file workers. Can one imagine automobile production managed in such a fashion: the workers of the Renault, Peugeot, Citroën, and Simca plants each deciding for himself what his production policy should be? In such a situation, prices are the only mechanism for transmitting and applying the national macrodecision. Contrary to all expectations, this mechanism, when it has not been hampered by political pressures, has functioned relatively well, sometimes even too well. For instance, the increase in the price of beetroot resulted in a rapid expansion in cultivation, which was soon followed by overproduction. Similarly, the artificially high price of corn allowed France to stop imports, but this price encouraged regions relatively unfavorable to the cultivation of corn (e.g., Beauce) to integrate it into their crop rotations and compete with regions gifted with a particularly favorable climate, such as the southwest. With abundant harvests and lower prices, this competition is becoming more painful for the two regions, one of which looks upon the crop as a vocation and the other of which is anxious to pay off recent investments. A policy that provided for regional decisions could have avoided this boomerang by not raising prices so high in the first place as to favor regional specialization.

At each stage and in each institution, the farmers would have their appointed place in decision-making agencies. Certain institutions would probably be entirely in their hands, since they already control a wide network of cooperative and farm credit associations. Moreover, they have created advisory and economic study services and farm management centers, which, if they were developed and coordinated, could study questions and prepare decisions from the point of view of agricultural producers.

These producers are in a very weak bargaining position;[2] they sell goods the production of which is highly variable and unpredictable, the consumption of which is inelastic, and which, being generally perishable, are difficult to store. Furthermore, they are situated at the beginning of the production, and this position leaves them little possibility for discussion. Finally, they are scattered physically and divided on issues, and have little strength to be used in applying economic pressure. To compensate for the weakness of this position, they must be assured a well-established power of decision within their organizations based on the holding of key positions and the means of making decisions competently, whether directly or through intermediaries. In particular, if a system of contracts or agreements among workshops were set up, political negotiation ought to operate to the benefit of the parties most burdened by the traditional limitations of agriculture.

The farmer will no longer be his own master as he was in the time of autarchic polyproduction, and he will partially lose the appearance of individual freedom that distinguishes a small, independent producer in a mass market. But he will regain this lost independence through effective participation in broad-based decisions that directly

[2]Latil, 1956; Fericelli, 1960.

determine his fate. At the present time, national macrodecisions are most often made in relation to political criteria. In determining a price for milk or wheat, economic imperatives are less important than political exigencies. The farmers do not complain of this, and with good reason, for they make up for their economic failings by their political strength. The dispersion that weakens them in the market makes them more effective in the Parlement. What they lose as producers they can easily regain as consumers. Since it is their family incomes that they are defending when they demand better prices, in the end it is fair that the economic decision be made on the basis of social, moral, and political considerations.

However, the political and professional representatives of the peasantry in Paris are not always faithful spokesmen of the small farmers and their true problems, so that the political overrepresentation of rural areas does not favor the farmer as much as one might expect. The political game among various parties and groups may sometimes even lead to a tacit agreement on the status quo and preclude any national decision, as was the case for farm extension and teaching. On the other hand, the peasants are well represented in agencies within the *départements,* but at present these have hardly any decision-making power. As agriculture occupies fewer workers, it will tend to lose its political overrepresentation. Above all, economic logic will prevail more and more in the determination of a farm policy — all the more so if the agricultural phases of production are integrated into complete circuits. Consequently, the creation of local and regional decision-making offices must be the essential objective of those who desire to give farmers real power of collective decision, the modern form of liberty.

To balance the financial power of manufacturers and farm entrepreneurs, farmers must clearly utilize their political strength and the intervention of public authority. Only this can make the agricultural Common Market operate in their favor without, for example, contributing to a further rise in the price of land. In France, only the government can hold in check international firms like Libby. The choice seems to have been quite easily posed for the past several years; however, the farmers, innovators in their own districts or *départements,* have had to be content with conservative measures from the government and the Parlement. But time is pressing, and the stakes will soon be set.

A massive professional exodus will be the condition and the consequence of this transformation, whatever social form it may take. Such a prediction, which is normal today, created an uproar only ten years ago. Anybody who dared to say it was taken for a prophet of evil and could not make himself heard in agricultural circles. And justly so, since in the past, rural exodus, a condition of agricultural progress according to the economists, in fact made way for the decline of the regions involved. Society became closed and static, agriculture became fixed in its habits, and peasants sought a lost past instead of thinking about the possibilities of the future. For ten years the mechanism has been working in reverse: a new generation of young farmers believes in the economic future and the nobility of the land as an occupation. They are taking advantage of the departure of their neighbors to expand, equip, and organize. Consequently they consider this exodus to be inevitable and even beneficial, and they demand that it be organized.

Economists predict that the active French population will amount to about fourteen million workers in twenty years. If we accept the fact that agricultural work will occupy between 5 and 10 percent of this active population, there will be a million farm workers, or a decrease of about two-thirds over the present number. The schematic calculation outlined above for ten dairy farms resulted in approximately the same proportion: seven workers take the place of twenty. Such a calculation for other products would doubtless lead to similar figures.

In the twenty years to come, this decrease in the number of farmers will be accomplished without much difficulty in regions where the farm density is already low, notably in the east, and those regions where the average age of the farmers is very high (e.g., the central regions). The young people who are preparing to take over the farms often represent less than a third of the working farmers. On the other hand, the highly-populated regions such as Brittany and the Vendée are going to pass through a very painful crisis, which it is important to make as easy for them as possible.

The decrease in the number of workers and the concentration of land will necessitate large-scale investments to remodel and equip the farm enterprises. Modern farmers expect this financing to come from the industrial and business sector. It is doubtful that the amortization and return for farm capital will remain as they are. One wonders as well if the economic and social cost of this conversion is economically justified and whether, from the point of view of the national economy, it would not be more advisable to employ these investments in other sectors and allow the change to take place slowly by letting agriculture itself finance this new modernization, as it did the previous one. Subsidies, legal reforms, a technological and commercial framework would suffice to make its task easier. In this way the farmers would have more chance to keep in their own hands the outcome of their activity.

In one way or another, the present revolution is going to continue, and there will be fewer and fewer farmers in the countryside, since the active farm population is decreasing faster than the rural population as a whole. Just as a century ago, the population of the countryside will consist mainly of nonfarmers. This statement seems contradictory, because for one hundred years we have been accustomed to use the words rural and agricultural, or countryside and agriculture, as synonymous. But this recent practice simply reflects the first rural exodus, which entailed the departure of nonpeasants (artisans, landlords, "managers," day laborers, and so on). The renaissance of the towns and small cities and the abandonment of the villages are the obvious proofs of this movement to anyone who walks through the countryside: a new rural society is being formed.

Until now we have spoken only of the productive agriculture organized into profitable workshops. But, whatever the economists say, there are several reasons for thinking that there will remain a "marginal" agriculture for subsistence, leisure, or luxury. A certain number of luxury food products such as *foie gras,* vintage wine, cheeses, "farm-fresh" chickens can only be made by artisanal peasant methods. And the society of abundance we are promised will include more and more buyers for these tasty and ostentatious delicacies; already there are Parisian restaurants and specialty shops that offer only products of traditional modes of cultivation and breeding (without fertilizers), the "nature foods."

The countryside has always been populated by those who combined the cultivation of a small piece of land with another principal activity. The rural industries of past centuries were in the hands of weaver-peasants; artisans and farm workers cultivated their own strips of land; the middle class of small towns, in addition to their offices and appointments and their small factories, held farm properties as well.

Today, worker-peasants are multiplying in many regions where
factories send their buses to pick up the peasants within a radius of
more than thirty miles. There are varying opinions about the implications of this double identity. Some see only a transition that permits
peasants to benefit from industrial salaries without giving up the security of the land, and think that normally this part-time farmer will
become a worker, that he will give up his farm and content himself
with a garden and a little poultry. Aside from the fact that urbanization and exodus are far from accomplished, forms of transition can
survive the conditions that brought them into being and can find new
functions. If the number of hours spent in the factory or the office
decreases significantly, it could be that office and factory workers
will continue to own land and will farm it to fill their leisure time
as much as to fill the pantry, and may even sell their neighbors a little
milk, fruit and vegetables, eggs, and chickens.

For their part, city dwellers are setting up their vacation homes
farther and farther from town, and to maintain them they are doing
some small-scale farming, in fruits or poultry, for example. This is
quite a costly procedure, of course, but it amortizes the invested
capital and serves some purpose. At the same time, it arouses the
farmers' bitterness toward the "amateurs" who are spoiling the profession — a problem serious enough to occupy the attention of the
Ministry of Agriculture. Moreover, city dwellers who come to the
country for two days per week or several months per year buy from
the neighboring peasants and thus contribute to the maintenance of
small-scale production. Finally, even if they have no gardeners or
caretakers, they require a multitude of services that help support
many people.

As marginal as they may seem, these forms of farm production and
rural life are not transitory. There is reason to believe that they will
in the future occupy a growing number of country people and an
appreciable segment of income. To counteract the unequal competition of these "handyman farmers," big producers will seek to protect
their status as farmers and monopolize aid from the administration
and farming contracts. But that will never prevent anybody from
giving a dozen eggs to his neighbor's wife.

To expect every person to have his specific task in a coherent and
effective system of production is a technocratic illusion. The more
effectively production is organized, the more likely it is to create subsidiary jobs, misfits, leisure time, and early retirement. It is common

knowledge that odd jobs and moonlighting are resuming importance. Moreover, our society is based less on production and increasingly on consumption, which gives rise to new service trades. In short, the constantly more elaborate rationalization of industrial society and the advent of affluence and waste must involve the creation of a "countersociety" of nonproductive consumers or worker-consumers, a whole population that lives without really working, or at least without producing.

Allowance must also be made for those who, physically or psychologically, cannot be integrated into too rational and organized a society. If they neither can nor want to live on the level demanded by industrial society, then they will normally find refuge in country life. These may be unstable persons unfit for rationalized tasks, or artists and artisans seeking calm and inspiration close to nature. All these people are difficult for economists to reckon with, yet they are increasingly numerous and will be sufficiently so in the future to populate this "countersociety" and give it its tone. For it is precisely this tone that city dwellers will come to seek in their leisure moments or in their old age; living on a small farm in the country provides retired persons and the various beneficiaries of social services with an interest and a source of income.

More or less consciously, the problems of the country and the land are always thought of in terms of agricultural production, while nature can be primarily a way of life. Only a century and a half ago, many country people were consumers rather than producers; if the government concerned itself with grain prices, it was not with the idea of increasing them to the profit of the producers, as is the case today, but to prevent their rising to the point where the country people of small means, who were consumers, would be reduced to starvation. It would obviously be paradoxical to try to bring back this population of beggars who lived so precariously. But the mountain people, who went off in the winter to work and earn their living in the city and returned in the summer to live on their land, followed the same seasonal rhythm as the great lords and the middle-class beneficiaries of ground rent.

It is not inconceivable that an affluent society may permit the return of the kind of life that alternates according to an annual, a seasonal, or a weekly cycle. Augé-Laribé feared the French countryside would become suburbanized; in fact, these will be neither suburbs nor "nonfarming rural" zones, as the Americans call them, but residential country populated by unemployed persons as well as the needy, by people who will not let the land lie fallow. These might be called "nonagricultural farm" regions, by antiphrasis. England furnishes suggestive examples of these new forms of country life and activities. We must try to think of the society of tomorrow from the point of view of the consumer rather than the producer as we have been accustomed to do, and to accept the fact that numerous rural regions will be consumers and not producers of alimentary products.

Country homes, productive agriculture, and subsistence or pleasure farming will disappear from certain regions devoted to extensive pasturage, and these regions will perhaps be infinitely more vast than we imagine today. What society and what social life will develop there? Some believe we must maintain a peasant population there by the use of subsidies, for they believe only such a population is capable of preserving and maintaining the countryside. Switzerland has made this choice for her mountainous regions. In other countries, this function would be more economically and effectively filled by forest rangers and stockbreeders. National parks and forests, or landscape agriculture and a folk peasantry? Formulated in these terms, the choice appears to have been made.

It does not in fact seem that the landscape requires a true rural society to maintain itself. This widespread opinion was born no doubt of the idea that social "erosion" inevitably leads to soil erosion. The example of many regions, notably around the Mediterranean, leads us to think that erosion is often favored by farmers and breeders; and we must note that in the American West the ecological equilibrium was disturbed by farmers. In a market agriculture the equilibrium between forest and range so dear to woodsmen can no longer be the product of peasant experience and stability; it is a delicate scientific and technical problem.

Tourism is bound to attract crowds in regions that are rugged and majestic. Having become a sufficiently important economic and social activity, tourism must assure the conservation of natural scenery. It is not the job of agriculture to entertain city dwellers. If they like to walk in verdant fields, intersected by quickset hedges and populated with white cows, they must pay for this scenery just as they pay for beaches and winter resorts. With the exception of a few sensitive souls nostalgic for a vanished peasant civilization, we would wager that an agriculture that provides scenery of this sort will find few patrons — unless "authentic" peasants in costume were transformed into bellhops and valets in luxury hotels like the Navajo Indians of the Grand Canyon in Colorado. In some regions favorable to the two activities, it will certainly be possible to combine agriculture and tourism and support a population and a society on these two resources. However, for the time being, the wish to "save" agriculture through tourism often leads to the dependence of tourism on agriculture.

In addition, industries and cities situated in nonfarming regions will extend their residential zones into the surrounding countryside. But this will be the extension of a diluted urban settlement and not the development of a new country society such as we have outlined above. Finally, we need hardly say, these different types will be blended into complex realities by making their mark on ecological structures inherited from the past and by assimilating the social traditions of each region of France. If the same model is imposed in Alsace, in the Vendée, in Périgord, and in Languedoc, the spirit and life of the large Alsacian village will have a very different flavor from the urbanity of Languedoc, and the countryside of Périgord will not resemble the Vendée.

Rural planning, which is spoken of so often but never properly studied, should be developed on the basis of this hypothesis, region by region, bearing in mind the traditional distribution of settlement and the traditional agrarian landscapes — aesthetic and functional masterpieces, the best of which must be preserved at all costs.

A thorough recasting of fundamental structures will be necessary in most cases. However, it would be useless to rush this process; it is preferable that the specialization of production and the organization of the workshops evolve slowly before a basic framework that might hamper future changes is set up. When technology makes it possible to foresee a form of agriculture without land, and land is reduced to its economic function, it is no longer realistic to encourage the purchase of land by peasants or to formulate complex legislation that will be out of date before it is applied. The attempts to fix optimal size for farms and the Penelope's web of land consolidation seem no more than obsolete patchwork at a time when all agrarian structures are being challenged.

Regions of dispersed habitation will continue to see a good number of their isolated farms fallen in ruins and their hamlets reduced to a single hearth. In regions of grouped habitation, villages will be reduced to hamlets with a few farms, and will have no other activity than agriculture. By a reverse process, towns and small cities will see their populations increase. Following this movement, priests and teachers will be concentrated in the county seats or the village centers, which will become the only gathering places for social life in the districts. The scale of rural society will thus be transformed, and the administrative framework of the French commune will lose its former importance.

The various forms that farm workshops may take in their localities have advantages and disadvantages that balance each other. Those who advocate dispersion extol the obvious convenience for daily work of buildings that are situated at a central point on the farm; but agglomerations of buildings are favorable to a modicum of social life. The question has been discussed in Germany, though it is not yet settled. In the Netherlands, the experience of the *polders* shows that the elaborate plans of the most competent experts and sociologists are thwarted by the inhabitants, who complain of the framework that is imposed on them and change it to their own liking. The odds are that in France regional habits will prevail over the reasoning of the sociologists and those who organize the work.

Compressed into villages or dispersed over the land, five to six hundred farm workshops would form a constellation, at the center of which would be situated a town or village center of four to six thousand inhabitants offering all the commercial, administrative, and cultural services necessary to a population, farming and nonfarming, totaling about ten thousand inhabitants. According to the topography, the type of lodging, the intensity and specialization of cultivation, the shops would be more or less numerous, the towns more or less populated, the territory as a whole more or less widespread.

Horticulture and arboriculture are conducive to a true "urbanization" of the countryside. In regions where many workshops will function without land, it is probable that they will group themselves in a town and that the outlands will not be heavily populated with farmers; the mechanized cultivation of cereals and forage crops requires few workers over a relatively short period of the year. The wheat producers of western Canada live in the city and spend their winters in Florida; it is hard to see why their French counterparts must live on their fields. Extensive animal breeding, for its part, will require vast land units.

Contrary to widespread opinion, a minimal population density is not a prerequisite of social life in a given area. Since the means of communication and transportation have improved, one can live ten or twenty miles from a center of social life without feeling as isolated as the Breton peasant lost at the end of his rutted road less than a mile from his church-steeple. The telephone, radio, and automobiles disturb isolation and conquer distances. On the other hand, if social life is to be maintained there must be many and varied people. A population of ten thousand persons, of whom less than one-third earn their living from agriculture, seems a satisfactory estimate. The other two-thirds would include administrators, merchants, educators, farm experts, representatives of the liberal professions, retired persons, and so on.

We are seeing the birth of a new rural bourgeoisie, which, after a half century, is going to revitalize small-town society and develop a way of life that will have much in common with that of the farmers of the area and with that of the inhabitants of the cities. Television and the phonograph will replace the piano. Struggles for prestige will again provide a subject for ironic humor and give spice to daily life. Associations of all sorts will multiply. Among younger people, dances have proliferated more rapidly than sports or cultural organizations, but each of the three will in future have its following.

Since they will often find it necessary to go into town, where the authorities, the merchants, the school, church, union, cooperative, and so on, are all located, farmers will participate in this social life. Whether or not they have their houses or workshops there, they will be "city people." Finally, several agricultural or industrial workshops for the processing of farm products or the making and repair of industrial products will furnish a source of income for industrial workers, and they will become less different from farm workers as their shops develop the same legal and social structures and are integrated in the same production process.

In the past, peasant civilization was in large part imposed on the citizens of small towns, who were thoroughly integrated into the life of the areas where they lived. In the future, on the contrary, the small towns will be at the outer reaches of complex urban networks centered on a great regional metropolis comprising several average cities. Recent statistics teach us that small and average cities grow faster than large ones. The entire network will be characterized by an urban type of life and what is sometimes called "mass culture."

Face-to-face society, confusion of roles, weak division of labor, and autarchy — these are the fundamental traits whose disappearance is already causing radical changes in the system of values and the pattern of social relations. These changes will work according to their own logic until new systems and new patterns are constructed.

More accentuated division of labor and differentiation of roles will fundamentally change the discipline that governs work. The necessities of the timetable and the imperatives of shorter cycles of production will make it possible to set up rules and restrictions in the daily life of the worker. He will no longer have to rely on his conscience, his courage, and his sense of a job well done. The moral philosophy of the father of a family will no longer be the worker's main standard of judgment and the farmer's criterion for management. Such a radical transformation in the moral exigencies of the job has already had deep repercussions on the farmer's mentality and personality.

Like the urban family, the peasant family is dividing the professional and educational roles between the mother and father in a new way. Either the father confines himself to manual labor, giving up to the mother his management functions and his paternal authority; or the father and mother form a team to manage the enterprise, since its success depends on their initiative and intelligence rather than on inherited patrimony.

It will become more and more common for a young man to choose the profession of farmer as he would any other. He will learn it in schools rather than from his father. Dividing his time between school and a "modern" family life, the little country boy will grow up in a situation similar to that of the young city boy, with whom he will share as well the society of contemporaries, the world of childhood. Having the same idols and reading the same children's publications, they will have the same values and ideals. The young farmer today is more different from his father than the latter was different from his ancestors of the eighteenth century, the Renaissance, and perhaps even classical antiquity. Hesiod and Xenophon, Virgil and Columella described a kind of life, a rural economy, and a type of man that belonged to the same breed as those of Olivier de Serres, Le Play, or Jean Giono.

The peasant village of the nineteenth century is thus opening itself to a broader society and to mass civilization. Social relations are no longer only personal, man-to-man; functional relationships are multiplying and institutions are becoming less human. The town clerk in an administrative unit of ten thousand inhabitants is no longer the neighbor and old school friend; he is an administrator with whom one is more or less acquainted, who receives people in his office and treats them as people under his jurisdiction.

In contrast to this modification there will obviously be a possibility of choice in social relations, which will no longer be determined solely by kinship or neighborhood. A man will be able to choose his friends and working companions; no longer will the nearest neighbor be the one who always aids him in certain jobs. The choices will be made in relation to social positions as well as by ideological and emotional affinity. The Centers for Technical Farm Studies prefigure these new relationships; rather than neighbors in the same village, they generally bring together farmers owning similar farms and having the same conception of the economic and social future, and often the same political or religious affiliation as well. It seems likely that it will be the same in the federations and contracts between workshops proposed above. Social control will be exercised less through personal interaction and will depend more on symbols and values developed and imposed by the broader society.

Nevertheless, the limitations of distance will continue to weigh heavily, and proximity will certainly remain a more decisive factor of organization than it is in the city. Moreover, the spread of sparsely settled areas will probably give greater importance to distance at the center of the megalopolis, and create relatively autonomous urban units. City life will become more countrified at the same time that rural society becomes urbanized.

However, to believe that rural society and personality will tomorrow be the same as those of large metropolises would be a simplistic illusion. Each rural society modernizes according to its bent, while acquiring common traits that obliterate the old individual characteristics. The direction taken and the mechanisms put into play are as instructive as the common image toward which these societies incline. Unfortunately we lack research data for diversified analysis.

Furthermore, all the preceding argument leads us to think that farmers and rural people will remain in some way different from city dwellers. But these differences will no longer indicate two basically contradictory civilizations; they will be differences in behavior norms, values, and personality traits that normally distinguish members of groups within the same society or civilization. Some think that farmers are in the process of acquiring class consciousness, and they encourage this tendency in the hope of seeing the formation of a "peasant class." It is a double error, since the peasantry is moribund, and class distinctions have less and less importance in the type of industrial society that is presently developing.

Neither a juxtaposition of small, autonomous societies (Karl Marx's "potatoes in a sack") nor a class, farmers will be simply a professional group among others, with their own peculiarities and interests. Working with biological material, dispersed over the countryside, in contact with nature, independent producers, having delegated a part of their decision-making power to superior corporate agencies, will doubtless have much in common with groups designated "intermediary" by certain statistical categories: new middle classes that combine salaried persons, liberal professions, and some merchants.

It would be easy to give a rough outline of the ideology that will motivate this group; it is already expressed quite clearly and simply in certain publications that consider themselves avant-garde. The exaltation of nature, a strong feeling of economic independence, and a cult of peasant traditions will nourish a deep conviction of the nobility of the profession, not to say its mission, which consists of feeding mankind. Insofar as it is colored by a deep concern with technicalities and economic efficiency, it will be an ideology of participation and progress. Those who fear or exalt the revolutionary spirit of the young peasants of today will soon be reassured or deceived, as the case may be.

Moreover, a clearer differentiation of social roles will lead to a greater diversification of systems of values, which will probably be reflected in politics by a decrease in moral and political argumentation in favor of economic and technical argumentation. Ideology itself will be distinguished more clearly from morality. In other words, the farmers will be less inclined to blame their economic difficulties on the malignance of governments or the injustice of the social system; they will seek economic causes and will try to remedy them, notably by using their political power. Thus, on all levels, morality will lose its instrumental role.

But, some will say, how are our traditionalist peasants going to shed the old self so abruptly and take on a new self? The peasant soul will survive the cataclysm that you forecast, if, indeed, it is to come. One has only to open a newspaper to dismiss this objection: there one sees article after article on progressive young farmers, on demonstrations, on conferences where the vocabulary of technical and economic efficiency has replaced the political and moral vocabulary that was in style only a few years ago.

On this point our studies are convincing: if economic structures are changed within a region, they will within a few years change the mentality of the inhabitants. It is striking to see the ease with which peasants formed in a traditional economic and social system can be moved to a modern system, given a few conditions — particularly that the coherence of the new system be rapidly established, visible, and comprehensible. It does not take the young farmers long to acquire "economic motivations," if only these have a meaning and are part of a coherent economic game that permits a glimpse of a successful future.

With astonishingly sure intuition they create entirely new institutions perfectly adapted to modern conditions, such as the C.E.T.A., S.I.C.A., groups of farms, and so on. But in reconstructing a new society on the dismantled structures of family, farm, and village, they sound the knell of the last vestiges of the peasantry in France, who will not survive their generation.

Thus, with them, the peasantry will itself be extinguished. And what will a world without peasants be like?

Appendix 1. On the Proper Application of Techniques in Rural Studies

"What I have said, I have said and not done."
(Gaston Dominici, at his trial)

The sociological study is one of the communications media created by industrial society, and it should be analyzed as such if its possibilities and limitations are to be understood. But this method of communication has a special function and meets with specific difficulties when it is used among the peasantry, which is still a relatively autonomous civilization deep within the broader society. Such mechanisms have always existed, and some have been analyzed in this book in connection with the diffusion of technological progress.[1]

Personal Contact

In the traditional peasant community, the notables (the mayor, the large landholder, the notary, the teacher) were invested with the function of interpreters between the peasants and the authorities. It is quite natural that the investigator should be placed by his rural respondent in this traditional communicator's role, which was also a role of authority. Traditional leaders participated in peasant society from a marginal position. The investigator, on the contrary, is usually a city dweller who is a stranger to the community he is studying; in this he resembles the civil servant or the politician. And whether he likes it or not, he gives the appearance of being in some sort of direct contact with a superior authority whom he is responsible for informing; he is a go-between through whom the peasant can make himself heard.

These traditional roles help to define the investigator's new role, in which he is, willy-nilly, confined by his respondent. Generally he accepts this situation and plays on the expectations it arouses by hinting, or even stating explicitly, that he has come to collect information and opinions intended to enlighten some authority. He serves a social function that the person concerned must, in his own interest, help him to fulfill correctly.

With the situation thus defined, the respondent can reject the dialogue completely or choose one of three attitudes. If he wants to

[1]For a general view of these problems, see seminar of May 11, 1963 (Appendix 2, No. 38), and Thomines-Desmazures, 1965.

please the authority to win its favor, he seeks to please the investigator by telling him the things he thinks will correspond to the latter's ideas. A second reaction is to try to make a good impression: to answer "well," to furnish the desired response in the course of the interview, which he thinks of as a kind of examination. The third is to complain, to air his grievances in the hope that a compassionate authority will help to better his miserable condition. These three attitudes are generally mixed in proportions that are not easily distinguishable and that vary in relation to the customs of the society being studied, the personalities of the respondent and the interviewer, and the survey technique used.

These attitudes are commanded by the way in which each peasant society is accustomed to deal with outside authorities. Relations with visitors are codified, and the individual's customary behavior normally guides him when he enters into personal contact with a stranger.[2] Avoidance is the simplest and most frequent reaction, but also the one the investigator circumvents most easily. Remarks like "Me? I have nothing to say" or "I don't know" or "I'm not educated" are often nothing but conventional assurances of modesty, forms of polite behavior toward someone who seems to be educated and full of learning. When the respondent does not completely refuse to answer but takes refuge in the evasive behavior that was part of customary social relations in the past, the whole conversation becomes bogged down, and the data gathered are dangerously and imperceptibly warped.

Often evasiveness is combined with the suggestion to go interview somebody else. It is then much more difficult to surmount, for the organization of the community is involved. "I can't answer you, but go see X or Y; they'll be able to tell you." This means: "I can't speak for everybody; others are given that responsibility by our society, and so they know what to say, but not me." In many societies, the stranger can establish contact only with the chief of the community and his lieutenants, and if he insists on speaking to other individuals it is up to the chief to designate them.

Michel Hoffmann's experiences[3] in the course of a number of opinion surveys conducted in Africa brings out the conflict between a "mass" technique and the hierarchical structure of a face-to-face

[2]Pitt-Rivers, 1954, pp. 32 ff.
[3]See Appendix 2, No. 38.

community. The random choice of a sample is in insurmountable contradiction with the hierarchical power structure of the community being studied: the chief would lose face, he would be renouncing his function, if he let the investigator have his way. In the course of a preliminary survey, when one asks a local authority (mayor or town clerk, for instance) for introductions to people for exploratory interviews, one is aways directed to people who will answer "well" — that is, precisely those one should avoid.

The evasiveness of the average man and the designation of a spokesman are stumbling blocks the rural investigator rarely comes up against in France if he is wise enough to take some elementary precautions. In country regions the percentage of refusals to answer is generally lower than in cities. Politeness requires people to receive a stranger, but carried to an extreme it can turn against the investigator; sometimes they decide to please him by telling him what they think he wants to hear. If the investigator is a farm expert, they will praise the benefits of modernization and progress. If he is a young man from a city university, they will extol to him the advantages of an education. Thus, they think, he will depart content and with a good opinion of the country and the people, which can always be useful.

To neutralize the guest with courteous hospitality is a traditional reaction of closed communities, and peasant villages have preserved this custom in many regions. It is in fact difficult to imagine that the visitor can be entirely neutral; he must bring with him some good or evil, and it is difficult to know which. I remember a conversation between two Iranian *rayats* on the occasion of our departure from their village in Fars: "He's leaving and he hasn't brought us anything," said one, to which the other retorted: "Yes, but he hasn't taken anything from us either." The stranger, if he has any appearance whatever of external authority, either takes or brings. Moreover, on him rests the reputation, good or bad, of the village; so it is important to gain his good will. The investigator who wants to overcome the pitfalls of politeness must clearly define the situation from the beginning. An introduction from recognized local authorities and a simple explanation of the possible usefulness of his work are sufficient in most cases.

In the peasants' experience, the survey interview is strangely reminiscent of a school examination. The interviewer, like the teacher, asks questions and is supplied with paper on which he writes down what is said. And one cannot imagine that his too-simple questions are as naive as they seem. Consequently, despite what he says, he is seeking not so much to learn as to judge. Now it is always disagreeable to be judged unfavorably, to get poor marks, especially if the interviewer is also going to ask one's neighbors the same questions. To have a poor mark is bad enough, but to risk being the lowest one in the class? No, not on any account! The investigator hears the question much more frequently in the country than in the city: "And what answer did the others give you?" In the country, the others are neighbors whom the respondent knows well, very often old school chums.

To force the respondent into the position of a good pupil who is seeking desperately to answer correctly, so that he will not be punished, is obviously not a good way to obtain valid information and sincere opinions from him. To reverse the situation, to make him understand that you have come to be informed and not to judge, is not an easy task for the interviewer. The timid and the anxious often succeed here better than others; they seem so inept, sitting there with their pencils and paper, that the peasant can look upon them as students rather than teachers, and, wanting to help them write a good answer, he tells them what he knows and thinks without ulterior motive. To listen without seeming to ask questions is a difficult art, and more so in the country than elsewhere.

For several years, surveys and investigators have been spreading like wildfire in country regions. More and more students are writing theses and dissertations. The idea of "statistics" is familiar, and people realize that those who gather them are not all tax inspectors. Farm organizations themselves sponsor studies by extension agents and active members, for administrative or educational purposes. Market studies as well are concerning themselves more often with country regions. Thus the role of interviewer is becoming clear and familiar to the peasants.

Communication and Opinion

The interview is a typically urban technique of social communication and a product of industrial civilization, where social relations are fragmentary and functional. To use it in traditional peasant societies, one must be aware of its strangeness and seek to reduce this to a minimum with the aid of a certain number of tricks: mainly by furnishing the respondent with the rules and instruments of the game, which are not as familiar to him as to the city dweller. In a peasant community everybody knows everybody else, and the inhabitants know all the aspects of each other's position and personality. Hence oral communication is of little use; indeed, it can be said to be useless for gathering information, since this can be done almost completely by observing everybody's behavior. It is pointless to say where you are going to the neighbor you meet on the road leading to a field; he knows you are going to that field and what you intend to do there.[4]

Similarly, it is needless to express one's sentiments orally in order to communicate them; they are betrayed by acts, dictated by situation, and shared or opposed by others.[5] Opinions and beliefs are sufficiently stable to be known by everybody. In fact, the individual is defined socially from childhood on by his family situation, and he is known personally as his character is being formed. During his early childhood, the young peasant is left to himself, and adults do not feel obliged to "communicate" with him. As he grows up, he is treated as a young adult.[6] Attitudes and beliefs are largely inherited from one's parents and those the child works out for himself rarely contradict those of his family.

Thus the peasant spends his life, faithful to himself and the image others have of him. He will never be able to modify this image by uncovering new aspects of his personality or position, since these are thoroughly familiar to everybody. Besides, to speak of himself and attach too much importance to his tastes and feelings incurs moral censure. Since normally one does not express oneself, it is not seemly to do so. Carried to the extreme, an absence of self-expression and communication can lead to pathological states and a true "social void."[7] Nevertheless what is unseemly in daily life can be accepted more easily in the exceptional situation of the interview with an unknown person,

[4]Maget, 1955.
[5]Mendras, 1967.
[6]Moscovici, 1961; Maurette and Gratiot-Alphandéry, 1956.
[7]Maucorps, 1966.

and this is why interviewers sometimes hear confidences one would deny an intimate friend.

Since he rarely needs to get acquainted with a stranger in everyday life, the peasant never needs to assert himself, to explain himself by expressing his opinions and feelings. In this he differs from the city dweller of industrial civilization, who must continually unmask himself to strangers in order to be able to maintain social relations with them. Almost never in a peasant's experience does a stranger ask him to put into words his opinions or feelings or his knowledge. Hence he does not know how to behave in the unfamiliar interview situation, and he finds himself defenseless in a social game he has never learned to play.

The main instrument of this game is obviously the capacity for verbal expression. Indeed, this varies very much within the city itself; the high civil servant's vocabulary and ease of speech are not those of the laborer. Those whose business it is to compose questionnaires know how hard it is to find words and expressions equally suggestive for all social strata. But, we must repeat, in everyday life city dwellers have more occasion than peasants to use conversation and words in order to communicate. Moreover, the average level of education is clearly lower in the country than in the city. Finally, the country person, once out of school, has less occasion to use his academic training than the city dweller and forgets it faster. We are speaking here only of ways of expression and not intelligence as measured by psychological tests, which has given rise to numerous studies and discussions; this is a different problem.[8]

Incapacity for expression derives not only from poor vocabulary and inexperience in handling words. It derives as well from the lack of the more or less abstract intellectual instruments codified by society into signs, symbols, stereotypes. Stimulated by advertising and the mass media, the city dweller manipulates a whole range of symbols in his daily life, with more or less success. He may be skillful or unskillful, but at least this manipulation is more habitual to him than to the peasant. On the other hand, the peasant resorts freely to analogy and symbolic imagery, which contribute much to the flavor of his speech. But his parable always has a special meaning, often ambiguous, which must be deciphered in its context and with its unique

[8]Heuyer and Piéron, 1954; Bretonnès, 1954.

coloration; while stereotyped signs and symbols, even used incorrec-
tly, are the small change of social communication, having in principle
the same value and meaning for all, and they are integrated into a
relatively homogeneous system of communication.

As newspapers, radio, and television penetrate into country
regions, they carry with them this common system and its instruments. The above remarks, therefore, refer to the recent past and
will largely lose their relevance in the near future. In the meantime,
the rural investigator in France is often surprised to see his
subjects play on both registers at the same time. Speaking of
his customary life, the peasant uses concrete and precise terms;
his judgments bear on personal experience, and his opinions
and behavior are suitable and coherent. On the contrary, when
he refers to the outside world he resorts to vague, abstract,
and often inadequate words that seem borrowed from an unfamiliar vocabulary. He expresses judgments and opinions that
are obviously not his own, and that in fact are often contradictory.
In short, he tries out a new language by repeating what he
has read in his newspaper or heard on the radio. When a respondent turns from a description of his technical problems to
discuss agricultural policy, the break in his speech is almost
always striking. For example, it often happens that the respondent
tries to attune himself to the interviewer's background and
speaks of the "improvement of rural housing" when he means
he is making repairs to his house.

The pretention to "fine language" is not found only in the
country, and to analyze its perculiarities we would have to study
the "urbanization" of country people's modes of expression. At
one extreme would be the peasant having only one register at
his disposal (which in certain regions he handles more easily
in local dialect than in pure French); and at the other extreme
one would find a complete fusion of the two registers, with the
urban predominant. To believe that one is "authentic" and the
other only an awkward veneer would be an error. It is important,
rather, to know in which fields and to what extent attitudes and
behavior are influenced by the urban register. For example, when
does the peasant speak in dialect and when in French? Is a
particular situation defined in one set of words more often than
in another? And from whose viewpoint? Does it follow that there

are significant differences in views or behavior?

We have suggested that peasants do not speak much, and yet there are some who cultivate the art of speech and conversation. In France this is the case notably in the Midi. In these regions, to speak well is a talent that permits one to be noticed on the village street or in the cafe, and to know how to tell a story is as important as to be able to compete with an adversary's wit and repartee. So, one might say, all the foregoing remarks are not valid for a whole portion of the French peasantry. Curiously enough, it seems that face-to-face logic operates even in this case, and the art of speech serves here more to conceal thoughts and feelings than to express them. It is not by speaking that people talk with each other and communicate their thoughts and feelings. Society has its own rules for this game; it is a show that people put on for each other, not a system of communication. The themes and the rhetoric are fixed, and the whole art consists in treating them skillfully, parrying the adversary's thrusts in order to attract public admiration.

There is no relation between this verbal prowess and an exchange of precise information and opinions appropriate to a given situation. It is well known that an ability to turn a phrase often leads to the twisting of one's thoughts and the distortion of analysis. And experience proves that conversationalists from the south are generally even more secretive than the less talkative mountain people. The rural investigator has learned the hard way that an open welcome and easy, colorful conversation can imply a protocol less likely to yield data than a difficult interview interrupted by embarrassing silences; one is pleasant and the other painful, yet it takes more time to gather useful data in a village in the French Midi than a village in the north.

Furthermore, being relatively stable, peasant society offers almost no choice of action to its members. When a choice must be made, the situation is so clearly defined and the options are so precisely delineated by tradition that the individual can form an opinion without hesitation. Throughout his life he has only to follow in the footsteps of his father. On the other hand, confronted with a new situation requiring a new decision, the peasant hesitates for a long time, carefully weighs the pros and cons, questions himself, seeks advice elsewhere, and waits until the last moment to make his decision.

It is also true that a new situation is rarely imposed on an isolated individual. Normally it involves the community as a whole, and thus it falls to the chief (or to the members in assembly) to analyze and define community opinion of the situation. The chief expresses the collective opinion, which will be ratified unanimously. It he does not know how to arrive at an opinion or decision that will earn the unanimous support of his village or tribe, he is not a good leader, and he has reason to fear for his power.[9] Of course, this "pure" situation is no longer found in France, but it is part of the role of leaders in a marginal position to know the world and guide the others in the community in their individual or collective relationships with the surrounding society. They no longer express the collective opinion, but they aid its formulation, because only they have at their disposal the necessary psychological and mental equipment to do so.

These observations finally lead us to ask ourselves what relationships exist among opinion, attitudes, and behavior in traditional peasant societies. Essentially, social psychology has defined its concepts and constructed its theory on the basis of data gathered in highly industrialized and urbanized societies, notably in the United States. If opinions are reactions to circumstances commanded by attitudes, the analysis of opinions permits us to detect attitudes and thus to foresee behavior to a certain extent. This is the schema appropriate to industrial society, which could be defined as an "opinion civilization," as opposed to traditional societies, which could be characterized as "attitude civilizations." In the former, in fact, opinions are one of the fundamental instruments of social relations and adjustment to continual change. The latter, on the contrary, function without need for opinions, since there is never a new individual situation.[10] In sum, it is hard to imagine that opinions can exist without being put to use or expressed, or to see the need for opinions on any subject in a totally stable, face-to-face society.

This hypothesis has been perhaps too briefly outlined here, but if it could be confirmed, the consequences for sociological and psychological research would be radical, since it would be absurd to go around collecting opinions from people who have none. This is a subject for basic research that could revitalize the

[9]Barth, 1964.
[10]Stoetzel, 1963, p. 157.

theoretical, methodological, and technical apparatus of sociology and psychology by introducing into them elements of intercultural comparison that have not yet assumed a sufficiently important place in these fields. Until such progress has been made, the rural investigator is obliged to take certain precautions that demand special training of him; and those who attempt opinion studies on a national level know that the material gathered in rural regions does not always have the same meaning as that obtained from city dwellers.

In the material derived from interviews, one can clearly distinguish opinions and information that refer to the surrounding society and are usually expressed in the "national" vocabulary (though sometimes in the "local" vocabulary as well). This category, naturally, includes everything that bears on the city, politics, economics. It represents the peasants' contribution to national public opinion, which influences them but of which they are a component. It is very difficult to know what relationships exist among these opinions, attitudes, and behavior. In certain fields they must be closely linked; in others they are relatively independent. Sometimes it seems even that no attitude or behavior corresponds to a stereotype. One must therefore exercise caution in interpreting the data.

Certain opinions on local affairs seem to be stereotyped; but, unlike those previously discussed, they are shared by almost all of the persons interviewed in a given population. They belong, for the most part, to a tradition that the individuals involved have more or less internalized, and that they would not dream of questioning. They are the opinions of which the anthropologist can learn directly from his informants, the things that go without saying, the norms and values common to the community as a whole. We earlier mentioned some examples.

Other opinions, on the contrary, vary significantly in relation to the social situations of individuals and reveal traditional social structures, e.g., contrasts between wealthy and poor, between pious and irreligious, and so on.

The logical relationships of compatibility or incompatibility that exist among these three spectra of opinion are probably the best indices for understanding the psychological mechanisms and behavior patterns of a peasant community.

The Interview

What instructions for the conduct of interviews can one draw
from these observations and the experience acquired by rural
investigators in France for the past several years? To put
together questionnaires on purely factual information or very
stereotyped opinions is no more difficult in the country than for
the various urban categories. One must know the vocabulary
and be sure that the interested parties have the information
and opinion one asks of them. Factual information is generally
easier to obtain in the country than in the city, if only the investigator has some familiarity with agriculture and local society.

One may meet almost any situation in the country; hence the
conscientious investigator must be informed about the life of the
people before setting out to question them, and some meager
familiarity with crop yields or techniques will permit him to
make the respondent realize that almost all his statements can
be verified. At the start of a study in a village of Epirus, it
became clear that by common agreement the peasants were
declaring only about half their resources and crop yields.[11] I
pointed out to the mayor that consultation with an agronomist
would permit the obvious and necessary corrections, and that the
credence of the study (preliminary to an investment project)
would thus be seriously diminished. My remonstrances brought a
rise in the figures declared so that they were no more than
about a quarter lower than the actual figures.

This procedure, while adequate for obtaining economic statistics,
may in other areas require one to undertake a complete study
of a community before setting out to question its members on
their attitudes and feelings. And the sociologist who wants to
get to the bottom of things must become an anthropologist in
order to do it right. Because of the syncretism of rural society,
the much-disparaged local monograph remains the best instrument
for understanding a peasant society not only as a whole but
even in its particular aspects, since these, if they are to be
properly analyzed, must be related to the whole.[12]

Once this necessity is recognized, survey practice still requires
the investigator to take drastic measures to outline the problems

[11]Mendras, 1961.
[12]See Appendix 2, No. 17.

or the sectors of analysis. Although it is harder to justify than in a mass society, this procedure is nonetheless necessary in peasant societies as well. Still, the investigator must always support the oral inquiry with observation and the use of available objective data (statistics, personal documents, descriptions, and so on). It is only by confronting opinion and behavior that we can infer attitude; the word and the deed must be reciprocally illuminating in the course of the inquiry itself. In urban society the partial study can be carried to its end, and reconstitution of various facts can await final synthesis; this is not possible in rural communities.

It is hence important to specify as closely as possible the instruments of oral inquiry best adapted to rural societies and the type of data one can expect of them. All investigators are agreed in thinking that the standardized questionnaire combining an obligatory series of open-ended or closed questions is not a good procedure for investigation in the rural environment. To be specific, the percentage of no-answer responses grows in proportion as one gets further from the city, and more, it seems for open-ended questions than for closed, since the latter more directly stimulate the response. The interview conducted with the aid of a series of open-ended questions, or the interview in clinical form ("non-directive"), starting with a very general question (such as, "Would you like to talk about the modernization of agriculture?"), seems less remote from rural habits. These furnish the best data, but data obviously more difficult to sift. They also require more experienced investigators, familiar with local farm problems. Along with the physical distances to be covered, these are limitations that weigh heavily on rural studies and make their cost much higher than that of urban studies.

Projective techniques in country regions generally give very poor or difficult-to-interpret results. Clinicians who deal with rural populations have a hard time utilizing instruments as classic as the Rorschach test or the Thematic Aperception Test. Attempts to use the TAT in rural communities in Europe and Africa (e.g., Dr. Ombredanne's "Congolese TAT") are often suggestive, and it would be desirable to adapt this test and experiment more systematically with it.[13]

[13]For an experiment in southern Italy, see Banfield, 1958; for France, see Bernot and Blancard, 1953, pp. 212–214, 390–400, and 425–441.

Confronted with blurred photographic plates that he is asked
to describe and interpret, the country person reacts with mis-
trust; he suspects a trap and often refuses to play along. If they
are more precise and clear, he describes the photos in detail
but refuses to interpret them or express the feelings or thoughts
they suggest to him. It would be helpful to know if this is a
simple defense reaction that could be surmounted by adjusting
the investigator and the instrument better to the respondent, or if
these pictures are really unevocative to peasants, as we suggest above.

Projective questions that require the interested party to play a
role or put himself in a hypothetical situation also produce very
poor results or meet a flat refusal. To the question, "If you
had six months to do nothing and a lot of money, what would
you do?" it frequently happens that the peasant responds simply,
"That's impossible. In this business we work, we can't take it
easy."[14] This recalls the experience of an American investigator
who asked a Turkish shepherd what he would do if he were
President of the Republic and received the answer, "Me, master of
the world?" — as if the question were absurd.[15] Yet any American
citizen would readily answer such a question.

On the other hand, the country person feels at ease in a
focused interview. He finds it normal that somebody should come
to talk with him about his problems and open a conversation
on a definite subject. The city dweller, however, generally finds
this situation strange. He wants to know precisely on what subject
he is to be questioned and what he must talk about; otherwise
he fears he is being manipulated and tends to remain on the
defensive. Once the conversation gets going, the rural respondent
follows the sequence of his ideas without being concerned
with the original theme. For him there is no one subject to be
treated, but rather a series of reflections that are interconnected;
and consequently he progresses from one subject to another
without being confined by intellectual frontiers. By the end of
the conversation it does not seem necessary to him to sum
up or to draw a conclusion. He stops because he has the
impression of having finished, because he is tired, or because
the interviewer asks him to stop.

[14]Mendras, 1958, pp. 77 and 86.
[15]Lerner, 1958.

By contrast, the city dweller wants the situation and the theme to be clearly defined at the outset, and then tends to treat his subject with respect for the rules of logic, trying always to be coherent. Whenever he can, he seeks to arrange his observations in categories, often dichotomous, in order to be able then to choose, as if he had to make a decision. At the end of the interview he wants to come to a conclusion that "sums up his thinking," and often he seeks the approval of the interviewer by asking him if he has treated his subject well.

The starting instructions do little to guide the rural respondent. It is the technique of the interviewer in conducting the conversation that is decisive. In fact, a peasant conversation always begins with some thoughts of a general nature, often statements of fact in which the two participants make each other's acquaintance, are put at their ease, and inspire mutual confidence. It would be crude and inelegant to announce immediately the subject of the conversation; it should not appear until later, when the swords have been crossed and the ritual thrusts have been made. Once caught up in the game, the respondent seeks to reflect, to question himself, to examine thoroughly his ideas and feelings. He has rarely asked himself about the problems now being submitted for his comment, and so he profits from the occasion to follow his interior monologue before a relatively neutral and understanding stranger who will return the ball to him and thus help him formulate and better control his feelings and thoughts. He often asks the interviewer to furnish him with material for thought and comparison by telling him of other experiences and other regions.

For him, each element has its significance and deserves to be weighed separately. He attaches little importance to coherence and can contradict himself with impunity. He aims to judge the whole experience not as the logical conclusion of a train of reasoning but as an overall view based on a few symbols. In this he resembles the buyer in the marketplace who, after examining the teeth, the hide, and the udder of the cow, stands back to judge its general form. Rambaud claims that peasants have a "capacity for historical reflection;" they think about their history, about the concrete, and tend to express their thoughts, even when general and abstract, in concrete terms and by imagery.

This has led some observers and investigators to say that they have encountered in peasants a sort of difficulty in abstracting and conceptualizing. However, an abstract idea can be communicated by analogies and concrete words as well as by abstract language. Abstract thinking is not always apparent.[16]

When an interviewer has occasion to return and visit a rural respondent, even a long time after the first conversation, the latter frequently recalls the first interview and says he has thought about it since. The interview leaves deeper traces in the country than the city; it is an event that can have distant and unexpected repercussions. Members of youth movements have understood this effect and have used large-scale surveys as an educational method and an instrument of agitation. The influence of surveys on the evolution of a rural community deserves detailed analysis, which is now in process in one multidisciplinary study undertaken in southern Finistère by the General Commission for Scientific and Technical Research (D.G.R.S.T.).

In basic research, the data must lead not only to an explanation and a theory of the realities studied but, probably more important, to the development of new ideas and classifications. Peasant societies are particularly rich in this respect, thanks to their anthropological peculiarity as compared with the industrial society that surrounds them. Still there is an essential difference between societies that anthropologists observe and those that rural sociologists study. In the former, investigations normally reveal myths and the symbols, more or less developed.[17] By contrast, when peasants are made to speak of their daily life and their social environment, the interviewer necessarily hears the theories, concepts, and categories of analysis of their own society. Some discerning observers reveal the most intimate mechanisms of the social system in which they live, and others are satisfied with a more conventional description; but in both cases the word usage, comparisons, facts cited, and anecdotes related all deserve close analysis. The researcher must then decipher the general meaning of particular observations in order to discover the concepts, define them, and name them. Once

[16]Hegel, 1963.
[17]Griaule, 1966.

this first task of interpretation is accomplished, a second abstraction is necessary to transform these concepts into concepts of theoretical analysis that can be joined to the body of scientific theories.

There is grave danger in transposing from one vocabulary to another ideas that are in fact irreducible, inasmuch as the social sciences are constructed essentially on an analysis of highly industrialized societies. We have seen, for example, to what confusion the idea of the social psychologist's role can lead when it is applied without precautions to rural studies. The other danger, nonetheless grave, would be to content oneself with ideas put forth by one's informants, especially when the latter express themselves well enough to give the ideas a name. A science makes progress from the day it replaces the vocabulary and ideas of common empirical knowledge with those constructed for its own use.

Appendix 2. Sources

I. Surveys and Studies by the Division of Rural Sociology of the C.N.R.S. (Center for Sociological Studies).

1. **Sundgau:** study of the attitudes of farmers toward modernization, conducted at the request of the Committee for Action of the *département* of the Haut-Rhin in 1954–55. Sample of 330 farmers (10 percent of those owning more than 20 acres); 55 interviews in depth and 245 questionnaire interviews.
Report: H. Mendras, "Les paysans et la modernisation de l'agriculture" (Paris, C.N.R.S., 1958), 150 pp. (Publications of the Center for Sociological Studies).

2. **Combrailles:** studies on the attitudes of farmers toward the farm crisis, conducted by Marcel Jollivet in 1956–57 at the request of the Regional Planning Committee of the Riom District. Sample of 80 farmers in three communes of the district of St. Gervais d'Auvergne (Puy-de-Dôme). Control study in the communes of Servant (Combrailles Bourbonnais) and Effiat (Limagne). Complementary agronomical and technical study conducted by André Brun, I.N.R.A.; complementary study of 45 women conducted by M.-T. de la Rivière.
Report: Marcel Jollivet, "Les réactions paysannes à la crise agricole dans les Combrailles," typewritten; and in *Economie rurale* (Oct.-Dec. 1966), pp. 15–28.

3. **Béarn:** study of the diffusion of hybrid corn in two districts of Nay (Basse-Pyrénées), conducted by J. C. Papoz, agricultural engineer, in 1959. Sample of 100 farmers. Interviews by means of questionnaires followed up by conversation.
Report: not published in its entirety. Appears in part in J.C. Papoz, "Enquête-pilote sur l'adoption de la culture du maïs hybride dans les cantons de Nay, Basse-Pyrénées," *Économie rurale,* XLV (1960), pp. 29–43.

4. **Léon:** survey of farm management and farmers' economic attitudes, conducted in collaboration with the Farm Economy office of the I.N.R.A. at Rennes (Director, Louis Malassis; responsible for the survey, J. Madec). Sample of 5 percent of the farmers in the agricultural region (276 questionnaires). Questionnaire on farm management followed up by a short sociological questionnaire.
Report: unpublished.

5. **Factor analysis** dealing with the 22 questions from the questionnaire, used in the four preceding surveys. 710 questionnaires. Conducted by Michèle Kourganoff under the direction of René Bassoul.

6. **Attitudes toward the land:** study conducted by Micheline Fairé in 1961 in collaboration with the Center for Research and Agricultural Studies in the district of Péage-de-Roussillon (Isère). Sample of 76 farmers selected according to a research plan.
Report: unpublished.

7. **Attitudes of winegrowers in Languedoc on wine and policies**

affecting wine growing: study conducted at the request of the Chief Study Commission on Alcoholism in 1963 by J. Duplex and R. Bassoul. Sample of 116 wine growers selected to represent flat and hilly regions, small and large farms in Hérault.
Report: unpublished.

8. **Agricultural organizations:** study of institutions, men, and ideologies conducted in 1955, prepared for use in round-table discussions of the French Political Science Association.
Report: H. Mendras, "Les organizations agricoles," *Revue française de science politique* (1955), pp. 736–760, and J. Fauvet and H. Mendras, *Les paysans et la politique dans la France contemporaine* (Paris, A. Colin, 1958), 533 pp.

9. **The demonstrations of June, 1961 and the agricultural policy of the Fifth Republic:** series of studies conducted by Yves Tavernier, research assistant of the F.N.S.P.
Report: Y. Tavernier and H. Mendras, "Les manifestations de Juin 1961," *Revue française de science politique,* XI (1962), p. 671. Y. Tavernier and G. Rimareix, "L'élaboration et le vote de la loi complémentaire d'orientation agricole," *Ibid.,* XIII (1958), pp. 389–425.

10. **Young farmers and their view of the future and their profession:** study conducted in 1963 by M. F. Wautelet with the collaboration of the M.F.A.R. Sample of 600 apprentices (boys and girls) distributed among 16 schools chosen to represent four types of French farm societies (Vendée, the north, Jura and Vaucluse). "Half of the students wrote papers on what they wished to do when they grew up and the other half essays on the theme, 'Describe the ideal life of a boy (or a girl).'"
Report: Graduate thesis, unpublished.

11. **Comparative attitudes of rural and urban inhabitants according to I.F.O.P. surveys:** comparative analysis of results of 50 studies by the I.F.O.P. under the direction of Michèle Kourganoff.

12. **Annotated bibliography** of 3000 titles on French rural societies. 500 titles were the subject of an analysis.
Report: Les sociétés rurales françaises, basic bibliography compiled by the Division of Rural Sociology under the direction of Henri Mendras (Paris, F.N.S.P., 1962), 124 pp.

13. **Rural exodus in France:** bibliography compiled in 1963 by Henri Mendras and Jean Duplex. Analysis of 300 works.
Report: Henri Mendras, "L'éxode rural en France, état des travaux." Doctoral dissertation.

14. **Images of the city and attitudes toward the surrounding society:** study conducted by J. C. and M. Kourganoff in a commune of southern Finistère. Sample of 200 persons.
Report: unpublished.

15. **Sociological atlas of rural France:** 65 maps representing demographic, economic, agronomical, political, and other characteristics at a local level.
Publication under the direction of Jean Duplex: *Atlas de la France rurale* (Paris, A. Colin, 1968).

16. **Nine comparative local studies** (1966): C (Manges), O (Beauce), N (Jura), A (Rouergue), B (Marche), M (Armagnac), G (Provence), R (lower Normandy), P (Pays Bigouden).

17. **French rural societies:** comparative analyses and methodological essays (1966, mimeographed, multiple pagination), based on data compiled for the two preceding works. All of these researches were conducted under Agreement 62 FR 053 of the D.G.R.S.T.

II. Unpublished Works

18. J. Maho, "Étude de la diffusion de l'information à Plozevet." Report on a D.G.R.S.T. study, 1963, 200 pp., mimeographed.

19. J. C. and M. Kourganoff, "Rapport d'enquête d'observation psychosociologique dans la commune de Plozevet, Sud-Finistère." Institut national d'études démographiques, 324 pp., typewritten.

20. R. Leveau, "Le Syndicat de Chartres, 1885–1914. Études du rôle des élites républicaines dans la transformation de milieu rural." Graduate thesis, 238 pp., mimeographed.

21. M. Moscovici, "Organisation familiale et changement social en milieu rural." Graduate thesis, Paris, 1965.

22. M. Moscovici, "Enquête pilote sur le passage de l'agriculture à l'industrie en milieu rural." Report for the Planning Commission, Committee on Productivity, March 1963, manuscript. A case study of professional mobility without significant geographic mobility (with the collaboration of M. Fairé).

23. **I.F.O.P.,** studies on farmers, specifically "Le moral des agriculteurs." Quantitative and qualitative studies. See Jollivet, 1966.

24. **Synergie-Roc,** various studies conducted at the request of the Ministry of Agriculture, the A.N.M.R., and others, specifically "Marche de la vulgarisation agricole, les attitudes a l'égard de la coopération et les S.A.F.E.R."

25. Thérèse Labbens, "Recherche documentaire en vue d'une sociologie des organisations agricoles." I.N.T.D. dissertation, 1960, 134 pp., mimeographed.

26. F. Leblond, "Les vétérinaires dans la vie nationale," I.E.O.P. dissertation, 1960, 122 pp., mimeographed.

27. M. T. de la Rivière, "Enquête sur le travail des femmes d'agriculteurs dans quelques exploitations familiales françaises," *Économie rurale,* XLIX (1961), pp. 11–27.

28. Gaston Lanneau, "Les attitudes sociales du paysan dans une zone de polyculture." Graduate thesis, Toulouse, 1964, 414 pp., typewritten.

29. R. Cabannes, "L'idée de progrès dans la presse agricole." Graduate thesis, Toulouse, 1964, 182 pp., typewritten.

30. P. Houée, "Développement agricole en Bretagne centrale." Graduate thesis, Poitiers, 1965, 2 vols.

31. Michel Greco, "Les Bretons à St. Denis." I.E.P. dissertation,

1965, 146 pp., typewritten. Study of the origins, social life, and adjustment of young workmen of Breton origin in St. Denis.

32. Guy Meyer, "Le développement socio-économique du canton de Pontacq." I.E.P. dissertation, Paris, 1960.

33. Y. Tavernier, "Le C.N.J.A." Dissertation, Paris, 1961, 220 pp., mimeographed.

34. G. Marzin, "Les tensions et les conflicts dans la région légumière du Nord-Finistère." I.E.P. dissertation, 1962, 103 pp.

35. A. Albenque, "État des techniques de production et de consommation dans l'agriculture et les arts ménagers." D.G.R.S.T., 1963, 206 pp., mimeographed. Multidisciplinary study of a Breton commune conducted under the direction of J. Fourastié.

36. C. Brittiaux, "L'administration des eaux et forêts." I.E.P. dissertation, Paris, 1963, 166 pp., typewritten.

37. "Economics and Anthropology." Report of a seminar at Burg Wartenstein under the auspices of the Wenner-Gren Foundation, 1960.

38. "L'enquête psycho-sociologue en milieu rural." Transcript of a seminar held May 11, 1963, by the Division of Rural Sociology.

39. "Sociologie rurale." Transcript of a course given at the I.E.P. in 1948–49 by Professors Cholley, Arbos, Moynier, Dumont, Marthelet, Le Bras, and Faucher. 400 pp., typewritten.

40. "Sociologie rurale." Transcript of a course given at the I.E.P. by J. Stoetzel in 1951–52. 291 pp., typewritten.

41. M. Bodiguel, "La diffusion des innovations en milieu rural: tracteurs et trayeuses dans deux communes bretonnes." Graduate thesis, Paris, 1966.

Appendix 3. Bibliography

The following list is in no way exhaustive. It is simply a compilation, for the reader's convenience, of works referred to in the text.

Arensberg, Conrad
"The Community as Object and as Sample," *American Anthropologist* (1961), 241–264.

Arland, Marcel
Le paysan français à travers la littérature (Paris, Stock, 1941), 191 pp.

Aron, Raymond
Dix-huit leçons sur la société industrielle (Paris, Gallimard, 1962), 377 pp.

Artaud, Marcel
"Le métier d'agriculteur," *Économie et Humanisme* (1944).

Augé-Laribé, Michel
Syndicats et coopératives agricoles (Paris, A. Colin, 1926), 211 pp.

Augé-Laribé, Michel
La politique agricole de la France de 1880 à 1940 (Paris, P.U.F., 1950), 483 pp.

Augé-Laribé, Michel
La révolution agricole (Paris, A. Michel, 1955), 437 pp.

Banfield, Edward
The Moral Basis of a Backward Society (New York, The Free Press of Glencoe, 1958), 204 pp.

Barjon, Louis
Le paysan (Le Puy, Mappus, 1945), 307 pp.

Barth, Frederick
Nomads of South Persia (Oslo, Universitetsforlaget, 1964), 159 pp.

Bedel, Maurice
Géographie de mille hectares (Paris, Grasset, 1937), 140 pp.

Bell, Daniel
Work and Its Discontents (Boston, Beacon Press, 1956), 56 pp.

Benedict, Murray R.
Can We Solve the Farm Problem? An Analysis of Federal Aid to Agriculture (New York, The Twentieth Century Fund, 1955), 601 pp.

Benoit-Guilbot, Odile
Les objectifs des entreprises moyennes et leur hiérarchie, C.N.R.S., Centre d'Études Sociologiques, 1966, 98 pp. mimeographed.

Benvenuti, Bruno,
Farming in Cultural Change (Assen, Van Gorcum, 1961), 468 pp.

Bernot, L., and Blancard, R.
Nouville, un village français (Paris, Institut d'ethnologie, 1953), 447 pp.

Bloch, Marc
"La lutte pour l'individualisme agraire en France au XVIIIe
siècle," *Annales d'histoire économique et sociale,* II, (1930),
329–383, 511–556.

Bloch, Marc
"Avènement et conquête du moulin à eau," *Annales d'histoire
économique et sociale,* VII (1935), 538–563.

Bloch, Marc
"Les transformations des techniques comme problèmes de
psychologie collective," *Journal de psychologie normale et pathologique,* XII (1948), 104–120.

Bourdieu, Pierre
"Célibat et condition paysanne," *Études rurales,* II (1962), 32–135.

Bourdieu, Pierre
"The Attitude of the Algerian Peasant toward Time," in Pitt-Rivers
(ed.) *Mediterranean Countrymen* (Paris, Mouton, 1963), 55–72.

Bretonnès, J.
"Les bases d'une étude psycho-sociologique sur l'épanouissement
de l'homme en milieu rural," *Revue du ministère de l'Agriculture*
(1954), 95–100.

Cassin, Eléna
"Symboles de cession immobilière dans l'ancien droit mésopota-
mien," *Année sociologique* (1952), 107–161.

Cépède, Michel
Du prix de revient au produit net en agriculture (Paris, P.U.F.,
1946), 447 pp.

Cépède, M. and Weil, G.
L'Agriculture (Paris, P.U.F., 1965), 527 pp.

Chombart de Lauwe, Jean
Bretagne et pays de la Garonne (Paris, Centre national d'information économique, 1946), 188 pp.

Chombart de Lauwe, Jean and Morvan, F.
Les possibilités de la petite entreprise dans l'agriculture française
(Paris, S.A.D.E.P., 1954), 151 pp.

Chombart de Lauwe, Jean and J. Poitevin.
Gestion des exploitations agricoles (Paris, Dunod, 1957), 222 pp.

Clément, Pierre
Le Salavès (Anduze, Languedoc-Éditions, 1953), 238 pp.

Coutin, Pierre
"Le remembrement des terres en Limagne," *Mélanges Ph. Arbos*
(Paris, Les Belles Lettres, 1953), 149–156.

Couty, Philippe
"Réflexions sur les procédés de recherche dans les enquêtes de
commercialisation," *Bulletin de liaison des sciences humaines*
(Paris, O.R.S.T.O.M., August 1966), 1–24.

Dahrendorf, Ralf
Homo sociologicus (Cologne, Westdeutscher Verlag, 1960), 71 pp.

Dampierre, Éric de
"Coton noir et café blanc, deux cultures du Haut-Oubangui à la veille de la loi-cadre," *Cahiers d'études africaines*, I (1960), 128–147.

Dauzat, Albert
Le village et le paysan de France (Paris, Gallimard, 1941), 219 pp.

Debatisse, Michel
La révolution silencieuse, le combat des paysans (Paris, Calmann Lévy, 1963), 277 pp.

Delatouche, Raymond
"Élites intellectuelles et agriculture au Moyen Âge," in *Recueil d'études sociales, publié à la mémoire de Frédéric Le Play* (Paris, Picard, 1956), 147–157.

Deléage, André
La vie rurale en Bourgogne jusqu' au début du XIe siècle (Mâcon, Protat, 1941), 2 vols., 774 pp.

Dion, Roger
Essai sur la formation du paysage rural français (Tours, Arrault, 1934), 162 pp.

Dombasle, Mathieu de
Annales agricoles de Roville, ou Mélanges d'agriculture, d'économie rurale et de législation agricole (Paris, Huzard, 1824), 8 vols.

Dorgères, Henry
Haut les fourches (Paris, les Oeuvres françaises, 1935), 220 pp.

Duby, Georges
L'économie rurale et la vie dans les campagnes dans l'Occident médiéval (Paris, Aubier, 1962), 2 vols., 823 pp.

Dumont, René
Économie agricole dans le monde (Paris, Dalloz, 1954), 595 pp.

Dumont, René
"Le prolétariat oublié et l'expansion agricole," *Esprit* (June 1955), 897–916.

Dumont, René
L'Afrique noire est mal partie (Paris, Éditions du Seuil, 1962), 287 pp.

Evans-Pritchard, E. E.
The Nuer (Oxford, Clarendon Press, 1940), 271 pp.

Faucher, Daniel
"Routine et innovation dans la vie paysanne," *Journal de psychologie normale et pathologique*, XLI (1948), 89–94.

Faucher, Daniel
Le paysan et la machine (Paris, les Éditions de Minuit, 1954), 280 pp.

Faucher, Daniel
La vie rurale vue par un géographe (Toulose, Institut de géographie, 1962), 319 pp.

Fauvet, J. and Mendras, H.
Les Paysans et la politique dans la France contemporaine (Paris, A. Colin, 1958), 532 pp.

Febvre, Lucien
Le problème de l'incroyance au XVIᵉ siècle (Paris, Albin Michel, 1942), 549 pp.

Felstehausen, H. H.
Economic Knowledge and Comprehension in a Netherlands Farming Community (Wageningen, 1965), 118 pp.

Fericelli, Jean
Le revenu des agriculteurs, matériaux pour une théorie de la répartition (Paris, Génin, 1960), 396 pp.

Fraisse, Paul
Psychologie du temps (Paris, P.U.F., 1957), 328 pp.

Friedl, Ernestine
Vassilika, A Village in Modern Greece (New York, Holt, Rinehart and Winston, 1962), 110 pp.

Friedmann, Georges
Villes et campagnes, civilisation urbaine et civilisation rurale en France (Paris, A. Colin, 1953), 481 pp.

Friedmann, Georges
Sept études sur l'homme et la technique (Paris, Gonthier, 1966), 215 pp.

Garavel, Joseph
Les paysans de Morette (Paris, A. Colin, 1948), 123 pp.

Gasparin, Agénor de
Cours d'agriculture (Paris, Librairie de la maison rustique), 16 vols.

George, Pierre
La campagne, le fait rural à travers le monde (Paris, P.U.F., 1956), 397 pp.

Géraud and Spitzer
"Le moral des agriculteurs," in *Revue française de sociologie,* VI (1955), 2–15.

Gervais, M., Servolin, C., and Weil, J.
Une France sans paysan (Paris, Éditions du Seuil, 1965), 128 pp.

Giono, Jean
Lettres aux paysans sur la pauvreté et la paix (Paris, Grasset, 1938), 92 pp.

Giono, Jean
Notes sur l'affaire Dominici (Paris, Gallimard, 1955), 153 pp.

Girard, A. and Bastide, H.
"Le budget temps de la femme mariée à la campagne," *Population,* XIV (1959), 253–284.

Godelier, Maurice
Rationalité et irrationalité en économie (Paris, Maspéro, 1966), 295 pp.

Grand, Roger, and Delatouche, Raymond
L'agriculture au Moyen Age, de la fin de l'Empire romain au XVIᵉ siècle (Paris, Éd. de Boccard, vol. 3, 1950), 740 pp.

Griaule, Marcel
Dieu d'eau, entretien avec Ogotemmeli, 2nd ed. (Paris, Fayard, 1966), 220 pp.

Griswold, Whitney
Farming and Democracy (New York, Harcourt, Brace, 1948), 227 pp.

Guillaumin, Émile
La vie d'un simple (Paris, Stock, 1942), 313 pp.

Guillaumin, Émile
Les paysans par eux-mêmes (Paris, Stock, 1953), 311 pp.

Gurvitch, Georges
La multiplicité des temps sociaux (Paris, Centre de documentation universitaire, 1958), 129 pp. mimeographed.

Halévy, Daniel
Visites aux paysans du Centre (Paris, Grasset, 1935), 350 pp.

Halévy, Daniel
La fin des notables (Paris, Grasset, 1930 and 1937).

Harper, Roland
"Comment changer le comportement des agriculteurs," in *Chronique sociale de France* (1954), 147–155.

Hazard, Paul
The European Mind, 1680–1715 (London, Hollis & Carter, 1953).

Hegel, G. W. F.
"Qui pense abstrait?," *Mercure de France,* CCCXLIX (1963), 746–751.

Heuyer, Piéron *et al.*
Le niveau intellectuel des enfants d'âge scolaire (Paris, P.U.F., 1950–1954), 2 vols., pp. 284–299.

Higbee, E.
Farms and Farmers in an Urban Age (New York, Twentieth Century Fund, 1963), 183 pp.

Hubert, H. and Mauss, M.
"La représentation du temps," in *Mélanges d'histoire des religions,* 2nd ed., (Paris, Alcan, 1929), 236 pp.

Jollivet, Marcel
"Les attitudes des agriculteurs des Combrailles à l'égard de la modernisation agricole," *Économie rurale,* LXX (Oct.–Dec. 1966), pp. 15–28.

Jollivet, Marcel
Les agriculteurs français, condition de vie et opinions (*Sondages,* 1966), 163 pp.

Juglart, Michel de
"Les aspects juridiques de l'entreprise agricole," in *Les aspects sociaux de la vie rurale* (Paris, Dalloz, 1958), 34–74.

Justin, Émile
Les sociétés rurales d'agriculture du XVIIIe siècle (1757–1793) (Saint-Lô, 1935), 371 pp.

Katz, E. and Lazarsfeld, P.
Personal Influence. The Part Played by People in the Flow of Mass Communications (New York, The Free Press of Glencoe, 1955), 400 pp.

Kerblay, Basile
"A. V. Cajanov, un carrefour dans l'évolution de la pensée agraire en Russie de 1908 à 1930," *Cahiers du monde russe et soviétique,* V (1964), 411–460.

Koyré, Alexandre
Études d'histoire de la pensée philosophique (Paris, A. Colin, 1961), 330 pp.

Labat, Emmanuel
L'âme paysanne, la terre, la race, l'école (Paris, Delagrave, 1919).

Labrusse, Bertrand
"La presse agricole," in Fauvet and Mendras, *Les paysans et la politique* (Paris, A. Colin, 1958), 303–317.

Latil, Marc
L'évolution du revenu agricole (Paris, A. Colin, 1956), 378 pp.

Lavergne, Léonce de
Économie rurale de la France depuis 1789 (Paris, Guillaumin, 1860).

Lefebvre, Henri
"Problèmes de sociologie rurale. La communauté paysanne et ses problèmes historico-sociologiques," *Cahiers internationaux de sociologie,* VI (1949), 79–100.

Lefebvre, Henri
Pyrénées (Lausanne, Rencontre, 1965), 109 pp.

Leites, Nathan
Du malaise politique en France (Paris, Plon, 1958), 192 pp.

Leites, Nathan
L'obsession du mal (Paris, undated), 667 pp. mimeographed.

Le Play, Frédéric
Les ouvriers européens (Paris, Dentu, Larcher, 1877–1879), 6 vols.

Lerner, Daniel
The Passing of Traditional Society (New York, The Free Press of Glencoe, 1958), 466 pp.

Le Roy Ladurie, Emmanuel
Les paysans de Languedoc (Paris, S.E.V.P.E.N., 1966), 2 vols. 1035 pp.

Leveau, Rémy
"L'enseignement et la vulgarisation agricole," in Fauvet and Mendras, *Les paysans et la politique* (Paris, A. Colin, 1958), 269–280.

Levesque, André
Le problème psychologique des migrations rurales en Ille-et-Vilaine (Paris, A.N.M.R., 1958), 215 pp.

Linton, Ralph
The Study of Man (New York and London, Appleton-Century, 1936), 503 pp.

Lionberger, Herbert
The Adoption of New Ideas and Practices (The Iowa State University Press, 1962), 163 pp.

Lionberger, Herbert and Hassinger
"Neighborhoods as Factors in the Diffusion of Farm Information in a Northeast Missouri Farming Community," *Rural Sociology,* XIX (1954), 377–384.

Maget, Marcel
"Les dates de mutations locatives de biens ruraux. Esquisses cartographiques d'après les recueils d'usages locaux," *Étude agricoles d'économie corporative,* II (1942), 317–344.

Maget, Marcel
"Remarques sur le village comme cadre de recherches anthropologiques," *Bulletin de psychologie,* VIII (1955), 373–382.

Mair, Lucy
"How Small Scale Societies Change," *Penguin Survey of the Social Sciences,* 1965, 20–35.

Malassis, Louis
Économie des exploitations agricoles (Paris, A. Colin, 1958), 302 pp.

Marriott, McKim
"La modernisation de l'agriculture dans les régions rurales sous-développées," *Chronique sociale de France,* II (1954), 123–134.

Marriott, McKim
"Village India," *A.A.A. Memoir* no. 83 (1955), 324–333.

Marx, Karl
The Eighteenth Brumaire of Louis Bonaparte (New York, International Publishers, 1964).

Maspétiol, R.
L'ordre éternel des champs (Paris, Librairie de Médicis, 1946), 589 pp.

Maucorps, P.
Le vide social (Paris/La Haye, Mouton, 1966), 207 pp.

Maurette, M. T., and Gratiot-Alphandery, H.
Loisirs et formation culturelle de l'enfant rural (Paris, P.U.F., 1956), 343 pp.

Meister, Albert
L'Afrique noire peut-elle partir? (Paris, Éditions du Seuil, 1966), 450 pp.

Mendras, Henri
Études de sociologie rurale, Novis et Virgin (Paris, A. Colin, 1953), 138 pp.

Mendras, Henri
Les paysans et la modernisation de l'agriculture (Paris, C.N.R.S., 1958), 142 pp.

Mendras, Henri
Six villages d'Épire, problèmes de développement socio-écono-mique (Paris, U.N.E.S.C.O., 1961), 92 pp.

Mendras, Henri
Les sociétés rurales françaises, éléments de bibliographie (Paris, Fondation nationale des Sciences politiques, 1962), 156 pp.

Mendras, Henri
La sociologie rurale (Paris, P.U.E. 1967).

Merton, R.K.
Éléments de théorie et de méthode sociologique (Paris, Plon, 1966), 524 pp.

Milhau, Jules
"La mentalité paysanne," in Milhau and Montagne, *L'agriculture aujourd'hui et demain* (Paris P.U.F., 1962), 340–370.

Miner, Horace
Culture and Agriculture (Ann Arbor, University of Michigan Press, 1949), 96 pp.

Mireaux, Émile
Une province française au temps du grand roi: la Brie (Paris, Hachette, 1958), 352 pp.

Moreau, R., and Reboul, J.
Le travail et la gestion des exploitations agricoles (Paris, CNCER, 1957), 70 pp.

Moscovici, Marie
"Les paysannes et la modernisation," *La Nef*, IV (1960), 65–73.

Moscovici, Marie
"Le changement social en milieu rural et le rôle des femmes," *Revue française de sociologie,* I (1960), 314–322.

Moscovici, Marie
"Personnalité de l'enfant en milieu rural," *Études rurales,* I (1961), 57–69.

Nadel, S.
The Theory of Social Structure (London, Cohen and West, 1957), 159 pp.

Naville, Pierre
L'automation et le travail humain (Paris, C.N.R.S., 1961), 743 pp.

Neufbourg, G. de C.
Paysans (Paris, Bloud et Gay, 1945), 190 pp.

Neufchateau, François de
Essai sur la nécessité et les moyens de faire entrer dans l'instruction publique l'enseignement de l'agriculture (Paris, Huzard, An X).

Nilson, Martin P.
Primitive Time Reckoning (Lund, C. W. K. Gleerup, 1960), 384 pp.

Norre, Henri
Comment j'ai vaincu la misère (Paris, Calmann Lévy Balzac, 1944), 235 pp.

Papoz, Jean-Claude
"Enquête pilote sur la culture du maïs hybride dans les cantons de Nay," *Économie rurale,* XLV (1960), 29–43.

Piaget, Jean
Le développement de la notion de temps chez l'enfant (Paris, P.U.F., 1946), 300 pp.

Pitt-Rivers, Julian
The People of the Sierra (London, Weidenfeld, 1954).

Redfield, Robert
A Village That Chose Progress (Chicago, University of Chicago Press, 1950).

Redfield, Robert
Peasant Society and Culture (Chicago, University of Chicago Press, 1956a), 162 pp.

Redfield, Robert
The Little Community (Chicago, University of Chicago Press, 1956b), 182 pp.

Rémond, René
"La morale de Franklin et l'opinion française sous la monarchie censitaire," *Revue d'histoire moderne et contemporaine,* VII (1960), 193–214.

Rimareix, G., and Tavernier, Y.
"L'élaboration et le vote de la loi complémentaire d'orientation agricole," *Revue française de science politique,* XIII (1963), 389–425.

Rivière G. and Maget, M.
"Fêtes et cérémonies de la communauté villageoise," in *Agriculture et communauté* (Paris, Libraire de Médicis, 1943), 75–95.

Rivière, M.-T. de la
"Enquête sur le travail des femmes d'agriculteurs dans quelques exploitations familiales françaises," *Économie rurale,* XLIX (1961), 11–27.

Rocheblave-Spenlé, Anne-Marie
La notion de rôle en psychologie sociale (Paris, P.U.F., 1962), 434 pp.

Rogers, Everett M.
Diffusion of Innovations (New York, The Free Press of Glencoe, 1962), 367 pp.

Rougier de Labergerie, J. B.
Recherches sur les principaux abus qui s'opposent au progrès de l'agriculture (Paris, 1788).

Roupnel, Gaston
La ville et la campagne au XVIIIe, Étude sur les populations du pays dijonnais (Paris, A. Colin, 1955), 359 pp.

Royer, Jean Michel
"De Dorgères à Poujade," in Fauvet and Mendras, *Les paysans et la politique* (Paris, A. Colin, 1958), 153–182 pp.

Rozier, Abbé François
Cours complet d'agriculture théorique, pratique, économique et de médecine rurale et vétérinaire (Paris, Marchaut, 1805), 11 vols.

Ryan, B. and Gross N.
"The Diffusion of Hybrid Seed Corn," *Rural Sociology,* VIII (1943), 15–24.

Salleron, Louis
Un régime corporatif pour l'agriculture (Paris, Dunod, 1937), 263 pp.

Sclafert, Thérèse
Cultures en Haute-Provence, déboisements et pâturages au Moyen Age (Paris, S.E.V.P.E.N., 1959), 271 pp.

Serres, Olivier de
Le théâtre d'agriculture et mesnage des champs (Paris, Huzart, 1804), 2 vols., 948 pp.

Stoetzel, Jean
La psychologie sociale (Paris, Flammarion, 1963), 316 pp.

Tarde, Gabriel
Les lois de l'imitation, 7th ed. (Paris, Alcan, 1927), 428 pp.

Tavernier, Yves
"Le syndicalisme paysan et la politique agricole du gouvernement (1958–1962)," *Revue française de science politique,* XII (1962), 599–646.

Tavernier, Y. and Mendras, H.
"Les manifestations de juin 1961," *Revue française de science politique,* XII (1962), 648–761.

Tavernier, Yves
"Les forces syndicales et politiques devant les problèmes fonciers," in Société française de sociologie, *Tendances et volontés de la société française* (Paris, S.É.D.É.I.S., 1966), 52–112.

Taylor, Lee and Jones, A. R.
Rural Life and Urbanized Society (New York, Oxford University Press, 1964), 493 pp.

Tchayanoff, Alexandre
"Zur Frage einer Theorie der nichtkapitalistischen Wirtschafts-systeme," *Archiv für Sozialwissenschaft und Sozialpolitik* (1924), 577–613.

Thabault, Roger
Mon village (Paris, Delagrave, 1945), 247 pp.

Thorner
"L'économie paysanne, concept pour l'histoire économique," *Annales E.S.C.,* XIX (1964), 417–432.

Tocqueville, Alexis de
The Old Regime and the Revolution (New York, Doubleday & Company, 1955).

Tocqueville, Alexis de
Recollections (New York, Doubleday & Company, 1970).

Van Den Ban
"Some Characteristics of Progressive Farmers in the Netherlands,"
Rural Sociology, XXII (1957), 205–212.

Van Den Ban
"Locality Group Differences in the Adoption of a New Farm
Practice," *Rural Sociology,* XXV (1960), 308–320.

Varagnac, André
Civilisation traditionnelle et genres de vie (Paris, A. Michel, 1942),
403 pp.

Vauban, S.
La dîme royale (Paris, Guillaumin, 1889), 208 pp.

Venard, Marc
Bourgeois et paysans au XVIIe siècle (Paris, S.E.V.P.E.N., 1957),
126 pp.

Warner, Charles K.
The Winegrowers of France and Government since 1875 (New
York, Columbia University Press, 1960), 303 pp.

Weber, Max
Gesamte Aufsätze zur Wissenschaftslehre (Tübingen, Mohr, 1958).

Weber, Max
Politics as a Vocation (Philadelphia, Fortress Press, 1965).

Weber, Max
The Protestant Ethic and the Spirit of Capitalism (New York,
Scribner, 1962).

Weil, Eric
"Tradition and Traditionalism," *Confluence,* II (1953), 106–116.

Weulersse, Jacques
Paysans de Syrie et du Proche Orient (Paris, Gallimard, 1946),
330 pp.

Williams, W. M.
The Sociology of an English Village: Gosforth (London, Routledge
and Kegan Paul, 1956), 246 pp.

Wilkening, E. A.
"Sources of Information for Improved Practices," *Rural Sociology,*
XV (1950), 19–30.

Westermarck, N.
"Le facteur humain et la réussite en agriculture," *Chronique
sociale de France,* II (1954), 135–146.

Wright, Gordon
Rural Revolution in France, Peasantry in the Twentieth Century
(Stanford University Press, 1964), 271 pp.

Wylie, Laurence
Village in the Vaucluse (Cambridge, Harvard University Press,
1957), 345 pp.

Yole, Jean
Les arrivants (Paris, Grasset, 1909), 352 pp.

Yole, Jean
Le malaise paysan (Paris, Spes, 1930), 296 pp.

Young, Arthur
Travels in France during the Years 1787, 1788, and 1789 (Cambridge, The University Press, 1929).

"L'information chez les agriculteurs," *Sondages,* I (1964), 1–77.

"La modernisation de l'agriculture en France," *Sondages,* XV (1953), 51 pp.

"La pression temporelle," *Sondages,* III (1953), 11–15.

Index